D0886746

Susan Deller Ross is professor of law at the University of Georgetown Law Center. She is a board member and director of the Women's Law and Public Policy Fellowship Program at the Law Center, as well as director of the Center's Sex Discrimination Clinic. Her publications include a law school casebook on sex discrimination, several articles on women's legal rights, and judicial training materials on child custody and visitation, and spousal support for the Women Judges Fund for Justice. Her litigation on behalf of women includes cases concerning wages, pension plans, pregnancy, sexual harassment, vocational training, and domestic violence. In the fall of 1991, she helped represent Professor Anita Hill in her testimony before the Senate Judiciary Committee concerning the Clarence Thomas nomination to the Supreme Court.

Isabelle Katz Pinzler has been director of the ACLU Women's Rights Project since 1978. She has done extensive litigation in the areas of civil rights, constitutional law, and employment law, including, in particular, the areas of women in the military and bias in standardized testing. Most recently, she successfully litigated the first case involving gender discrimination in standardized testing and the first successful discrimination challenge to the SAT, *Sharif v. N.Y.S. Education Department* (New York, 1989). Before joining the ACLU, she served as deputy director of the National Employment Law Project and as a staff attorney with the Law Reform Unit of the Legal Aid Society of Cleveland.

Deborah A. Ellis is legal director of the NOW Legal Defense and Education Fund. In 1992, she argued before the U.S. Supreme Court in a case challenging Operation Rescue blockades. Formerly the legal director of the ACLU of New Jersey and a staff attorney at the ACLU Women's Rights Project, she has taught women and the law courses as an adjunct professor at Yale College, Rutgers School of Law, and New York University School of Law. She is a cum laude graduate of Yale College and New York University School of Law and served as a law clerk to Federal Judge Frank M. Johnson, Jr.

Kary L. Moss was a staff attorney with the Women's Rights Project from 1988 to 1992. Before joining the ACLU, she served as a law clerk in the United States Court of Appeals for the Second Circuit. She has published extensively about governmental efforts to punish women for their prenatal behavior and about accessing health care for low-income women.

Also in this series

THE RIGHTS OF ALIENS AND REFUGEES
THE RIGHTS OF AUTHORS, ARTISTS, AND OTHER
  CREATIVE PEOPLE
THE RIGHTS OF CRIME VICTIMS
THE RIGHTS OF EMPLOYEES
THE RIGHTS OF INDIANS AND TRIBES
THE RIGHTS OF LESBIANS AND GAY MEN
THE RIGHTS OF OLDER PERSONS
THE RIGHTS OF PATIENTS
THE RIGHTS OF PRISONERS
THE RIGHTS OF SINGLE PEOPLE
THE RIGHTS OF STUDENTS
THE RIGHTS OF TEACHERS
THE RIGHTS OF YOUNG PEOPLE
THE RIGHT TO PROTEST
YOUR RIGHT TO GOVERNMENT INFORMATION
YOUR RIGHT TO PRIVACY

AN AMERICAN CIVIL LIBERTIES UNION HANDBOOK

THE RIGHTS OF WOMEN

THE BASIC ACLU GUIDE TO WOMEN'S RIGHTS

THIRD EDITION
Completely Revised and Up-to-Date

Susan Deller Ross
Isabelle Katz Pinzler
Deborah A. Ellis
Kary L. Moss

General Editor of the Handbook Series
Norman Dorsen, President, ACLU 1976–1991

SOUTHERN ILLINOIS UNIVERSITY PRESS
CARBONDALE AND EDWARDSVILLE

96 95 94 93   4 3 2 1

Library of Congress Cataloging-in-Publication Data

The Rights of women : the basic ACLU guide to women's rights / Susan
    Deller Ross . . . [et al.]. — 3rd ed., completely rev. and up-to-
    date.
        p.   cm. — (An American Civil Liberties Union handbook)
    Previous ed. (1983) entered under Ross, Susan Deller.
    Includes bibliographical references.
    1. Women—Legal status, laws, etc.—United States.   I. Deller
Ross, Susan.   II. American Civil Liberties Union.   III. Series.
KF478.Z9R67   1993
346.7301′34—dc20
[347.306134]   92-34244
ISBN 0-8093-1898-9   CIP
ISBN 0-8093-1633-1 (pbk.)

*This book is dedicated to
Steve, Jim, Andy, and Doug
with grateful appreciation
for all their support*

Contents

Preface ix

Acknowledgments xi

Introduction xiii

I. Constitutional Rights: The Concept of Equal Protection, State Equal Rights Provisions, and the Equal Rights Amendment 1

II. Employment Discrimination 18

III. Parenting and Work 93

IV. Family Law 115

V. Reproductive Freedom 178

VI. Liberty Rights During Pregnancy 209

VII. The Criminal Justice System 221

VIII. Education 248

IX. Insurance 284

X. Public Accommodations and Private Clubs 292

XI. The Military 297

XII. Homelessness 305

XIII. The Legal System 311

Preface

This guide sets forth your rights under present law and offers suggestions on how they can be protected. It is one of a continuing series of handbooks published in cooperation with the American Civil Liberties Union (ACLU).

Surrounding these publications is the hope that Americans, informed of their rights, will be encouraged to exercise them. Through their exercise, rights are given life. If they are rarely used, they may be forgotten and violations may become routine.

This guide offers no assurances that your rights will be respected. The laws may change, and in some of the subjects covered in these pages, they change quite rapidly. An effort has been made to note those parts of the law where movement is taking place, but it is not always possible to predict accurately when the law *will* change.

Even if laws remain the same, their interpretation by courts and administrative officials often varies. In a federal system such as ours there is a built-in problem since state and federal laws differ, not to speak of the variations among states. In addition, there is much diversity in the ways in which particular courts and administrative officials interpret the same law at any given moment.

If you encounter what you consider to be a specific abuse of your rights, you should seek legal assistance. There are a number of agencies that may help you, among them ACLU affiliate offices, but bear in mind that the ACLU is a limited-purpose organization. In many communities there are federally funded legal service offices that provide assistance to persons who cannot afford the costs of legal representation.

In general, the rights that the ACLU defends are freedom of inquiry and expression; due process of law; equal protection under the law; and privacy. The authors in this series have discussed other rights (even though they sometimes fall outside the ACLU's usual concern) in order to provide as much guidance as possible.

These books have been planned as guides for the people directly affected: thus the question-and-answer format. (In some areas there are more detailed works available for experts.) These guides seek to raise the major issues and inform the nonspecialist of the basic law on the subject. The authors of these books are themselves specialists who understand the need for information at "street level."

If you encounter a specific legal problem in an area discussed in one of these handbooks, show the book to your attorney. Of course, he or she will not be able to rely exclusively on the handbook to provide you with adequate representation. But if your attorney hasn't had a great deal of experience in the specific area, the handbook can provide helpful suggestions on how to proceed.

Norman Dorsen, General Editor
Stokes Professor of Law
New York University School of Law

Acknowledgments

Many people have been helpful in the preparation of this book. We would like to especially thank Claudia Withers, for her help on "Employment Discrimination"; Joan E. Bertin and Elisabeth A. Werby, who coauthored the section on workplace hazards in the parenting and work chapter; Melanie S. Griffin, for her help on the section on domestic violence in the family law chapter; Sally Goldfarb, for her assistance also on "Family Law"; Ellen Vargyas and Jacqueline Berrien, for their help on "Education"; Marcia Youngman, for her assistance on "Insurance"; Priscilla Ruth MacDougall, for her help on the section on names in "Family Law"; Kitty Kolbert, Julie Mertus, and Rachael Pine, who coauthored the chapter on reproductive rights and Dawn Johnsen, for her invaluable comments and expertise; Alexa Freeman, Brenda Smith, and Ellen Barry, for their help on the section on women in prison in "The Criminal Justice System"; Carolyn Becraft for her help on "The Military"; and Kristin Morse, for her help on "Homelessness."

Nancy Tainiter, a law student at Cardozo Law School, and Elisa Velasquez, a law student at New York Law School, were wonderful cite-checkers; Jessica Brown, Peggy Chase, Paula Krauss, and Carl Lewis were instrumental in preparing the manuscript for publication.

This is the third edition of *The Rights of Women*. It is built upon the foundations of the two earlier editions. We, therefore, gratefully acknowledge the assistance of the following people on the previous editions.

The first edition: Ruth Bader Ginsburg, Barbara Babcock, Ann Freedman, Judy Potter, Nancy F. Stanley; (then) Georgetown University law students Dayle Berk, Betty Branda, Lois Frankel, Sandy McCandless, Max Richtman, Faye Stank, and Grey Wilson; and Bruce Green, Ruth Rowse, Alexandra Buek, Eleanor Lewis, Jeffrey Orleans, Eve Paul, Harriet Pilpel, Nancy Stearns, and David Zugschwerdt.

The second edition: Diane Dodson, Sheila Mooney, Donna Lenhoff, Janet Benshoof, Lourdes Soto, Ann Teicher, Suzanne Lynn, Madeline Kochen, Isabelle Pinzler, Wendy Williams, Kathy Bonk, Nancy Stanley, Diana Steele, Janice Siegel, Betsy Brinson, Ellen Leitzer, Mary Catherine Kilday, Margie Kohn, Holly Knox, Laurie Woods; Professor Sylvia Law and the (then) students of the Arthur Garfield Hays Civil Liberties Program at NYU School of Law who worked under her direction: Pat Hennessey, Mitchell Bernard, Ellen Levine, Stefan Presser, Anita Cava, Sharon Blackman, Richard Betheil, Richard Zall, Elaine Fink, Karen Freedman, and Jed Ringel; and particularly Ann Barcher, the coauthor of the second edition.

Introduction

Throughout United States history, much of the discrimination women have faced, while rooted in custom and stereotypes, was also supported and reinforced by the legal system itself. When Elizabeth Cady Stanton and Lucretia Mott called the first women's rights convention at Seneca Falls, New York, in 1848, one of their major concerns was a legal system that profoundly discriminated against women. They detailed these "unjust laws" in the Declaration of Sentiments adopted by the convention. The law, they observed, deprived all women of the right to vote, "this first right of a citizen." Laws also prohibited women from engaging in many occupations and professions, including the practice of law.[1] The law was particularly harsh to the married woman. It deprived her of all rights, rendered her "civilly dead," and made her husband her "master." It also gave the husband ownership of his wife's property, including the wages she earned,[2] and full guardianship of their children in case of divorce, as well as the power to deprive her of liberty and to beat her.

Of course, most such unjust and inhumane laws have disappeared from the books. It took a bitter seventy-year fight, but women eventually gained the vote with the ratification in 1920 of the Ninteenth Amendment to the Constitution. Women won other rights too, including increased control over property and wages and the right to custody of their children in divorce.

But not all sex-based laws had disappeared by the middle of the twentieth century. Into the 1970s there continued to be laws that mandated a woman could not work extra hours to earn overtime pay when a man could, that a husband should have sole control over property owned jointly with his wife, that a working wife could be denied fringe benefits when a working husband got those benefits automatically, that a young woman was entitled to parental support only until she turned eighteen while a young man could receive such payments until the age of twenty-one, or that a woman had to take her husband's name upon marriage. Government officials could and did decide that female high-school students had to take homemaking and could not play on the tennis or football team, that a girl who ran away from home was a juvenile delinquent but the boy who did so was a normal, high-spirited kid, and that a poor woman who wanted to enter a government training program had to wait until all poor men had the chance to do so.

Because of the prevalence of such discriminatory laws and practices—and because at that time there appeared to be little chance that courts would invalidate them—women activists in the 1970s sought the Equal Rights Amendment (ERA) to the United States Constitution. The ERA was designed to do away with all sexually discriminatory laws and practices. It proclaimed simply:

> Equality of rights under the law shall not be denied or abridged by the United States or by any State on account of sex.

The amendment, first proposed in 1923 and long dormant, gained political momentum with the rebirth of the feminist movement and was approved by Congress in 1972. A decade later, on 30 June 1982, the ERA was officially declared dead—having failed by a narrow margin to gain ratification by the necessary thirty-eight states.

Feminists, of course, decried this loss. But the demise of the ERA masked the larger victory of the women's movement. In the same decade in which the ERA went down to defeat, sex discrimination law in this country was completely transformed. Under the pressure of the women's movement and because of changes in the role of women in society, the Supreme Court reexamined and changed its interpretation of the Constitution; sex discriminatory laws and practices once automatically approved by the Court as constitutional are now likely to be declared invalid.[3] Feminist pressure produced results in other areas as well. Congress and state legislatures rewrote old laws to eliminate sex discriminatory provisions and passed new laws to outlaw sex discrimination in such diverse areas as employment, education, credit, and housing. And federal and state agencies began more seriously enforcing laws against discrimination on the job. In short, despite the loss of the ERA, the 1970s gave us the legal structure for eradicating discrimination.

Thus, this book explains in detail how women can use the laws on the books in the continuing struggle to gain real equality in the family, the marketplace, the workplace, and academia. For the law is now, in most cases, a tool for helping women— not the source of women's oppression it once was. And that is an important measure of the progress women have achieved in their slow march toward equal rights.

Despite these profound changes in the legal system, however, legally sanctioned discrimination still persists well into the 1990s. The right to choose to terminate a pregnancy is under grave threat from a conservative Supreme Court; it has a majority appointed by Presidents Reagan and Bush, who acted to implement the Republican party pledge to put anti-abortion judges on the Court. State laws may discriminate against women due to pregnancy. Poor women and women of color continue to suffer a disproportionate share of the burden resulting from twelve years of conservative legal and economic policies. Blatant, legally required, sex discrimination persists in the military, where most jobs are designated for "men only" and enlistment criteria are more stringent for women than for men. And sex discrimination is still the legally tolerated norm in insurance rates.

These continuing challenges from the legal system to women's equal status demonstrate how important it remains for women to work together to change society, including its laws. They also indicate how vital it is for women to increase their representation on all of the nation's courts and legislative bodies. For until women constitute 50% of the institutions that make our country's laws, women simply cannot be assured that those laws will truly reflect their interests. Once that goal is achieved, women may finally have the equal status in society which Elizabeth Cady Stanton and Lucretia Mott first hoped for in 1848.

NOTES

1. *Bradwell v. Illinois,* 83 U.S. 130 (1873).
2. Technically, the husband owned the wife's personal property outright and had the right to manage and control her real property, which included the right to use or lease it and to keep any rents or profits from it for himself. Babcock, Freedman, Norton, and Ross, *Sex Discrimination and the Law: Causes and Remedies,* at 561–62 (detailing as

well all aspects of a married woman's unequal status under the common-law system).

3. In fact, the Supreme Court has now ruled that many of the sex discriminatory laws detailed above in the text are unconstitutional. *See e.g.*, *Kirchberg v. Feenstra*, 450 U.S. 455 (1981)(invalidating Louisiana statute making husband "head and master" with sole control of community property owned jointly with his wife); *Wengler v. Druggists Mutual Insurance Co.*, 446 U.S. 142 (1980)(invalidating Missouri law giving all working husbands, but only some working wives, death benefits for their surviving spouses); *Stanton v. Stanton*, 421 U.S. 7 (1975) and 429 U.S. 501 (1977)(invalidating Utah law under which parental support was paid for young women only up to the age of 18 but for young men up to the age of 21).

THE RIGHTS OF WOMEN

I

Constitutional Rights: The Concept of Equal Protection, State Equal Rights Provisions, and the Equal Rights Amendment

This first chapter on constitutional rights explains how to use the Constitution to change those state and federal laws and the actions of government officials that still discriminate on the basis of sex. For while the incidence of such laws and practices has dramatically decreased, many remain. Although there is no ERA to attack such discrimination, there are a wide variety of other weapons to use, including the Constitution itself—now vastly changed by the Supreme Court interpretations of the 1970s. Thus, there will often be many ways to address a particular problem, but women should always consider an additional approach based on the federal or state constitutions.

EQUAL PROTECTION

What constitutional doctrine can be used to get rid of sex discriminatory laws and government practices?

The relevant doctrine is generally referred to as "equal protection" and is derived from the Equal Protection Clause of the Fourteenth Amendment to the Constitution. The key language in the amendment provides that:

No State shall . . . deny to any person within its jurisdiction the equal protection of the laws.

What does the Equal Protection Clause mean?

The Equal Protection Clause is generally used to combat discriminatory laws and practices. Historically, the principal concern has been with discrimination directed against African Americans: segregated public schools, denial of voting rights, and segregated public accommodations. But the concept of equal protection has also been used to protect the rights of other groups: aliens, ethnic minorities, and women.

Technically, the Equal Protection Clause prohibits discrimination because the courts have interpreted the phrase "no State shall deny any person the equal protection of the laws" to mean in effect "no State shall deny any person the protection of *equal laws.*" In other words, a state legislature may not treat its citizens differently. The state must pass laws that apply equally to African Americans and whites, to Latinos and Anglos, and that do not single out any one group for favored treatment over another group. If a state legislature does pass a law favoring one group defined by an impermissible classification such as race, the courts will declare that law invalid.

This summary explanation of the meaning of equal protection bears qualification. Not all classifications of people violate equal protection. In fact, most do not. In a variety of contexts, state laws can and do single out different classes of citizens for different treatment. For example, residents of a state for more than a certain period (up to thirty days) are qualified to vote in state elections; those who have resided in the state for less than the stated time cannot vote in state elections. People over the age of sixteen who have passed a state driver's test may drive; people under age or sixteen, depending on state law, and those who have not passed the test (even if they could have) may not drive. Such distinctions are valid under the Equal Protection Clause.

Does the Equal Protection Clause prohibit discrimination by private individuals or private institutions?

No. The guarantee of equal protection is limited by the concept of *state action*. The Fourteenth Amendment provides that "no *State* shall deny . . . equal protection." The courts have interpreted those words to mean that only federal, state, and local governments are forbidden to discriminate. The prohibition covers a broad range of governmental activities—from passing discriminatory laws to engaging in discriminatory practices—but it is still limited to action in which the government is implicated. Thus, if a public school official decides to bar women from a physics class, even though there is no law requiring him or her to do so, this would be a prohibited *state practice.* But if a private school official made the same decision, it would not violate the Equal Protection Clause.[1]

State action sometimes reaches more activities than the above discussion indicates because some courts have found "state action" present when a government involved itself with or supported the activities of a private institution. And a private institution fulfilling functions normally considered governmental may under some circumstances be deemed to engage in state action. Thus, if the government provides most of the funds for building a private hospital, or if a private company owns a town where all of its employees live, the courts may say that both the hospital and the town are imbued with state action, even though they are nominally private institutions. The hospital and the company town will have to measure up to the standards of equal protection.

Understanding the state action concept is important for two reasons. First, where there is no state action, women will need other laws—such as Title VII, the federal law barring employment discrimination—to protect them against discrimination. Second, where there is state action, women may be able to challenge discriminatory practices although no law prohibits the specific practices. For instance, the women students who succeeded in integrating the originally all-male University of Virginia at Charlottesville were able to do so because it was a state school. Thus, women must be aware of the state action requirement when considering constitutional challenges to sex discrimination.

What tests has the Supreme Court used to determine whether a state law violates the Equal Protection Clause?

The Supreme Court has used three distinct tests. These are neither precise nor capable of mechanical application. In a shorthand way, they are often referred to as the "reasonableness" test, the "strict scrutiny" or "suspect classification" test, and the "intermediate test." Each test looks at (1) the government's purpose in passing the law and (2) the relationship between the purpose and the classification (black or white, man or woman, eighteen and over, or under eighteen) used to accomplish that purpose.

1. The Reasonableness Test. The test the Supreme Court has used in the majority of cases is basically a test of reasonableness. Did the state have a reasonable purpose in passing the law? Is there some difference between the two classes of people that makes it reasonable to treat them differently? If the answer to both questions is yes, the law is valid.

While the approach sounds fair, it has proven virtually meaningless because of the Court's refusal, in most cases, to apply the test to the facts in any serious sense. The Court will even make up or accept a spurious purpose for the law in order to justify differential treatment. A classic example of manipulating "state purpose" to uphold a state law as reasonable occurred in a famous sex discrimination case. In 1949 the Supreme Court said that Michigan could prohibit all women from holding bartender jobs without violating the Equal Protection Clause because the state's purpose was to prevent moral and social problems, and prohibiting women from bartending was a reasonable way to prevent those problems. Both steps in this reasoning were fallacious. The Court assumed without proof that Michigan had this purpose, and it ignored the more obvious state purpose, which was undoubtedly to permit male bartenders to monopolize the industry. The law therefore should have been invalidated—for the desire to treat equals unequally cannot be a reasonable purpose under the Equal Protection Clause.

The Court's second step was to assume—again without supporting facts—that women bartenders cause "moral and social problems," which men bartenders do not cause and which will be prevented if the state keeps women from holding these jobs. At first blush, this reasoning may have a certain logical appeal. Women cause problems; if you remove the women, you remove the problems. The logic falls apart when one realizes that the Court was indulging in pure speculation. How do we know there really were any problems? Even if problems existed, is it likely that women were the sole cause? The phrase "moral and social problems" was probably a euphemism for illicit sex. If this is the problem, why not exclude men from bars rather than exclude women from bartending? Better yet, why not simply demand that bar owners take measures—directed equally against both the male and female participants—to prevent illicit sex bars and any attendant disruption? The Court's analytical weakness in examining this law lay in its willingness to make up nonexistent facts to support its assumptions and in

its refusal to examine alternatives. In short, when the Court
"applies" the reasonableness test, it generally mentions the test
as a cover for the fact that it is ducking the real issues, thus
giving states free rein to discriminate.[2]

2. The strict scrutiny or suspect classification test. The second test developed by the Supreme Court to decide whether
a state law violates the Equal Protection Clause is the most
stringent test, at the other end of the spectrum from the rational
basis test. It is a test that the Court has generally applied to
racially discriminatory laws or to laws affecting certain fundamental rights, such as the right to vote. Consequently, experts
say that use of the test is triggered by a law that sets up a
"suspect classification" (e.g., treating blacks and whites differently) or by one that affects fundamental rights. The test itself
is called "strict scrutiny" because the Court examines the law
very closely. The questions are (1) Does the state have a compelling purpose of "overriding public importance" in the law?
(2) Is the classification established by the law necessary to
accomplish that purpose? That is, both the law's purpose and
the differences between the two classes of people affected by
the law are looked at very critically.

It is extremely difficult to show that a law is valid under this
test. For example, most states cannot prove that their purpose
in passing a law was of "overriding public importance" rather
than merely "reasonable." Similarly, it is much more difficult
to prove that a particular way of categorizing people is "necessary" in order to achieve the state's purpose than that it is a
reasonable way to do so. Consequently, the Supreme Court
tends to find laws unconstitutional when it uses this test. For
this reason, women's rights advocates long pushed to have the
Court consider sex a "suspect classification," thus requiring use
of the strict scrutiny test when examining laws or practices that
discriminate on the basis of sex. The Court, however, has
repeatedly refused to do so.

An example of this approach is found in the Supreme Court's
analysis of a Florida law that made sexual conduct between an
African American person and a white person illegal, although
the same conduct was not illegal if the two persons were either
both African American or both white.[3] The state of Florida
argued that its purpose in passing the law was to maintain
sexual decency. But the Supreme Court could not find any

differences between persons engaging in interracial sex and those engaging in intraracial sex that made it necessary to single out the first group for criminal punishment. In other words, the classification—treating the two groups differently—was not necessary in order for the state to achieve its claimed purpose of maintaining sexual decency. Therefore, the law was invalid because it denied, without a valid reason, the protection of equal laws to persons who engaged in interracial sex.

3. *The intermediate test.* In 1976 the Supreme Court announced a third equal protection test that, thus far, has applied primarily, though not exclusively, to sex discrimination cases. This test is situated between the rational basis test on the one end and strict scrutiny on the other; thus, the test is referred to as the "intermediate" or "middle tier" test. It provides that classifications by sex are constitutional only if they (1) serve "important government objectives" and (2) are *closely and substantially related* to the achievement of those objectives. When deciding whether any law that treats people differently because of their sex is constitutional, the Court now asks two questions: Does the law further an important goal of the government? Is the different treatment of men and women closely and substantially related to the achievement of that goal? (If the law could be written to deal with the problem along functional lines without referring to sex, the answer to the second question is probably no.) If the answer to either of these questions is no, the law is unconstitutional.

The Supreme Court first applied the new test in *Craig v. Boren.*[4] The case involved an Oklahoma law that prohibited the sale of 3.2 beer or "near" beer (with a lower alcohol content) to young men under twenty-one years old, but to young women who were under eighteen. The male plaintiff argued that it violated the Equal Protection Clause to treat eighteen- to twenty-year-old men and women differently. Oklahoma attempted to justify the law to the Supreme Court as a measure to improve traffic safety—a worthy state objective. After examining Oklahoma's statistics on "driving while intoxicated," the Court concluded that the statistical differences in the behavior of young men and women were too insignificant to justify denying beer to the young men. Thus, although driving safety might be an important purpose to Oklahoma, treating men and women differently in allowing them to buy 3.2 beer was not really closely and substantially related to the accomplishment of the state's purpose. Other efforts—such as improved education about the dangers of drinking and driving, and better enforcement of drunk-driving laws—would have a more direct effect on traffic safety.

What relevance do these equal protection tests have to women's rights?

Prior to the development of the intermediate test, the Supreme Court's decision about which test to apply almost invariably determined the outcome of the case. If it used the reasonableness test, the state law was valid. If it used the strict scrutiny test, the law was invalid. Since in the past the Court almost always used the reasonableness test when examining sexually discriminatory laws, it almost always upheld these laws. Moreover, the Court has never declared sex a suspect classification, like race, that would automatically require "strict scrutiny." In May 1973, the high water mark, four of nine Justices voted to apply this stringent standard to a sexually discriminatory military benefits law.[5] A majority did not emerge for this position, perhaps because some Justices were waiting at the time to see whether the Equal Rights Amendment passed before applying the strict scrutiny standard.

Meanwhile, the intermediate test ensures that the Court will take a more critical look at sexually discriminatory laws than it did in the past when it simply used the reasonableness test and usually found the laws valid. For example, the intermediate test was used by the Court in a 1979 decision to strike down an Alabama statute that required only husbands to pay alimony to their ex-spouses. (See discussion of this case in chapter 4, "Family Law.") Although the intermediate test is an improvement over the old reasonableness test, it still allows the Court a great deal of latitude in deciding cases. It provides no guarantee in the 1990s—particularly as the courts, especially the Supreme Court, become more conservative and less concerned with the protection of civil rights and civil liberties in general—that sexually discriminatory laws will be struck down.[6]

Does the Equal Protection Clause prohibit pregnancy-based discrimination?

No. The Equal Protection Clause does not protect women

against what is probably the most persistent and difficult form of sex discrimination: pregnancy discrimination. In 1974 the Supreme Court did an extraordinary thing. In a case called *Geduldid v. Aiello*,[7] the Court held that under the Constitution discrimination on the basis of pregnancy is *not* sex discrimination. The case involved a California state mandated disability program that replaced workers' wages for every type of physical disability that prevented them from working except for disability periods arising from normal pregnancy and delivery. It is not clear how the Court would rule on a state law that specifically burdened pregnant women, as opposed to one that denies them a benefit. Congressional actions making pregnancy discrimination equivalent to sex discrimination in the employment context (see chapter 2) may make a difference in some outcomes. The Court, however, has so far refused to extend equal protection clause prohibitions to pregnancy discrimination. The Court has also refused to view abortion rights cases as violating the Equal Protection Clause or as constituting sex discrimination, seeing them instead in terms of the right to privacy. (See chapter 5, "Reproductive Freedom.")

Are there other major areas where the Supreme Court has refused to apply the usual equal protection test in sex discrimination cases?

Yes. The Supreme Court has refused to apply equal protection analysis to cases in which the government claims a national security interest, including almost all cases involving the military. Specifically, in 1981 the Supreme Court refused to invalidate the all male draft registration which was challenged on grounds of sex discrimination.[8] Issues concerning women and the military are discussed more fully below in chapter 11, "The Military."

Is there any way women can assert their constitutional right to equal treatment without the ERA?

Definitely. Women can continue to bring lawsuits challenging unequal treatment under the Equal Protection Clause of the Fourteenth Amendment. No lawsuit is guaranteed to win, but the chances are much better than they were twenty years ago. Nor are all courts the same. Some federal and state court judges are much more likely than others to give women relief.

The Supreme Court of California, for example, has adopted the "strict scrutiny" test of equal protection for laws discriminating against women, so it should be easier there and in some other state court systems to win lawsuits based on the state constitution's equal protection clause.

Is it possible to assert the right to equal treatment without bringing a lawsuit?

Legal rights can be asserted in informal discussions and negotiations with officials or even in demonstrations and publicity engendering events. Merely raising a question of the legality of the actions of public officials will sometimes have a positive effect on those actions: public officials do not like to be accused of discrimination. And an indication of a readiness to pursue lawsuits may convince officials that a person is serious about a claim for fair treatment.

Are there any other federal constitutional rights women can use?

Many other sections of the Constitution will be useful in fighting important women's issues. For example, the right to privacy is derived from several amendments and has been used to establish the right to practice birth control and to choose abortion and thus the right for women to control their own bodies. The Due Process Clause of the Fourteenth Amendment may be invoked in a number of situations. But this chapter has focused on the concept of equal treatment because that problem has pervaded most of the issues that have concerned women in the last twenty years. It is thus essential to understand equal protection in order to recognize its application to different problems—and to apply it vigorously when necessary.

Does the Constitution address the more subtle barriers to women's equality?

No. The Constitution, as interpreted by the Supreme Court, addresses itself to overt intentional discrimination.[9] It does not deal with the myriad of subtle and complex barriers to women's equality, such as societal sexism, the lack of pregnancy and other disability leave policies, the lack of decent and affordable child care, and programs to care for the elderly and the ill. These are burdens that fall disproportionately on women and

burden them in the struggle for social, political, and economic
equality in this society, but they must be addressed through
legislative and other political action.

STATE EQUAL RIGHTS PROVISIONS

**Are there any state constitutional provisions that prohibit
sex discrimination?**

Yes. Sixteen states—Alaska, Colorado, Connecticut, Hawaii,
Illinois, Maryland, Massachusetts, Montana, New Hampshire,
New Mexico, Pennsylvania, Texas, Utah, Virginia, Washington, and Wyoming—have adopted equal rights provisions in
their state constitutions.[10]

Also, New Jersey in effect adopted an equal rights amendment in 1947 when it amended the equal protection provision
in its constitution to apply to "persons" instead of "men."[11]
Similarly, California interprets the general equal protection
clause in its constitution to prohibit most forms of sex discrimination.

Women in these states may sometimes be more successful
in combating discriminatory state laws and practices if they rely
upon their state equal rights amendment rather than federal
constitutional provisions.

**Why can a state equal rights amendment offer more protec-
tion than the federal constitution?**

In our federal-state system of government, state courts are
free to interpret their own constitutions in ways that provide
more protection than the federal constitution; one way to think
of this is that the federal constitution and laws are a floor, but
not a ceiling. Because the federal Equal Rights Amendment
has never been enacted, the federal constitution does not bar
all sex-based distinctions in the law but only those that fail the
"intermediate scrutiny" test.

However, a state with an equal rights amendment has specifically recognized that sex-based distinctions should not be
permitted and thus will ordinarily be more likely to strike down
sex-based laws under the state ERA than the federal court
would be under the federal equal protection clause.

What is the standard of review used by courts for state ERAs?

Many state courts employ a higher standard of review in sex discrimination cases brought under the state's ERA than the federal courts use in equal protection cases. The higher standard of review used by some state courts for state ERA claims makes it easier to challenge discrimination in those states. The actual standard of review used differs depending on how the court in that state has interpreted its ERA.

High courts in three states—Maryland, Pennsylvania, and Washington[12]—have ruled that all sex-based classifications are prohibited because the ERA imposes a standard higher than the traditional strict scrutiny standard used for racial classifications, an absolute standard that eliminates sex as a factor in determining legal rights. (The only exception is in discrimination based on physical characteristics—see the question below on ERAs and reproductive rights.) For example, the Pennsylvania Supreme Court declared in one of its first cases interpreting the ERA that "[t]he thrust of the Equal Rights Amendment is to insure equality of rights under the law and to eliminate sex as a basis for distinction."[13]

In eight states—Colorado, Connecticut, Hawaii, Illinois, Massachusetts, New Hampshire, Texas, and Virginia—courts have ruled that sex discrimination should be treated like race discrimination and therefore consider sex a "suspect" classification and apply a strict scrutiny test.[14] The use of this test results in the invalidation of all gender-based distinctions, except, in some states, those based on physical characteristics. The two states mentioned above that do not have an ERA, California and New Jersey, offer this level of protection under the general equal protection clause in their state constitutions. In fact, California's broad interpretation of its constitution in 1971 led the way for the United States Supreme Court to begin invalidating laws that discriminated on the basis of sex.[15] In New Jersey, courts have said that its equal protection clause offers "comparable or superior protection" to the Fourteenth Amendment.[16]

Utah uses only the intermediate standard of review, identical to the federal standard under the Fourteenth Amendment.[17] Alaska uses a "sliding scale" determined by how the court assesses the importance of the rights asserted and how suspiciously the court views the classification scheme.[18] It is applied in such a way that gender based statutes usually are invalidated.

In three states with an ERA—Montana, New Mexico, and Wyoming—there has not yet been enough litigation under the ERA to define a standard.

Can state ERAs be used to prohibit nongovernmental discrimination?

Six state ERAs—Colorado, Hawaii, Illinois, New Hampshire, Virginia, and Wyoming—expressly apply only to instances where governmental action is involved.[19] On the other hand, Montana's ERA is very broad and specifically prohibits discrimination by "any person, firm, corporation or institution."[20] In the other states, no state action is expressly required but in practice courts do not extend the ERA to cover all private discrimination. However, there are strong policy reasons[21] why a state ERA should prohibit more private discrimination. Advocates thus argue, sometimes successfully,[22] that less state involvement is required under state ERAs than under the federal constitution and that a state equal rights provision may regulate private conduct that cannot be reached under the Fourteenth Amendment.

Can state ERAs be used to prohibit discrimination that is unintentional?

Perhaps. In the preceding section of this chapter it was noted that the federal Equal Protection Clause applies only to situations of intentional (or facial) discrimination. It is not yet clear whether the same limitation will be true for state ERAs. Although some state courts have suggested that unintentional policies that have a disproportionate effect on women may be challenged under the state ERA, there have not yet been any instances where such a theory has been successfully used.[23] One commentator has persuasively argued that state ERAs should apply to all types of discrimination.[24]

What kind of cases have been brought under state ERAs?

The largest number of cases have arisen in the area of family law, perhaps because family law is considered the domain of state courts and state laws. For example, state ERAs have been used to invalidate different age minimums for marriage for men and women,[25] provide reciprocal grounds for divorce for husbands and wives,[26] expand the obligation for spousal support at divorce,[27] and invalidate common law presumptions that household goods acquired during marriage belong to the husband.[28] State ERAs have also been used to improve educational opportunities, both in the classroom and in athletic programming. For example, advocates used the Pennsylvania ERA to successfully challenge the "men only" admissions policy of a city high school.[29] The Pennsylvania ERA was also used to challenge the exclusion of women from the Pennsylvania Interscholastic Athletic Association (PIAA); in the years since this ruling in the early seventies, the number of female participants has increased in basketball, soccer, track and field, gymnastics, softball, field hockey, and lacrosse.[30] The Washington state ERA was also used to obtain better funding for female athletic programs at a state university.[31]

State ERAs have also been used to eliminate economic discrimination. For example, in Pennsylvania the ERA was used to eliminate gender differences in insurance rates.[32] And in Colorado it was used to challenge an employer health insurance policy that excluded from coverage medical expenses associated with normal pregnancy.[33]

Can state ERAs be used to expand reproductive rights?

Unfortunately, state ERAs have not been as successful in challenging restrictions on abortion. This is because some courts have decided that the ERAs do not apply to true physical differences between the sexes and thus, for example, have upheld the denial of Medicaid funding for abortions, as happened in Pennsylvania in 1985.[34] Another problem is that the right to abortion has been defined as a privacy right rather than as an equality right. However, as the Supreme Court becomes more willing to restrict abortion rights, state ERAs may increasingly become a source of protection for the right to choose. So far a few states have used state ERAs, often in conjunction with other state constitutional provisions, to challenge Medicaid funding restrictions.[35]

Can ERAs be used in other forms of advocacy besides litigation?

Yes. In some states the passage of the ERA spurred the state legislature to undertake a comprehensive reform of state laws to assure conformity with the ERA. For example, after the ERA was enacted in New Mexico, the legislature established an equal rights committee that reviewed all New Mexico laws and recommended revisions to eliminate discriminatory provisions; many of these revisions were eventually enacted.[36]

Furthermore, the presence of an equal rights amendment in a state can be a valuable tool in legislative and administrative advocacy. For example, the women's coalition in Montana, the first (and so far only) state to pass a law prohibiting gender-based insurance rates, used that state's equal rights amendment as one of the policy reasons why the legislation should be adopted.

NOTES

1. The decision might of course violate other laws. See chapter 8, "Education," for a discussion of Title IX of the Education Amendments of 1972.
2. In the late 1980s the Supreme Court began to indicate some willingness to apply a rational basis test with some bite to it. In a case called *City of Cleburne v. Cleburne Living Center*, 473 U.S. 432 (1985), the Court invalidated a zoning ordinance that barred a group home for retarded adults from a residential area. The Court held that "[t]he State may not rely on a classification whose relationship to an asserted goal is so attenuated as to render the distinction arbitrary or irrational." 473 U.S. at 446.
3. *McLaughlin v. Florida*, 379 U.S. 184 (1964).
4. 429 U.S. 190 (1976).
5. *Frontiero v. Richardson*, 411 U.S. 677 (1973). The Court invalidated the requirement that women in the military prove their husbands' dependency in order to get medical and housing benefits, while men received them automatically for their wives. The decision's sweeping language—women's legal status was once like that of slaves;" "romantic paternalism" has "put women not on a pedestal, but in a cage"—should have added to its impact but was never accepted by the full Court.
6. See, for example, *Rostker v. Goldberg*, 453 U.S. 57 (1981) (upholding federal law providing that men but not women must register for the draft); *Michael M. v. Superior Court of Sonoma County*, 450 U.S. 464 (1981)(upholding California statutory rape law making boys and men but not girls or women criminally liable for consensual sex with an

opposite-sex partner who is under the age of 18); *Geduldig v. Aiello*, 417 U.S. 484 (1974)(upholding California law providing workers' disability benefits to all disabled men, but not to women workers disabled by childbirth). And these were decisions of the Burger Court which still had a substantial liberal wing, not of the Rehnquist Court which increasingly does not.

7. 417 U.S. 484 (1974).

8. *Rostker v. Goldberg*, 453 U.S. 57 (1981).

9. *Personnel Adm. of Massachusetts v. Feeney*, 445 U.S. 901 (1980).

10. Alaska Const. art. I, § 3; Colo. Const. art. II, § 29; Conn. Const. art. I, § 20; Haw. Const. art. I, § 3; Ill. Const. art. I, § 18; Md. Const., Declaration of Rights, art. 46; Mass. Const. pt. 1, art. I; Mont. Const. art. II, § 4, N.H. Const. pt. 1, art. II; N.M. Const. art. II, § 18; Pa. Const. art. I, § 28; Tex. Const. art. I, § 3a; Utah Const. art. IV, § 1; Va. Const. art. I, § 11; Wash. Const. art. XXXI, § 1; Wyo. Const. art. I, §§ 2, 3, art. VI, § 1.

11. N.J. Const. art. I, ¶ 1. In *Peper v. Princeton University Board of Trustees*, 77 N.J. 55, 78 (1978), the New Jersey Supreme Court affirmed that the change from "men" to "persons" in the 1947 constitution granted women "rights of employment and property protection equal to those enjoyed by the men." *See* Note, *Rediscovering the New Jersey E.R.A.: The Key to Successful Gender Discrimination Litigation*, 17 Rutgers L.J. 253, 270-75 (1986)(discussion of 1947 constitutional convention).

12. *Rand v. Rand*, 374 A.2d 900, 903 (Md. 1977); *Henderson v. Henderson*, 327 A.2d 60 (Pa. 1974)(per curiam); *Darrin v. Gould*, 540 P.2d 882, 888 (Wash. 1975)(en banc).

13. *Henderson v. Henderson*, 327 A.2d 60, 62 (Pa. 1974)(per curiam).

14. *Civil Rights Comm'n v. Travelers Ins.*, 759 P.2d 1358 (Colo. 1989); *Page v. Welfare Comm'r*, 365 A.2d 1118 (Conn. 1976); *State v. Rivera*, 612 P.2d 526, 62 Haw. 120, 124 (1980); *People v. Ellis*, 311 N.E.2d 98 (Ill. 1974); *Attorney General v. Massachusetts Interscholastic Athletic Assn, Inc.*, 393 N.E.2d 284 (Mass. 1979); *Buckner v. Buckner*, 415 A.2d 871 (N.H. 1980); *In Interest of McLean*, 725 S.W.2d 696, 698 (Tex. 1987); *Mahan v. National Conservative Political Action Committee*, 315 S.E.2d 829, 832 (Va. 1984).

15. *Sail'er Inn, Inc. v. Kirby*, 485 P.2d 529, 539 (Cal. 1971). This decision struck down a provision of the state's business and professional code that prohibited the hiring of women as bartenders.

16. *New Jersey Shore v. Estate of Baum*, 417 A.2d 1003 (N.J. 1980). The only gender-based classifications that have been upheld are the limitations of statutory rape to females. *E.g.*, *State v. Thompson*, 430 A.2d 246 (N.J. Super. 1981).

17. *Pusey v. Pusey*, 728 P.2d 117 (Utah 1986)(invalidating a maternal preference in custody disputes).
18. *Keyes v. Humana Hospital Alaska, Inc.*, 750 P.2d 343, 357 (Alaska 1988).
19. *See generally* Avner, *Some Observations on State Equal Rights Amendments*, 3 Yale L. & Pol'y Rev. 144, 149–50 (1984); Heins, *The Marketplace and the World of Ideas: A Substitute for State Action as a Limiting Principle Under the Massachusetts Equal Rights Amendment*, 18 Suffolk U.L. Rev. 347 (1984).
20. Mont. Const. art. II, § 4.
21. The main reason is that the federal state action doctrine is based in part on federalism concerns and is narrowly construed to protect the states' traditional jurisdiction over private actions. *See* L. Tribe, *American Constitutional Law* 1691 (1988). That rationale is irrelevant to the interpretation of a state constitution.
22. *Burning Tree Club, Inc. v. Bainum*, 501 A.2d 817, 822 (Md. 1985); *Darrin v. Gould*, 540 P.2d 882, 891 (Wash. 1975) (en banc) (finding state action because the interscholastic sports system used public funds); *see Hartford Accident & Indemnity Co. v. Insurance Commissioner*, 482 A.2d 542, 549 (Pa. 1984).
23. There have been very few cases brought under state equal rights amendments that apply a disparate impact theory, although some courts have suggested that such a theory may be possible. *E.g.*, *Snider v. Thornburgh*, 436 A.2d 593, 601 (Pa. 1981).
24. Segal, *Sexual Equality, the Equal Protection Clause, and the ERA*, 33 Buffalo L. Rev. 85 (1984). In support of her position, Segal points to the fact that commissions established by states to guide the process of statutory compliance with constitutional equal rights provisions have defined the scope of their mandate to include facially neutral laws that have a potentially discriminatory impact.
25. *Phelps v. Bing*, 316 N.E.2d 775 (Ill. 1974).
26. *George v. George*, 409 A.2d 1 (Pa. 1979).
27. *Holmes v. Holmes*, 127 Pa. L.J. 196 (Ct. Common Pleas 1978).
28. *DiFlorido v. DiFlorido*, 331 A.2d 174 (Pa. 1975).
29. *Newberg v. Board of Public Education*, No. 5822 (C.P. Phila. County, August term, 1982). This particular case illustrates the usefulness of a state ERA since the same admissions policy at the same school had been challenged earlier, unsuccessfully, under the federal equal protection clause. *Vorchheimer v. School District of Philadelphia*, 532 F.2d 880 (3d Cir. 1976), *aff'd by an equally divided court*, 430 U.S. 703 (1977).
30. *Commonwealth v. Pennsylvania Interscholastic Athletic Association*, 334 A.2d 839 (Pa. Commw. Ct. 1975). *See also* Avner, *Some Observa-*

tions on State Equal Rights Amendments, 3 Yale L. & Pol'y Review 144, 163 & n. 90 (1984).

31. *Blair v. Washington State University*, 740 P.2d 1379 (Wash. 1987).

32. *Bartholomew v. Foster*, 563 A.2d 1390 (Pa. 1989).

33. *Colorado Civil Rights Comm'n v. Travelers Insurance Co.*, 759 P.2d 1358 (Colo. 1988).

34. *Fischer v. Department of Public Welfare*, 502 A.2d 114, 121 (Pa. 1985).

35. *Right to Choose v. Byrne*, 91 N.J. 287, 306 (1982)(denial of Medicaid funding "denies equal protection to those women entitled to necessary medical services under Medicaid"). In *Moe v. Secretary of Administration & Finance*, 417 N.E.2d 387 (Mass. 1981), the Massachusetts Supreme Judicial Court found that the state could not restrict public funding but based its ruling on privacy rather than the state ERA.

36. *See* Avner, *Some Observations on State Equal Rights Amendments*, 3 Yale L. & Pol'y Rev. 144, 146 & n.8 (1984).

II
Employment Discrimination

Despite many advances in the role of women in the American workplace since the enactment of the Civil Rights Act of 1964,[1] women continue to experience sex discrimination in employment. Statistics on the sex segregation of workers and on the undervaluation of women's wages, as well as the individual experiences of many women, suggest that many employers in the United States discriminate against women workers on a regular basis. This costs women a lot of money and is illegal as well, but it frequently saves employers money. Because of that harsh fact, few of these employers will stop discriminating if they can avoid doing so.

One of the goals of Title VII of the Civil Rights Act of 1964 was to overcome this pervasive employment discrimination against women. Nevertheless, women that represent a large and ever-growing proportion of the work force often remain confined to low-paying, low-status jobs with little or no opportunity for advancement. Some of the modest advances of the 1960s and 1970s are, despite new legislation, threatened with serious erosion because of the Reagan-led backlash of the 1980s.

Women have begun to fight against this reality, but many do not fully understand the mechanisms used to discriminate or the legal weapons available to attack them. To some extent, laws already on the books enable women to mount a major and systematic attack on discriminatory employment patterns throughout the United States with the aim of opening up more meaningful and better-paid jobs for all women. In some instances new or revitalized laws will be necessary before women can achieve true equality in the workplace. This chapter seeks to give women the basic information necessary to understand the present situation, to explain the laws that make discrimination illegal, to advise how to enforce them, and to suggest some strategies for their effective utilization. Chapter 3 will go into more detail about the vital issues of work and family.

What is job discrimination?

The answer to this question may appear obvious—but it isn't. Discrimination of the most conspicuous kind is shown by the employer who openly brags that he or she pays female sales-clerks less than male clerks or who tells a talented secretary that she'll never be promoted to a managerial position because he or she can't stand bossy women. But such blatant examples do not begin to tell the story. A Senate committee has described how discrimination in employment operates:

> In 1964, employment discrimination tended to be viewed as a series of isolated and distinguishable events, for the most part due to ill-will on the part of some identifiable individual or organization. It was thought that a scheme that stressed conciliation rather than compulsory process would be most appropriate for the resolution of this essentially "human" problem, and that litigation would be necessary only on an occasional basis in the event of determined recalcitrance. This view has not been borne out by experience.
>
> Employment discrimination, as viewed today, is a far more complex and pervasive phenomenon. Experts familiar with the subject generally describe the problem in terms of "systems" and "effects" rather than simply intentional wrongs, and the literature on the subject is replete with discussions of, for example, the mechanics of seniority and lines of progression, perpetuation of the present effects of pre-act discriminatory practices through various institutional devices, and testing and validation requirements. In short, the problem is one whose resolution in many instances requires not only expert assistance, but also the technical perception that a problem exists in the first place, and that the system complained of is unlawful.[2]

Women, too, must adopt this broader perspective. In the past, they have often complained about symptoms, not root causes. The emphasis has been on the individual, a specific woman who doesn't get a particular job or promotion. Or they have stressed the importance of equal pay for equal work. But attacking these obvious forms of discrimination will do little to change women's basic lot in the employment world. If women are serious about improving the situation, their major efforts must be directed toward something deeper.

What major concepts define job discrimination?

Before analyzing specific employment practices that discriminate against women, three basic factors operative in sex discrimination cases should be made clear.

First, any effort devoted exclusively toward solving the problem of an individual woman is likely to have minimal impact. By definition, discrimination is a class problem necessarily affecting large numbers of women—whether they be fifty women in a small company, five hundred thousand women in the AT&T system, or the millions of women workers nationwide. To illustrate, if an employer refuses to promote Susan Smith because she is a woman, that employer is really saying that all women in Susan's position are ineligible for the promotion. Susan's efforts should attack not only the particular decision not to promote her but also the general policy that fails to promote women. Unfortunately, women often neglect to fight the general policy. If a woman complains about discrimination, she understandably focuses on her own job opportunities. Those in a position to help her often adopt the same focus rather than translate her complaint into its broader framework: a policy of discrimination against the class of females. This means that women who are afraid to risk their jobs by complaining or who fail to perceive the discrimination go unhelped. When another woman complains, the whole process must be repeated. Moreover, it is far more difficult to prove discrimination against a particular woman than discrimination against many women. Companies can always find specific reasons for not promoting Susan Smith—she was late to work three days in a row or she failed to sharpen her employer's pencils. When the employer must give reasons for a failure to promote all women, the excuses are harder to manufacture.

Thus, the first rule should be to look for the way any sex discrimination problem affects other women. In legal terms, this generally means litigating on behalf of classes of women—class action lawsuits. Even before litigation, the problem must be visualized as one encountered by a class of women. It is not enough to help the individual while leaving the job market situation unchanged for other women.

A second basic point in examining employment bias is to regard sex segregation of jobs and the wage discrimination that accompanies it as the prime target rather than simply equal pay for equal work. Equal pay has been a rallying cry for women. The first major federal legislation against sex discrimination, the Equal Pay Act, embodied this concept. According to public opinion polls, most people now believe in equal pay. But equal pay for equal work is not the real problem. Women are paid less than men for doing the same work, of course, but most women don't do the work most men do. In 1988 women were still 99% of all secretaries, 99% of all dental assistants, 97% of all childcare workers, 95% of all nurses, and 90% of all telephone operators.[3]

The salaries in those jobs that remain predominantly female won't be raised by equal pay laws because there are so few male dental assistants, child care workers, nurses, telephone operators, and secretaries. If a given employer has no male employees who get paid more than female employees for the same work, there is no way for the women in those jobs to claim they are getting unequal pay under the Equal Pay Act.

The statistics above show that some jobs are almost always performed by women. Women are also almost totally *excluded* from many male-dominated jobs, many of them higher paying. For example, the same 1988 statistics showed that men were 99% of all auto mechanics and carpenters, 98% of all firefighters, 97% of all pilots, and 95% of all welders. With some occasional exceptions, women also tend to be excluded from the upper-level white collar jobs in administration and business management. We must learn to recognize this situation for what it is: sex segregation of the job market. Certain jobs are typed female—generally low-paying repetitive jobs. Other jobs are male—often paying more and in many cases offering a chance to be creative as well. Sometimes the sex-typing of the job changes: prior to the advent of typewriters, secretaries were predominantly male; indeed the vestigial word for the rare female in that job was *secretress*. But jobs are very frequently sex-typed, one way or the other, and whenever the job turns out to be female, it also turns out to be low-paying.

To summarize, the legal standard of "equal pay for equal work" requires that there are men workers to compare with women workers, that both do work that is substantially the same, and that both work in the same place. Only if all conditions are present does the employer have to increase female wages to the level of male wages. If women and men are segregated into very different, or unequal, kinds of work, a demand for equal pay is futile. Since workers *are* segregated by sex in this country, women must switch their focus from equal pay, as it is now defined, and concentrate instead on the integration of jobs and on increasing the wage level of the "female jobs."

Integrating jobs will open up more interesting work to women, who will then command the higher pay that goes with such work. Real integration will also help change the wage structure because as men enter traditionally female jobs the pay level of these jobs should rise. The classic example is the rise in pay and status of secondary school teachers and social workers as men entered these fields.

It is not enough, however, to hope for a better wage structure as a side effect of integration. The wage structure itself must also be attacked in order to help, right now, the women who have already been shunted into the low pay of "women's work." Traditionally female jobs do not pay less because the work is inherently worth less; they pay less in part because women do this work. Where the wage structure itself is discriminatory, women must seek court decisions that will end wage segregation by forcing employers to raise the pay scale for traditionally female jobs. (See questions and answers on pay discrimination when jobs are segregated below.) Of course, this will also have the effect of attracting more men to these jobs, thus promoting job integration. The pattern goes full circle.

Another fundamental concept is that many employment policies are illegal, even though they appear to be fair on the surface and even though the company never *intended* to discriminate. An example of such a policy is the decision of a large company to upgrade the educational level of its labor force by hiring only college graduates. This appears to be fair policy—it seems to apply equally to everyone, female and male, black and white— and it may be that in the company has no intention of discriminating. But is it a fair policy? First of all, until very recently more men received college educations than women. And the percentage of whites with college educations far exceeds the percentage of blacks. Thus, the effect of the policy is the exclusion of a disproportionate number—relative to the labor force as a whole—of women and of blacks from jobs with the company. The effect, not the intention, of the policy is discriminatory. Furthermore, it is important to point out that the company may not have a bona fide reason for discriminating in this way. It may have never conducted a study to see whether a college education is really necessary to do the jobs. In fact, many current employees—persons hired before the new policy was established—probably do not have college degrees, which indicates that a college degree is not necessary. These two factors—the discriminatory effect of the policy and the lack of any real business need for it—render the policy as unlawful as the practice of an employer who refuses to promote a secretary because he or she can't tolerate women in positions of authority. In 1971 the Supreme Court ruled in *Griggs v. Duke Power Company* a case involving discrimination against blacks, that a policy of the kind just described is illegal.[4]

Another example of such a policy is a company's refusal to hire unwed parents. Again, the policy appears at first blush to be evenhanded. But it affects more women than men because it is easier for men to hide the fact that they are unwed parents and because women more often have the custody and care of children born out of wedlock. An employer, moreover, would be hard pressed to show that the legitimacy of one's children affects work performance.

Lawyers often refer to this concept as the *neutral rule* or *disparate impact* doctrine, by which they mean that any employment policy appearing to be facially neutral but which in fact adversely affects employment opportunities of women or of a minority group is discriminatory. Under the *Griggs* ruling, if the employer has no provable business justification (which lawyers refer to as *business necessity*) for a policy, it constitutes illegal discrimination. This legal concept is at the very core of antidiscrimination law and is used over and over in different situations against different employment policies.

Unfortunately, in 1989 the Supreme Court handed down another decision, *Wards Cove Packing Company v. Atonio*,[5] that made it much more difficult for women, racial minorities, and others affected by this type of "disparate impact" discrimination to prove their cases in court. In *Wards Cove*, the burden was on the women or minorities who suffer the discrimination to show that the policies or practices that disproportionately exclude them from the workplace are not a business necessity. Furthermore, the 1989 decision held that the practice in question need not be related to the ability to perform the job successfully; it need only advance some "legitimate goal" of the employer. Fortunately, Congress overwhelmingly passed the Civil Rights Act of 1991 to overturn this and several other such decisions that undermined the Civil Rights Act of 1964. Thus, the important disparate impact doctrine is now once again the law. For further details, see the section below on The Civil Rights Act of 1991.

In conclusion, three general approaches should be kept in mind when attacking discriminatory employment practices. The first is to look for the way discrimination affects a large class of women, not just an individual. The second is to strive for the elimination of sex segregation of jobs and undervaluation of women's wages. And finally is to target not only obviously discriminatory policies, but to carefully examine apparently neutral policies for discriminatory effects. With these basic concepts in mind, we can turn to the specifics of job discrimination.

Under what laws is it illegal to discriminate against women workers?

Four major federal laws and a myriad of state and city laws forbid such discrimination. The federal laws are Title VII of the 1964 Civil Rights Act (generally referred to as Title VII), as amended by the Pregnancy Discrimination Act of 1978 and by the Civil Rights Act of 1991; the Equal Pay Act; Executive Order 11246 (as amended by Executive Order 11375); and the Age Discrimination Act of 1967. Teachers have additional relief under Title IX of the Education Amendments of 1972[6] (see chapter 8, "Education").

What is the most important law prohibiting sex discrimination?

Title VII of the 1964 Civil Rights Act is the most far-reaching law and has the greatest potential for bringing about change in employment practices. In fact, the three key concepts of job discrimination—its class effects, the necessity to challenge sex segregation, and the "neutral rule doctrine" are all concepts that developed under Title VII.

TITLE VII OF THE 1964 CIVIL RIGHTS ACT

Is it ever explicitly legal to limit jobs to persons of one sex?
Rarely. This question arises because of a particular provision in Title VII that allows an employer to hire people of one sex only if it can prove that being a person of that sex is a "bona fide occupational qualification." In legal jargon, this provision is referred to as the BFOQ, and it is the only legal justification for limiting a job to members of one sex. When a woman tries to get a "man's job," (or, for that matter, when a man applies for a "woman's job") the employer opposing the claim will sometimes contend that being one sex or the other is a BFOQ for that job.

After an initial period of uncertainty about whether Title VII protects women in a meaningful way, it seems the BFOQ actually does not have much practical significance despite frequent references to it. Judges have usually found that a contested job can be reserved for men or reserved for women only in very rare cases. In general, the employer must show that the job duties one sex cannot perform are part of the very "essence" of the business and that all or substantially all of the members of the excluded sex cannot perform these job duties, or that it is impossible to make individual determinations. In *Dothard v. Rawlinson*,[7] for example, the Supreme Court approved an all-male BFOQ for the position of guard in Alabama's maximum security prisons. The reason: Alabama's prisons were found to be "constitutionally intolerable" places of "rampant violence," a "jungle atmosphere" with sex offenders scattered throughout the inmate population. The Court reasoned that in this setting women guards would be peculiarly subject to sexual assault and thus unable to do their job of maintaining order. Whatever one thinks of this stereotypical reasoning, this case has not created a dangerous precedent for women's ability to obtain previously all-male jobs since few employers, even among prison administrators, meet the "standard" of the Alabama prisons![8]

The BFOQ defense has been successful, however, in a few

cases where the employer has asserted it based upon considerations of the privacy and modesty of its customers or other third persons. These include jobs such as washroom attendants or certain kinds of nurses.[9] In a variation on the privacy theme in another case, prison officials successfully argued for the exclusion of male guards in a women's prison as necessary to the rehabilitation of the female inmates, many of whom had suffered sexual abuse at the hands of men.[10]

Apart from these exceptions, courts have taken a very narrow view of the BFOQ defense. A typical example of this narrow judicial approach to the BFOQ occurred when a lower federal court declared that only when a sexual characteristic itself is necessary to do the job can the employer refuse to hire people of the opposite sex.[11] The court used the example of a wet nurse. Someone who employs wet nurses can refuse to hire men in general, without considering their individual characteristics, since having breasts is necessary to do the job. Female sex in this rare instance would be a BFOQ.

Acting jobs are mentioned frequently as suitable candidates for requiring one sex as a BFOQ on the ground that one sex may be necessary to make a role seem authentic or genuine. This example has never been tested in court, however, but if we remember Shakespeare's day, when boys were used to portray women in plays, even this example may not be accepted by the courts.

Wage Discrimination

When men and women are segregated into different jobs, but the jobs are worth the same to the employer, can the employer pay the women less than the men?

Despite the fact that job segregation is illegal, it persists. And while it is extremely important to integrate one-sex jobs, such integration is likely to take many years to accomplish. In the meantime it is also important to attack the wage structure of all-female jobs if we want to change women's low economic status in the job market. Almost thirty years after passage of the Civil Rights Act, national statistics show women workers have made very little progress in increasing their low salaries as compared to men—on the average, women now earn 65 cents for every dollar earned by a man. (Until very recently it

was 59 cents.) Many discrimination experts believe the reason
is the historic and systematic undervaluation, on the basis of
sex, of wages in all-female jobs. Whether this is illegal is not
clear, although the Supreme Court removed one important
stumbling block to the goal of making it illegal in a 1981 case,
County of Washington v. Gunther.[12] (As we shall see, however,
several lower courts have placed other barriers in the way of
women challenging discriminatory wage setting rules.) Alberta
Gunther and three other women prison guards at the Washington County jail in Oregon sued their employer under Title VII
for paying them less than male prison guards. The lowest-
paid man earned more than the highest-paid woman, and the
plaintiffs claimed that at least part of the differential was based
on sex. The county defended the suit by showing that the
women guarded fewer prisoners and therefore spent more time
doing clerical tasks than the men did. In other words, although
the men's and women's jobs were roughly similar, they were
not the same job. The Equal Pay Act, by its terms, would not
reach a sex-based wage differential of this sort, because the
statute is narrowly drawn to outlaw unequal rates of pay based
on sex only where a man and woman are performing essentially
the same job. The county argued that Title VII should be
interpreted in the same narrow way and that the women should
therefore lose their lawsuit.

The women guards contended that wage discrimination can
occur even where men and women are segregated into different
jobs. In their case, for example, they claimed the county had
evaluated the work of all guard jobs and that the evaluation
showed the women should be paid approximately 95% of the
male rate. Instead, the men received full value under the
evaluation while the women received less than full value at
only 70% of the male rate rather than the 95% they should have
received. They claimed the failure to pay them full value was
based on their sex and that Title VII was written more broadly
than the Equal Pay Act and could be interpreted to cover the
practice.

The Supreme Court agreed with the women, ruling that
nothing in Title VII requires a showing that a man and woman
are performing the same job, or "equal work," before the
woman can prove the existence of sex-based discrimination in
her wages. The importance of the case lies in its firm rejection

of the view that Title VII is no broader than the Equal Pay Act. However, many troubling issues remain to be resolved. The Court sent Alberta Gunther and the other guards back to a lower court for a chance to prove their claim that men got full evaluation value while women got less. But the Court specifically said that even if the women proved these claims, the Court was not ready to rule on whether such facts violate Title VII. The Court also refused to say whether courts can use statistical techniques or other methods to quantify the effect of sex discrimination on wage rates.

How can women prove they are being underpaid on the basis of sex when they are doing different work from that of men?

Although the Supreme Court's *Gunther* decision seemed to pave the way for further action on a variety of forms of wage discrimination, the problem that remains is how to prove that particular women's jobs are worth the same as the more highly paid men's jobs and that some portion of a wage differential is due to sex discrimination. On this problem the Court expressed no opinion except to allude to various methods strongly opposed by some employers. Court decisions since the *Gunther* ruling have not been particularly encouraging where women have sought to prove discrimination through the use of job evaluation studies.

Nevertheless, it is crucial to understand job evaluation because it remains an important tool for analyzing whether women have pay equity. Job evaluation is essentially the process of analyzing jobs and then awarding points to each job for various factors such as its skill, physical effort, responsibility, and working conditions. To illustrate, for the factor of responsibility, a job requiring the employee to supervise no employees might get 0 points, while supervising 1 to 5 employees would merit 5 points, and 6 to 100 employees, 10 points. Or for the factor of physical effort, no lifting would merit 0 points, lifting 10 to 15 pounds at irregular intervals, 5 points, and lifting 15 to 50 pounds regularly, 10 points. A host of similar questions are asked for all jobs, and the points are added for each job. As a result, the persons holding the jobs with the highest number of points should get the highest salaries.

In the lawsuits decided since the *Gunther* case involving

these evaluations, the employers chose not to adhere to the point rating after completing it. The most famous case involving job evaluation plans was brought by the American Federation of State, County, and Municipal Employees (AFSCME) challenging the wage-setting mechanisms of the state of Washington. In *AFSCME v. Washington*,[13] the union brought a Title VII sex-based compensation case on behalf of state employees who worked in job categories that were at least 70% female. The state had generally set salaries for its workers after conducting surveys of prevailing market wages for the jobs in question. In 1974, however, the state commissioned a study to find out if a wage disparity existed between workers employed in jobs held predominantly by women and those in jobs held predominantly by men. The study revealed, based upon job points for the factors of knowledge and skills, mental demands, accountability, and working conditions, that workers in female-dominated jobs were paid approximately 20% less than workers in male-dominated jobs of equal worth (i.e., having equal points) to the employer. Two similar studies in later years revealed similar results.

When the state refused to implement immediately an equal-worth pay scheme, the union brought suit and won in the trial court on the grounds of both intentional discrimination and the neutral rule or disparate impact theory. Unfortunately the court of appeals reversed the decision on both grounds. The appeals court ruled that the union could not use the neutral rule theory because it could only be applied to a "single practice," and basing pay on "market rates" was not such a practice.[14] The appeals court also ruled that the state had not engaged in intentional discrimination. The court said that it could not infer intentional discrimination from evidence that women and men had been segregated into different jobs and that women were paid less than men for jobs with the same point totals. The court concluded that an employer should be able to rely on the market to set wages and should not be bound to implement a job evaluation study. After the *AFSCME* decision, the parties agreed to a settlement. The workers did not get back pay, but the state agreed to a $482 million upgrade of the salaries of 34,000 employees. Since the *AFSCME* decision, however, other lower courts have issued similar rulings.[15]

Perhaps the most discouraging aspect of the *AFSCME* case

is that the appeals court opinion was written by Judge Anthony Kennedy who is now Justice Kennedy of the Supreme Court. Ultimately the Supreme Court will have to clarify this issue. The Court might close off certain kinds of wage discrimination cases—by ruling, for example, that job evaluation plans cannot be used to show that certain all-female jobs are being paid less than different all-male jobs on the basis of sex or that the disparate impact theory cannot be used in wage discrimination cases.

Is there another way to try to prove that women's wages in all-female jobs are depressed because of sex discrimination?

Yes, and this method may prove to be more successful in Title VII lawsuits than job evaluation studies. In 1986 the Supreme Court accepted the use of a statistical method for proving wage discrimination in a case involving black employees who had been underpaid because of their race. The case was *Bazemore v. Friday*,[16] and the method used by the plaintiffs was regression analysis, a way of sorting out the effect of various factors on salary. The plaintiffs' regression examined the influence of race, education, tenure, and job title, and showed that race did affect salary. After the *Bazemore* decision, women faculty at Yeshiva University also used a multiple regression analysis to prove that they were underpaid based on their sex compared to male faculty doing work in a different kind of department; men were concentrated in the higher paid clinical departments while women were in the lower paid preclinical departments.[17] Thus, this method may offer hope to other women as a method of addressing systemic wage discrimination through litigation. For further information on the use of regression analysis to prove sex discrimination in wages, readers should consult Clauss, "Comparable Worth—The Theory, Its Legal Foundation, and the Feasibility of Implementation."[18] Of course, anyone who is attempting to address serious wage inequities through litigation will need the help of experienced Title VII litigators as well as a large number of committed women coworkers.

What other steps can be taken by women who want to attack this form of wage discrimination?

Women can take many steps besides filing charges with

the Equal Employment Opportunity Commission (EEOC) and starting lawsuits. (See the Enforcement section below for instructions for filing such charges). On the national level, if the Supreme Court ever adopts a rule that makes it impossible to show that a sex-based undervaluation of women's wages in sex-segregated jobs violates Title VII, an amendment to Title VII should be pressed, based on laws of Canada and three of its provinces that explicitly require equal pay for work of equal value. On a state level, women can file lawsuits under state fair employment practice laws and strive for amended state laws. They can also push their unions to take action or, in the absence of unions, organize with other women to bargain with their employer. Other suggestions include a request for a job evaluation plan, where there is none to date, and close scrutiny of existing job evaluation plans. Scrutiny is necessary to determine whether some job elements common to men's jobs (e.g., weight lifting) have been overrated in value and other job elements common to women's jobs (e.g., the manual dexterity, speed, and attention to detail needed for typing) have been underrated. Close attention is also needed to see that all elements of women's job are given points or that men are not given points for tasks they do not perform. These cautionary notes illustrate some of the ways job evaluation plans can be skewed against women. So while the plans can be helpful, women must be aware of their negative side and must therefore be fully involved in the job evaluation process to ensure that the results accomplish something.

Are there any organizations that can provide help on this issue?

A coalition of women's and labor groups was formed in the early 1980s to push for fair wages. It is the

National Committee on Pay Equity
1126 16th St., N.W.,
Suite 411
Washington, D.C. 20036
(202) 331-7343

NCPE acts as a clearinghouse and has a wealth of publications on the subject. Its publication "Legislating Pay Equity to Raise Women's Wages: A Progress Report on the Implementation of the Ontario, Canada Pay Equity Act," has important information on Ontario's 1987 law requiring private and public employers to establish pay equity between male and female workers with *similar* jobs by using job evaluation studies. The Ontario law is also noteworthy in requiring all employers to take action to achieve pay equity without waiting for women workers to file complaints of discrimination. While the law does not reach all wage inequities because it is limited to situations where men and women perform similar work, it is broader than the U.S. Equal Pay Act, which requires pay equity only where men and women have the *same* jobs. Thus, it is a law that might profitably be copied in the United States at the state or local level. The NCPE can also provide information on other organizations that work on the issue of pay equity and wage discrimination.

Sexual Harassment

Is sexual harassment in the workplace illegal?

The testimony of Professor Anita Hill at the confirmation hearings for Supreme Court Justice Clarence Thomas dramatically brought the problem of sexual harrassment into public focus. Of course, working women have long been aware of this pervasive problem. Unwanted sexual advances, employment decisions based on acceptance or rejection of sexual favors, called *quid pro quo harassment*, and offensive remarks and pictures in the workplace, known as *hostile environment harassment*, are all-too-common features of women's employment, as Professor Hill made so clear in her testimony before the Senate Judiciary Committee on the Thomas nomination to the Supreme Court. A survey done in 1976 showed that 88% of the working women responding had experienced sexual harassment on the job.[19] More recent studies have shown little, if any, improvement in this picture.[20] The problem is serious—especially for women entering nontraditional employment with mostly male coworkers. Adressing the problem, the Supreme Court—in a case called *Meritor Savings Bank v. Vinson*[21]—clearly articulated that both forms of sexual harassment mentioned above are violations of Title VII.

What is the definition of sexual harassment on the job?

The EEOC has issued guidelines that define sexual harassment as follows.

Unwelcome sexual advances, requests for sexual favors, and other verbal or physical conduct of a sexual nature constitute sexual harassment when (1) submission to such conduct is made either explicitly or implicitly a term or condition of an individual's employment, (2) submission to or rejection of such conduct by an individual is used as the basis for employment decisions affecting such individual, or (3) such conduct has the purpose or effect of unreasonably interfering with an individual's work performance or creating an intimidating, hostile, or offensive working environment.[22]

Thus under the guidelines, in order to establish a violation of Title VII, a victim of harassment must show *one* of three things: (1) that she was forced to submit to sexual harassment in order to get or keep her job—even if this is "just understood" and not explicitly stated; (2) that submitting to or rejecting the harassment was the basis for an employment decision that affected the victim—the victim refused sexual advances and was fired, demoted, transferred, or given less favorable working conditions; (3) that the harassment itself was intended to or did interfere with the victim's work or created "an intimidating, hostile, or offensive working environment," whether or not there was any other unfavorable job action. It is important to remember that a woman's simply being subjected to a work environment that is offensive to her is enough basis for filing charges with the EEOC.

If a woman is subjected to sexual harassment but does not lose her job, can she get some kind of monetary award for "pain and suffering" and as punishment of the employer?

Yes, under the Civil Rights Act of 1991. In a major step forward, Congress finally decided that women can get damages for intentional employment discrimination, including sexual harassment cases. This is especially important in cases of hostile environment sexual harassment, in which women suffer no loss of wages. Before the new law was passed, the only remedy for women in that situation was a court order that the harassment cease and the employer enforce rules against it.

The new law allows women to sue for both compensatory damages (i.e., "pain and suffering") and punitive damages. Unfortunately, Congress also set a maximum limit on the amount of damages an individual woman can recover—a "cap" that does not apply in cases regarding race, national origin, and most religion claims. For further details, see the section on the Civil Rights Act of 1991 below.

In some states, however, women can recover full damages for sexual harassment, without any cap, under various legal theories. For example, women working as flag persons on an Iowa road construction crew were awarded $35,000 in damages under the Iowa Civil Rights Act for a "barrage of offensive conduct" waged by their male coworkers.[23] In Washington, D.C., a woman who worked as a marketing coordinator for an architecture and interior design firm sued under the D.C. Human Rights Act and also asserted claims based on breach of contract and intentional infliction of emotional distress, because her supervisor repeatedly asked her to provide sexual favors to clients and potential clients. She won $150,000 compensatory damages, $100,000 punitive damages, and attorney's fees and costs, for a total recovery of $489,500.[24] And a New Jersey woman was awarded $1500 under state law from each of five coworkers and supervisors who repeatedly mocked her with remarks about her virginity and marital status, posted offensive cartoons, blocked her way physically, and subjected her to other offensive actions.[25]

Can an employer be held liable for harassment by supervisors and coworkers even if he or she was unaware of it?

Although the Supreme Court did not directly address this issue in *Meritor Savings Bank,* it did say that courts should follow the general laws about agency. Using that approach, lower courts have generally found the employer liable for anything supervisors do, even if the company does not know about it or has rules against it. If an employer fires an employee for refusing sexual advances, the company will have to pay. The answer is less clear in the case of sexual harassment (usually of the hostile environment type) by coworkers, customers, or clients. In that instance the employer may be held liable, but only if he or she knows or should know what is going on. This would be the case if the employee complained to management about what was happening or if it was obvious to see.

What steps should women take to protect themselves against sexual harassment?

Although the Supreme Court has fully recognized sexual harassment as a form of employment discrimination, lower courts are often still reluctant to impose liability. They may feel that men are entitled this behavior, that women flirt and invite advances, or that men do not know what is prohibited conduct. In this climate, in addition to filing charges with the EEOC, it is important to take steps that might help eradicate the conduct.

First, a woman must say no in very clear terms. If the first refusal does not eliminate the problem, she then must inform management *in writing* of the problem, asking them to take steps to end it and indicating that the conduct in question violates Title VII. A lawyer or advisor should be consulted at the earliest possible stage. Copies of all correspondence to and from management and immediate, detailed notes about conversations with anyone about the subject should be kept. These documents and notes may be important later on if the situation comes down to her word versus his or if the company tries to deny knowledge of the problem, thereby avoiding liability under Title VII. Finally, charges should be filed with the EEOC if all else fails, or as soon as the victim is denied a promotion, fired, or given a bad evaluation.

Work Conditions

May a company give "light work" to women and "heavy work" to men?

No. Companies historically indulged in this practice; however, since light work is generally paid less than heavy work, there is obvious discrimination against women. The practice was one of the first that women workers attacked under Title VII. One famous case involved the Colgate-Palmolive Company. Before Title VII was passed, Colgate-Palmolive completely segregated its women workers into light work and its men workers into heavy work, with the highest pay for light work less than the lowest pay for heavy work. After the new law passed, the company decided to allow men to do light work (giving them an advantage in times of layoff), but did not let women do the more highly paid heavy work. A federal court found this to be illegal and ordered that the women be paid all the money they had lost by their segregation into light work. [26]

May a company deny jobs, promotions, or overtime work to women because of state "protective" labor laws?

No. The so-called protective labor laws are a series of state laws passed since the beginning of the twentieth century to regulate women's—but not men's—work. It has become increasingly evident that these laws restrict more than protect women. Some forbid women to hold certain jobs, such as bartender or miner. Others assume that women do not want to work long hours or nights and consequently forbid them to do so. Still others, based on the assumption that all women are physically weak, declare that no woman may lift moderate or heavy weights or work before and after childbirth. Of course these laws do not prohibit the unpaid housewife from working under such conditions; only the paid worker is "protected." And many of the "protections" are inapplicable to the least desirable "female" jobs—night work is seldom closed to charwomen. These facts provide a clue to the real effect of such "protective" laws. Companies use them to deny women jobs, and women workers have used Title VII to attack this practice.

The most famous case involved Lorena Weeks, a worker at Southern Bell Telephone, who bid for the more lucrative switchman job. The company denied her bid, claiming she would have to lift a thirty-pound fire extinguisher, which the Georgia law on weight lifting for women forbade. (The company conveniently forgot that she already had to lift a thirty-five-pound typewriter.) After several years of litigation, Lorena won the job, and $30,000 as well, to compensate her for lost wages. [27]

Other women have challenged laws forbidding overtime work (at lucrative overtime pay rates) and closing certain jobs to women, and they have all won their lawsuits even though the companies argued that male sex was a BFOQ for the work or jobs the women were trying to get. The federal courts have flatly rejected this claim and have ordered the companies to stop using these laws to discriminate against women workers. And the courts have been joined by the EEOC, the federal agency that administers Title VII. In convincing employers or unions of the illegality of such laws, the best legal precedents to show them are the EEOC regulations,[28] the *Weeks* case, and the case of *Rosenfeld v. Southern Pacific Railroad Company*,[29] which determined that an employer must give individual women the opportunity to show that they are physically qualified for a job involving physical strength and may not refuse to hire all women on the basis that many women could not meet the physical requirements.

May a company refuse to hire women because it must provide them with seats or lunch breaks under state labor laws, which may be expensive to provide?

No. An EEOC ruling asserts that not only must the company hire women in these circumstances but it must also provide these benefits to men.[30]

Other items provided for by state laws of this kind are ten-minute rest periods, restrooms, a minimum wage, and premium pay for overtime work. The last two provisions are generally available for men workers; in fact, the federal minimum wage and overtime pay law covers both men and women, and at a higher rate than all but one state law. But some men workers are not covered by the federal law and should benefit from the few state laws making such benefits available to women only—an obvious category is male agricultural workers. In Wisconsin a group of such workers brought suit to extend the state female minimum wage to men.[31] California male employees sued unsuccessfully for rest periods as provided for women under a California law;[32] the state legislature later provided the benefits, even though the men had lost their lawsuit.

The courts may greet favorably the attempts of men in other states to change such women-only laws, as indicated by a federal appellate case in Arkansas. The Potlatch Forests company thought it saw an opportunity in Title VII to stop paying women overtime as required by the state law. It sued the state to have the law declared invalid. The court refused to do so, pointing out that Potlatch Forests could easily comply with both the state law and Title VII by paying men the premium overtime rates, too.[33] But other courts may interpret the law differently. In California, a state law requiring overtime pay only for women was declared invalid under Title VII.[34] The court refused to save the legal protection of the statute by extending the benefits to men. The Supreme Court refused to review either the Arkansas or the California case, so there is no final word on which interpretation should be adopted by other courts.

Women in states with labor laws applicable to women should keep in mind the distinction between laws that protect workers and laws that protect men's jobs from female competition. Laws that hinder women workers should be attacked; laws that benefit them should be extended to cover men as well.

Should any of the protective state labor laws for women be preserved?

No. First, some of these labor laws—maximum hour and weight limitations, for example—are so restrictive that they have been attacked over and over again by blue-collar women workers across the country. Both the courts and the EEOC have found the laws invalid because they discriminate against women. Second, laws that women workers are not attacking, like the overtime pay or rest period laws, should be preserved by giving the same benefits to men workers. This has already been done under Title VII to some extent and should also be carried out by legislation in every state that still has such laws on the books. These laws would then address such important problems as, for example, the need for maximum hour laws so parents can get home to their children. The best solution to this problem would be new laws providing that overtime work must be voluntary for all workers.[35] A voluntary overtime law would penalize neither the man who wanted to get home to his children nor the woman who wanted double-time pay to put her child through college.

May a company refuse to hire or assign women of childbearing age or capacity for jobs where they will be exposed to substances or procedures that are allegedly hazardous to fetuses?

No. See chapter 3 (Parenting and Work) for an extended discussion of this issue.

May a company hire men and women only for separate departments in a plant?

No. This is just another form of illegal sex segregation.

Is it legal for a company to forbid transfers between departments when it once segregated those departments by sex in initial hiring but no longer does so?

No. Usually the "men's" department will have higher pay scales than the "women's" department. The no-transfer policy appears to be evenhanded because it applies equally to all workers, but very few men will want to transfer to a department where the pay is less; conversely, many women will want to transfer to more highly paid work. This is an example of a neutral rule that has disparate impact; more women than men will be adversely affected by a policy which, in effect, locks women into low-paying jobs.

Can a company and a union negotiate a seniority system that discriminates against women?

No, but there is one severe limitation on women's ability to challenge discriminatory seniority plans. The Supreme Court has held that discriminatory seniority plans are illegal only if the parties that negotiated them *intended* for them to discriminate. In other words the neutral rule or disparate impact doctrine does not apply to seniority systems.[36] Another serious problem has been corrected by the 1991 Civil Rights Act. In 1989 the Supreme Court ruled that women seeking to challenge a facially neutral seniority plan conceived to discriminate against them must file discrimination charges when the plan is first adopted. The case, *Lorance v. AT&T Technologies*, was brought by Patricia Lorance and other women workers who had worked at AT&T Technologies.[37] Until the late 1970s, the company had a system of plantwide seniority in case of layoffs. At that point, women began, for the first time, to be permitted to transfer into the higher-skilled, higher-paid, formerly all-male "tester" jobs. In 1979 the company and the union entered into a new seniority agreement. Under this new plan, workers in the tester jobs would lose their plantwide seniority for the first five years in that job. As a result, when layoffs came in 1982, women like Patricia Lorance who had years of plantwide seniority lost their jobs while men who had worked for the company for a much shorter time, but had held the tester job longer, kept theirs. The women claimed that the seniority system had purposely been set up that way in order to protect the more junior men at the expense of the more senior women.

They filed charges of discrimination and took their employer and their union to court. When the case got to the Supreme Court, it held that the women should have filed their charges when the plan was first adopted in 1979 and should not have waited until they actually felt its effect by losing their jobs in 1982. This unjust result has now been repaired by the Civil Rights Act of 1991. See the section on the Civil Rights Act of 1991 below.

Hiring

Can an emloyer refuse to hire employees below a certain height or weight if the standard is applied to men and women alike?

No. This is another example of the neutral rule or disparate impact doctrine and one the Supreme Court specifically declared illegal in the case of *Dothard v. Rawlinson.*[38] Under the Civil Rights Act of 1991, it will be continue to be illegal. For further details, see the section on the Civil Rights Act of 1991 below.

In *Dothard*, in addition to an explicit ban on women guards in some prisons there was a requirement that all guards be 5 feet 2 inches tall and weigh 120 pounds. This had disparate impact on women, i.e., it adversely affected their employment opportunities. Over 41% of all women cannot meet this standard, but less than 1% of all men are similarly ineligible. The Court ruled that the requirement discriminated against women because of this differential impact, and then rejected Alabama's defense that the height-weight standard was needed to pick strong guards. If strength is required, the Court stated, employers should test directly for strength, rather than rely on the inexact proxy of a certain height and weight. Since that decision, many other courts have invalidated height and weight rules, especially for police jobs.

May a company or employment agency place help-wanted ads in sex-segregated newspaper columns?

No. This practice is blatantly illegal.

Is it legal for newspapers to segregate help-wanted advertising columns by sex?

Strangely enough, this is sometimes legal even though it is

illegal for any company to *use* the columns. Title VII applies only to labor unions, employers, and employment agencies. Only if a newspaper acts as an employment agency when it publishes want ads can a court say that the newspaper violates Title VII. Some federal judges have decided that newspapers are not employment agencies for this purpose and that they may segregate columns without violating the federal law, although another judge has disagreed.[39] In any case, to the extent that this now rare practice persists in the 1990s, there are other ways to force change.

First, many states have laws similar to Title VII that do cover newspapers. Women have used these laws successfully to force the *New York Times* and the *Pittsburgh Press* to stop their discriminatory practices.[40] They can also be used in other localities.

The second method is a roundabout but perhaps effective way of using Title VII. Women could sue, in one lawsuit, all the companies and employment agencies that place ads in segregated columns. This class action lawsuit would pit the class of all women job applicants against the class of all companies and agencies using one paper's sex-segregated want ads. Because women would be suing a class, the judge could order everyone in that class to stop using the columns. And if no one could use the columns, the newspaper would be forced to stop the practice.

Once the want-ad columns are integrated, may an ad itself specify or suggest that only men or only women need apply for a particular position?

No. This practice is just as discriminatory as sex-segregated columns. Theoretically, under the BFOQ provision of Title VII, there might be some jobs for which the company could advertise in this way. But as already explained, the BFOQ provision is very limited, so as a practical matter ads should not use discriminatory language, such as "boy," "girl," "man," or "woman."

May a company or employment agency give job applicants employment tests if it gives the same tests to all applicants and grades them all in the same way?

It depends. If the proportion of women who pass the test is

the same as the proportion of men who pass, the test is perfectly legal. However, if fewer women than men or men than women pass, the test may be illegal under the neutral rule or disparate impact doctrine. Under the rule in *Griggs v. Duke Power Co.*[41] and the EEOC guidelines,[42] a court can order a company to stop using a test unless it can prove the test validly predicts who would perform the job better. Proving this is called validating the test and is required by the EEOC guidelines. In conducting a validation study, the employer must consider alternative methods of employee selection that will help select capable employees without eliminating a disproportionate number of women or men. It is useful for women to understand how this form of discrimination was treated under the *Griggs* rule and how it will presumably be treated under the new Civil Rights Act of 1991.

The EEOC definition of tests has been extremely broad and basically includes any formal, scored technique to assess job suitability. Women have launched few major challenges to the use of these tests, and testing is usually viewed solely as a problem for minorities. However, women test less well than men in areas such as mathematics, science, weight lifting, and mechanical aptitude—areas that women have systematically been conditioned to ignore as unfeminine. And although a physical strength test has, in fact, been successfully challenged in a case involving firefighters,[43] other cases have been less successful in challenging such requirements since the courts found them to be job related.[44]

Some studies have shown also that graders will devalue an article if they think it is written by a woman;[45] thus any test involving evaluation of written essays by a grader who knows the sex of the test taker should be examined for sex bias. The same is true for evaluations of face-to-face interviews. Thus women need to be aware of and ready to challenge sex bias in testing. (See also chapter 8, "Education," on bias in educational testing.)

Can a company refuse to hire women because it doesn't want to build a women's restroom?

No. Absurd as it seems, companies that have never hired women really do use the argument that they can't hire women now because it would cost too much money to install a toilet for them. So far, cost has not deterred courts from ordering a company to stop discriminating, and the EEOC doesn't give credence to this "restroom" argument either. This should be a sufficient response to any company's objections on this subject, but there are a number of practical alternatives that could be suggested in this situation such as the construction of separate entrances and a new wall in the middle of an existing bathroom, the installment of a portable restroom unit in the corner of an unused room, or the placement of a lock on a small bathroom so that only one person (of either sex) could use it at a time.

May a company recruit for jobs by encouraging its present employees to bring in their friends as applicants?

If the jobs are segregated by sex and sex stereotyped, this practice may have the effect of perpetuating the segregation. The company has an obligation to correct sex segregation, so it must take affirmative steps to ensure an integrated pool of applicants for every job.

What steps can a company take to ensure an integrated pool of applicants?

There are no hard and fast rules as long as the remedy is adequate. Basically, the company must do what it takes to accomplish the result. This means changing advertising and recruiting methods and educating company personnel. For example, if the company's advertising and brochures show men and women segregated by sex in different jobs, the company must change the materials. Bell Telephone companies historically maintained rigid sex segregation in all telephone company jobs, and their advertising reflected this. After the EEOC launched a major investigation into their practices, the telephone companies changed their ads, and pictures of a woman working high up on a telephone pole appeared in major magazines along with pictures of a male operator. This is just one example of the kind of action that needs to be taken to achieve the ultimate goal of attracting both men and women applicants for all jobs.

The EEOC issued guidelines[46] on affirmative action in 1979 and, despite repeated attacks on the concept of affirmative action throughout the 1980s, these have remained intact. They outline the steps employers may take to overcome the effects of any past or present discriminatory employment practice. In 1979 the Supreme Court upheld the EEOC's position that employers need not be found in violation of Title VII before they can implement these affirmative action programs.[47] The EEOC's guidelines set forth a three-step process for employers: self-analysis of employment patterns by the employer, determination of a reasonable basis for taking action, and reasonable action designed to solve the problem.

Can training programs—whether for management or for blue-collar skilled craftwork—exclude women?

Under the law, no, although in practice this is done over and over again. Training programs are often a good place to begin an attack on segregated jobs because management's claim of not finding qualified women applicants has no validity when it refers to a program designed to give people those qualifications.

Indeed, women are advised to push for affirmative action particularly in training programs since the Supreme Court has explicitly approved it in this context. In an effort to correct the absence of blacks in higher-skilled jobs, a company in Louisiana started a new training program for both whites and blacks, with a guarantee that the blacks would get some of the training slots. When the company chose a black who had less seniority than a white for this training program, the white sued, called the company's action reverse discrimination. The Supreme Court disagreed. The company's action was a reasonable way to correct the results of past discrimination against blacks that had led to the virtual absence of blacks in the higher-skilled jobs. While this case involved race discrimination, the same theory should apply to sex discrimination.

Is it illegal for a company to hire or promote a higher percentage of male employees than female employees?

It depends. A statistical difference in the percentage of women, compared to men, hired or promoted by a certain employer, taken alone, is not enough to prove a violation of Title VII. Women wishing to challenge the employment practices of such an employer would have to show that women were not hired or promoted in proportion to their representation in the available pool of qualified people or that there was some sort of unjustified neutral rule or practice causing women to be eliminated from the pool. In technical or professional fields where more men than women have the necessary qualifications, the practice would probably survive; but it should not in jobs or fields that require only the general background equally available to men and women in our society. Employers in some jobs for which they have only hired men often argue that women are not interested in these jobs and do not apply for them in numbers anywhere equal to the men. In such cases it is important to be able to show that women have applied or at least tried to apply and have been discouraged or turned away.

Can an employment agency deal with persons of one sex only?

No. This would be legal only for those rare jobs for which one sex is a BFOQ.

If a company requests an employment agency to send a man to fill a certain job, is it legal for the agency to comply with this request?

No. The fact that someone else urges the agency to discriminate does not give it a license to do so. The agency must consider and refer women applicants for the job as well as male applicants. Other illegal agency practices include discriminating in employment counseling, accepting discriminatory job orders, and publishing discriminatory ads.[48]

Unions

May a labor union limit its membership to males or refer only the male members for most jobs?

Theoretically, no. But the notion that blue-collar, skilled craft jobs are male jobs is so deeply ingrained that even the governmental agencies that are supposed to eradicate sex discrimination long disregarded the obvious fact that these highly paid jobs are among the most male-monopolized jobs in our society. The government has allocated major resources to eradicating racial discrimination in this area, but has allowed the even more pervasive sex discrimination to go unchallenged. Women, too, are raised to believe that only men should hold these jobs, but they must reeducate themselves and challenge the barriers. For one thing, women might more than double their incomes if they do so, an incentive particularly important for women with little formal education who are now trapped in low-paying, dead-end jobs.

Several groups of women who understood this reality decided to change it. They sued the U.S. Department of Labor to force the department to carry out its responsibility for enforcing Executive Order No. 11246, which prohibits contractors who receive federal funds from discriminating against women in the skilled craft jobs that constitute the bulk of some contractors' work. Rather than fight, the department decided to settle the lawsuit. Under the resulting court order, the department was required to issue periodic numerical goals and timetables for training and hiring women at all levels of the skilled craft trades.[49] Each federal contractor must meet these goals or explain why it did not. The goal for training and hiring women for 1980 was 6.9%, but the goals have not been updated. Theoretically, if a contractor does not meet that goal in each job category, it is subject to the penalties of Executive Order No. 11246. And if the contractor argues that it cannot meet the goal because the unions are not cooperating in referring or providing women for the jobs, the union is referred to EEOC for Title VII review. But in fact, even with the court order, the Labor Department does little to enforce these goals and timetables. Much more pressure is needed in this area.

What are the rights of women workers with regard to marriage and family?

This is a very important topic and is discussed in a separate chapter, chapter 3 on Parenting and Work.

Retirement

Are different retirement ages or benefits for men and women legal?

No. There have been several court decisions requiring equal treatment,[50] and the EEOC guidelines take the same position.[51] The following policies have all been declared illegal.

Companies sometimes forced women to retire earlier than men, to the disadvantage of women who wanted to keep on working, and they sometimes gave women an option to retire earlier, to the disadvantage of men who would like to leave earlier. Sometimes men were allowed to retire at the same age as women but with a lower pension than the women were allowed. Another similar practice led to a major Supreme Court decision. The Los Angeles Department of Water and Power for a long time charged women employees more than men for equal pension benefits upon retirement. As a result, women had lower take-home pay than men. The rationale for this practice: the average woman lives longer than the average man. In 1978 the Supreme Court declared that this was illegal because it prejudges and penalizes any individual woman who does not fit the average.

In 1983 the Supreme Court ruled that another variation on the same theme—giving women lower monthly pension benefits than men—was equally illegal.[52] At the same time, however, the Court accepted the insurance industry argument that women should only get equal benefits for that portion of their benefits attributable to wages earned after the Supreme Court decision. This result allows insurance companies to postpone paying equal benefits until sometime well into the twenty-first century, when the women who first started working in 1984 retire—for only their pensions will be entirely based on post-1984 wages. Women who started work earlier—for example in the mid 1950s—will have a large portion of their benefits attributable to pre-1983 wages, and thus will receive much lower pensions than men with the same work history. Thus, the older the woman, the more discrimination the Supreme Court permitted in her pension checks. In the early 1980s there were repeated efforts to pass legislation (usually referred to as H.R. 100) that would have prohibited sex discrimination in all pensions and insurance, but the bill was ultimately defeated due to the lobbying efforts of the insurance industry. Passage of such a law remains a high priority of many feminist groups.

Insurance

Is it legal to provide health insurance coverage only to employees who are "head of household"?

The Supreme Court has not spoken on this issue. However, so far the lower courts that have dealt with this practice have permitted it as a business necessity despite the fact that it is a neutral rule that usually has discriminatory impact on women, i.e., the practice would exclude more women than men from health benefits. They have ruled—on the basis of flimsy evidence and arguments—that the costs of providing health insurance to all workers is so prohibitive that employers are free to make this sort of distinction.[53]

If a company can prove that it costs more to provide some kinds of insurance to women than to men, may it give women smaller benefits than men?

No, under EEOC guidelines and a Supreme Court decision,[54] Title VII forbids averaging costs by sex, just as it would forbid averaging costs by race. Averaging is a way of attributing to the individual the experience of the group even when the individual does not conform to average group behavior. Title VII says women are to be judged as individuals, and the cost for the group is therefore irrelevant. Employers and insurance companies have contested this concept, but the EEOC guidelines have prevailed.

May a labor union use its bargaining power to negotiate contracts that discriminate against women?

No, under the law, although unions do it all the time. Besides suing such labor unions, women members will undoubtedly find that an excellent remedy against this practice is to seize some power for themselves in the unions so that women do the negotiating, too.

Are there any other illegal employment practices that have not been mentioned?

Hundreds. The practices detailed here are designed to give the reader some sense of the kind and degree of discriminatory employment practices, but the list could go on and on. The best guide is simply to trust one's own judgment as to what is discriminatory, tested by the judgment of a lawyer or experienced advisor. Under Title VII, discrimination can be classified under one of two headings: practices discriminatory on their face, which are judged by the standards of the BFOQ; and apparently neutral practices, discriminatory in effect, which are judged by the standards of business necessity. Whenever a woman senses that she has been discriminated against, she should do something about it, whether or not she has the information needed to prove it and whether or not some court has already declared the practice illegal. Proving the facts and changing the law are up to those charged with responsibility for investigation and presentation of her claim. The woman's responsibility is to identify the practice and to demand strict adherence to, and vigorous enforcement of antidiscrimination policy.

What federal agency administers Title VII?
The Equal Employment Opportunity Commission, often called the EEOC.

Enforcement—Nonfederal Employees

How does a woman enforce her rights under Title VII?
The first step is to contact the nearest EEOC field office—in person, by writing, or by phone. In person a complainant will be asked to fill out a Charge of Discrimination form. The type of information requested may include name, address, and telephone number, the name of the respondent (the employer or union), its address, phone number, and number of employees (there must be at least 15), the basis of the alleged discrimination (sex, race age, etc.) or the date of the most recent discriminatory act, and the details of the discrimination. A letter should outline the complaint, giving this type of information. The details should include a brief description of what was done to the complainant (or to a group of women) that was unfair and how men were treated differently. The EEOC will send the employer a copy of the charge within ten days; then it will begin an investigation of the charge.

What action does the EEOC take after receiving the charge?
In a state or city that passed a law against sex discrimination in employment, usually called a fair employment practice law (FEP law), the commission's first step will normally be to send a copy of the charge to the state or city FEP agency. The EEOC does this because Title VII requires that any person filing a charge with the EEOC must first file the charge with her local or state FEP agency. To ensure that this is done, the EEOC files the charge for the complainant. At one time the EEOC

was required to wait up to sixty days to begin its investigation of the charge in order to give the FEP agency a chance to investigate first. At the end of this time, the EEOC would either review the state or local agency's finding (if the investigation was complete) or begin its own investigation. Now, however, the EEOC and most state and local agencies have entered into work-sharing agreements. Officially these agreements divide upcoming charges into various categories. These divisions of responsibility are different in various parts of the country.

If the EEOC has primary responsibility for the kind of charge a complainant has filed, it will notify the state agency of the charge and will proceed to investigate without waiting to allow the state or local agency to act first. If the state agency has primary responsibility for the kind of charge the complainant has filed, the EEOC will allow it to investigate the charge first. The EEOC usually takes no further action until it reviews the findings and orders of the state agency. However, if the state agency does not begin investigation or if it begins to investigate but it appears that there will be a long delay before the matter is resolved, the complainant should request the EEOC take over responsibility as the law provides. The EEOC will also take over from the beginning if the charge is against the state agency itself or if it is necessary to get immediate or temporary court action while the charge is being investigated and processed. The practical result of many work-sharing agreements is that, regardless of the category of the charge, whichever agency receives the complaint first investigates it.

The EEOC will sometimes review a state agency decision, but not always. Depending on the reputations of the complainant's area EEOC and state agency, she may have a preference about which one conducts the investigation of her complaint. A local women's organization can explain how the work-sharing agreement between the EEOC and local state agency operates. If the office that first receives the charge investigates, the next step is to ask which agency is more responsive. This information will help a woman decide whether to file her complaint with the EEOC or state agency first. If she files with the state first, she should file also with the EEOC just to protect her rights. If she is not satisfied with the state investigation, she can and should ask the EEOC to review it (otherwise, the EEOC probably will not do so).

If a woman decides to file with the state agency, or if her charge is sent there, she should cooperate fully with the investigators. The agency's final findings and orders are considered very seriously when the EEOC reviews them, and they are almost always adopted without further investigation.

How does the EEOC investigate a charge?

An EEOC investigator is assigned to the case and will ask the complainant questions and interview the respondent; the investigator may talk to witnesses and may review records. The complainant may be requested to give additional information, including the identity and whereabouts of any witnesses who will support the details of incidents that gave rise to the charge or preceded it, the complainant's work history with the respondent, a job description and the reasons the complainant was given or the respondent will give for its action(s), and ways in which the complainant was treated differently from others. The type of information sought by the EEOC is most often the type relevant to individual cases of discrimination as compared to classwide discrimination. A complainant should always be as cooperative as possible with the investigator, but it may be necessary to direct the investigator's attention toward the larger, classwide issues.

In the course of an investigation the respondent will also be asked to provide specific information concerning the issues raised in the charge, as well as the identity and whereabouts of witnesses who will support its version of the facts, information about the business operation and the workplace, and of course personnel records. If the respondent is uncooperative, the EEOC has the power to issue a subpoena to obtain the necessary evidence. If the respondent still refuses to comply, this can be enforced in court.

Based on the evidence gathered, the investigator prepares a recommended determination for the office director as to whether there is cause to believe that there was discrimination. Based on that recommendation, the director will issue, and the complainant will receive, a Letter of Determination that will state whether or not the director believes the allegation made is supported by the evidence.

If the director does find cause to believe the discrimination occurred the letter will say this and will invite the respondent to meet with the EEOC to work out an agreement for providing relief. If such an agreement cannot be reached, the investigative file will be reviewed at the EEOC headquarters, and the EEOC (in cases of state or local employers, the Department of Justice) will either bring a suit on the complainant's behalf or will formally notify her of her right to sue on her own behalf.

If the director does not believe some or all of the allegations in a complainant's charge, the Letter of Determination will say this and will notify her of her right to request that EEOC headquarters review that determination. If such a request is not made within fourteen days the determination will become final on the fifteenth day, and the investigation will end. The Letter of Determination should include a Request for Review Form. If a complainant does not request review at that time, she can still go to court herself to enforce her rights. It is advisable to request such a review, especially if the case involves complicated or class-based facts. If a review is not requested within fourteen days, and the request is accepted, a final EEOC determination will be made after that review and its results will be sent to the complainant when it is complete.

What is a Notice of Right to Sue?

There are basically four different situations in which a complainant may receive a Notice of Right to Sue from the EEOC. Regardless of the reasons for receiving such a notice, it is important to remember that a complainant has only ninety days to file suit in federal court from the day she receives the notice.

The first situation warranting Notice of Right to Sue is when a charge is dismissed. EEOC regulations call for the dismissal of a charge if (1) the investigation shows that the law (Title VII, for example) does not apply to the case,[55] (2) the EEOC cannot complete the investigation because they cannot locate the charging party, (3) the charging party does not cooperate in the investigation, or (4) the charging party does not accept a settlement offer that the EEOC deems would afford full relief from the harm alleged. This last one can be tricky if the complainant and the EEOC have very different views about what would constitute full relief. If such a problem arises, a complainant should consult an attorney.

The second reason for receiving a Notice of "Right to Sue" is that the EEOC finds no violation with respect to all the allegations in the charge. Before this happens the complainant should be given an opportunity to provide more evidence and then fourteen days (as outlined above) in which to request EEOC headquarters to review the determination. A complainant has ninety days to file suit from the day that the determination becomes final—either after the fourteen-day period is over if she does not ask for a review or after the final EEOC action at a later date if she does ask for review.

The third circumstance for receiving a Notice of Right to Sue is when the EEOC does find a violation but either fails to obtain relief and/or simply decides to bring a suit on the complainant's behalf. Whether or not to bring a lawsuit is up to the EEOC commissioners and may or may not have anything to do with the merits of the case. It is simply their decision. Since the beginning of the Reagan years and into the Bush administration, the commissioners have shown a marked preference for individual cases and against systemic or class-type cases. So although the EEOC may appear to be bringing more suits in recent years they are actually getting relief for fewer people and are failing to address the larger issues of systemic discrimination. This tendancy perpetuates the notion of discrimination as an individual aberration in a mostly nondiscriminatory society and ignores the more extensive sexism and racism of many employers and other institutions.

The fourth way to receive a right to sue letter is to ask for one. A complainant has a right to receive such a notice at any time after 180 days have passed from the date the charge was filed or the EEOC took jurisdiction over it from the state FEP agency, whether or not the investigation is complete. But, a complainant should not request this letter unless an attorney recommends she do so.

How long does it take the EEOC to resolve a complaint?

It is difficult to say, although very long periods of delay common in the early years of the EEOC seem to have abated somewhat. No one quite knows why; it may be just as much because of slipshod investigations and quick dismissals as because of any increased efficiency. In any event, once a complainant's charge has been assigned to an investigator, she can contact that investigator and find out about the progress of the case.

If the EEOC is not handling a complaint rapidly enough or to the complainant's satisfaction, is there any action she can take?

Yes. A complainant has an automatic right to bring suit 180 days after the EEOC acquires the power to act on her charge (that is, 180 days from the time she filed a charge with the EEOC where there is no state FEP or 180 days after the EEOC assumes responsibility for a charge that was handled first by a state agency). If a complainant wants faster action than the EEOC can give and finds a lawyer to take her case, she can request the EEOC letter giving her the right to sue (the Notice of Right to Sue). Although technically she is not entitled to a right-to-sue letter before the 180 days are up, the EEOC will sometimes give the letter upon request if the EEOC will not be able to process your charge within 180 days. *This notice should not be requested until a complainant has a lawyer since she or he must start the lawsuit within ninety days of the complainant's receipt of the notice and will need time to prepare the case.*

Are there time limits to watch out for?

Definitely, and they are extremely important. A person can lose a lawsuit simply by failing to comply with certain time requirements under Title VII, regardless of the facts of the case.

The first time limit involves the date a complainant files her charge with the commission. Title VII says this must be done within 180 days of the act of discrimination if there is no state or local FEP agency. If there is a state or local agency, a complainant must file with the EEOC within 30 days after the state or local agency finishes with her case or within 300 days of the date of the act of discrimination, whichever is earlier. (It is best to file with the EEOC right away, even when filing with the state or local agency first.)

Regardless of missed deadlines, it may still be possible to comply with this requirement. Several courts have said that if the discrimination is of a continuing nature, such as a policy the company has never countermanded, then a charge is always filed within the time limits. Actually, almost every form of discrimination can be viewed as continuing. Therefore, it is better to describe discrimination as continuing, rather than limiting a charge to a particular date. Thus, if the company refused to promote a woman on 11 August 1993 because she is a woman, she can regard the situation in two ways. She can say she was were personally discriminated against on 11 August 1993, or she can say that the company has a continuing policy of refusing to promote women into certain jobs, which she became aware of on 11 August 1993.[56]

Another reason to file a charge as soon as possible is to increase the amount of a monetary award in a lawsuit. Under Title VII, a woman can win back wages, that is, the amount of money she would have earned if she had not been discriminated against. But she can collect back wages only for a period of time dating from two years prior to filing the charge up to the end of her lawsuit. The later the charge is filed, the later the date from which the judge will compute the back pay due. For instance, if a woman files a charge on 1 January 1993 and ultimately wins her lawsuit, she will collect back wages from 1 January 1991 up to the date she wins the lawsuit, and the company will be ordered to increase her future wages to what she should be earning. If she waits to file until 1 September 1993, the back wages will be computed from 1 September 1991, and she will lose eight months of back wages that she is entitled to.

Another time limit posed by Title VII involves going to court. A complainant has only ninety days after the day she receives her EEOC right-to-sue letter to file the court complaint that starts the lawsuit. Therefore, the notice should not be requested until she has a lawyer and makes certain the lawyer understands that the complaint must be filed within the time period, or she will lose the case. (If by some chance this happens, the lawyer has been extremely negligent, and another lawyer should be consulted to consider whether to sue the first one for malpractice.)

Who can file a charge of discrimination with the EEOC?

Anyone who believes she has been discriminated against can file the charge, or an organization can file on her behalf. Women workers who are afraid the company will find out and fire them if they file charges should ask an organization to file for them. However, the organization filing the charge must get the women's authorization, and the EEOC will check to see that it did so. If an organization files, the EEOC will ask for the workers' names and addresses, but will keep this information confidential.

While labor unions are commonly considered organizations, under Title VII they are also considered "persons." Since any injured person can file a charge, a union can file a charge on behalf of itself or on behalf of one or more of its members. A woman's union may therefore file a charge against her employer challenging a discriminatory action or policy that has affected her without getting her authorization or submitting her name to the EEOC.

Whom can the charges accuse of discrimination?

Four kinds of entities can be charged: an employer, a labor union, an employment agency, and, in some cases, a joint labor-management committee controlling apprenticeship or training. The employer must have at least fifteen employees to be covered by Title VII, and the labor union must have at least fifteen members. The only important exception to the fifteen-employee rule is the United States government, which is not covered by Title VII in the same way that other employers are covered. (Questions on federal employees are discussed a little later in this chapter.)

Are school teachers and employees of state and local governments protected by Title VII?

Yes, as long as the school boards and governments have at least fifteen employees. These two groups were added to the coverage of Title VII by amendment in 1972. Rights of employees of state and local governments and school teachers are the same as those of other employees covered by Title VII, with one difference: only the Justice Department can sue on their behalf, and not the EEOC. But these employees can still bring their own lawsuits.

Will a woman's employer or union find out if she files a charge?

Yes. Ten days after someone files a charge with the EEOC, it sends a notice of the charge to the employer or union, and the notice includes the name of the person filing the charge. To avoid this, women can have an organization file on their behalf, but the company will usually find out the names of the women at some stage because the EEOC will have to discuss remedies for specific people with the company.

If a company fires someone who files a charge against them, or if some other retaliatory action is taken, is there anything that can be done about it?

Yes. Retaliation for filing a charge of discrimination is just as illegal as the discrimination itself. If a woman's company retaliates, she can file another charge with the EEOC and sue the company for back wages. If she needs to get her job back or end any other retaliation immediately, she can request that the EEOC bring a lawsuit to accomplish this. Under the 1972 amendments to Title VII, the commission has the authority to bring lawsuits for what is called "temporary or preliminary relief"—i.e., relief pending final disposition of the initial charge. If the EEOC won't help, she can ask her lawyer about bringing a suit to force the company to reinstate her.

Will women be able to afford the court costs and attorneys' fees for a Title VII lawsuit?

Title VII provides that the court may award court costs and attorneys' fees to the successful party. Although courts have frequently awarded both items to successful plaintiffs, they almost never require an unsuccessful plaintiff to pay the company's fees. The awards of attorneys' fees have sometimes been very large—substantial awards have ranged from $20,000 to $225,000. But the courts are making it more difficult for lawyers to collect these fees, and even when they do it often takes years. Because of these problems, many attorneys are reluctant to take on discrimination cases unless the client can pay something along the way. The attorneys' fees provisions were included in the Civil Rights Act of 1964 in order to encourage private lawyers to take discrimination cases, but because of narrow interpretations of the fees' provisions by some judges, many lawyers cannot afford to take the cases. Various provisions of the Civil Rights Act of 1991 are designed to alleviate this problem.

In order to secure a private attorney, a woman may be asked to pay the lawyer on a contingent fee basis. This means that lawyers will take their fee from a portion of her recovery on the case, especially if she cannot advance much of the money. A better approach is to make it clear that the lawyer should first attempt to get a separate award for attorneys' fees; and if that does not cover the value of the work, the lawyer can then make up the difference between the award and the value on a contingent fee basis. (Careful time records should be kept for the attorney's fee award.) Of course, a contingent fee will not even be suggested if the likely recovery is not large. As for court costs, she probably will have to reimburse the lawyer for these as the case progresses, even though ultimately she can expect to win them back if she prevails.

How should women go about finding a Title VII lawyer?
The best source of information may be the local EEOC office, which maintains a list of Title VII lawyers.

What can women read in order to understand more of the legal technicalities about Title VII?
It cannot be overemphasized that laypersons are capable of reading and understanding the statute and regulations, which set forth in more detail all the procedures described above. Women should also read the cases cited in the notes at the end of this chapter and any pertinent law review articles. The statute (Title VII) is found in 42 U.S.C. § 2000e *et seq.* The regulations are found in 29 C.F.R. pt. 1601 (the section dealing with procedures) and pt. 1604 (the section dealing with sex discrimination). A convenient place to find all federal laws and regulations dealing with sex discrimination in employment is a book produced by the Commerce Clearing House, Inc. (CCH), *Employment Practices Guide.* Another publisher, the Bureau of National Affairs (BNA), has a similar book, *Fair Employment Practice Manual.* A law librarian can help locate these works.

Enforcement—Federal Employees

Are federal employees covered by Title VII?
Yes, but to enforce their rights they must follow different procedures than other employees.

What agency enforces the Title VII rights of federal employees?
The EEOC was given the responsibility for enforcing the

Title VII rights of federal employees under President Carter's Civil Rights Reorganization Plan of 1978. That responsibility was transferred from the Office of Personnel Management (the old Civil Service Commission) as part of the effort to consolidate Title VII enforcement within one federal agency.

Does Title VII define discrimination against federal employees differently from discrimination against other employees?

This question arises because federal employees are not covered by the same section of Title VII as are all other employees. The section that outlaws employment discrimination against federal employees was added to Title VII in 1972 and requires federal employees to follow different procedures from other employees. Given this separation of employees into two groups, it becomes important to know whether the definition of what constitutes discrimination for other employees is the same for federal employees. The answer is that courts have been using the same definition of discrimination for both groups. Therefore, for the purpose of challenging sex discrimination in federal employment, women should use the standards of what constitutes employment discrimination under Title VII that have already been set forth above and should likewise look for the same remedies.

Do federal agencies have any obligation under Title VII to develop affirmative action programs?

Yes. This is a separate requirement imposed only on the federal government. Thus the government has two duties under this law: (1) it must not discriminate, and (2) it must develop affirmative action programs to increase opportunities for minorities and women. Both duties also arise under Executive Order No. 11478, which has been in effect for a longer time. (See "The Executive Order" later in this chapter for more detail on the meaning of affirmative action.)

Each federal department or agency must draw up national and regional Equal Employment Opportunity (EEO) plans, which are reviewed annually by the EEOC. Each agency must also prepare periodic progress reports on its program, again with review by the EEOC. When the EEOC finds that these affirmative action plans or the progress under them are inadequate, it has the authority to require improvement or impose corrective action. Finally, a special requirement to set up training and education programs to encourage maximum advancement by every employee has also been imposed by Title VII.

In 1978 Congress added to these Title VII affirmative action requirements for the federal government by requiring the development of a special Federal Equal Opportunity Recruitment Program (FEORP). The purpose of this program is to eliminate underrepresentation of minorities and women in specific federal job categories. Federal guidelines issued by the Office of Personnel Management (OPM) now require every federal agency to step up recruitment of minorities and women in every job category where their underrepresentation is identified. Reports on recruitment plans must be submitted to the EEOC with the agency's annual EEO plan, and the plans may be reviewed by both the Office of Personnel Management and the EEOC.

Women employees of the federal government should demand that they have a say on these EEO and recruitment plans in order to ensure that the plans become a real instrument for change.

What procedures should be followed by a federal employee to assert her Title VII right not to be discriminated against?

In rough outline, she must first consult with an Equal Employment Opportunity (EEO) counselor in her agency or department, who will try to resolve her complaint informally. If the counselor cannot do so, the employee should file a formal, written complaint of discrimination with the agency, which will be followed by an agency investigation and, if the employee so requests, a hearing. The agency then reaches a decision.

If the employee is unhappy with the result, she may appeal the employing agency's decision either to the EEOC or, in special cases, to the Merit System Protection Board (MSPB). The EEOC or the MSPB, as the case may be, can order the agency to pay lost wages and correct the discrimination, including hiring or reinstating the injured employee. If the employee is still unhappy with the results, she can start a Title VII lawsuit against the agency, either at this stage or at several earlier stages. Occasionally an employee gets a satisfactory result from the administrative process, but the agency refuses to give her the relief ordered. In that case she may have to go to court to enforce the EEOC order.

A special note about the MSPB appeal procedure is in order. The Civil Service Reform Act of 1978 split up the old Civil Service Commission into two agencies—the MSPB and the Office of Personnel Management (OPM). The MSPB generally handles appeals from employment decisions involving claimed violations of the civil service law. If a federal employee charges that some adverse action, such as a discharge, suspension, reduction in rank or pay, or unsatisfactory performance evaluation, is both discriminatory and in violation of civil service laws, her case is considered a mixed case and her initial appeal must go to the MSPB rather than to the EEOC. Those cases that just involve a claim of discrimination are appealed only to the EEOC.

May an organization file a complaint of discrimination with a federal agency on behalf of an individual?
Yes, but it must be with the person's consent.

May a woman be represented by another person during the procedures before the agency and the EEOC or MSPB?
Yes. An employee may be represented by someone else at any stage of the proceedings. The representative does not have to be a lawyer, although this probably would be beneficial.

Are there any time problems of which federal employees should be aware?
Yes. The original contact with the EEO counselor must be within 90 days of the discriminatory action, although the counselor may make exceptions to this rule. (Prior to passage of the Civil Rights Act of 1991, the time limit was 30 days.) The employee has only 15 days after her final interview with the EEO counselor (which will follow the informal conciliation efforts) to give the employing agency a formal, written complaint. Later, if she wants to appeal the agency's final decision on her written complaint to the EEOC or MSPB, she must do so within 20 days of the agency's decision. Finally, if she chooses to go to court, rather than appeal to the EEOC or the MSPB, she has 30 days from the employing agency's final decision to

do so. If she appeals first to the EEOC or MSPB and then goes
to court, she likewise has 30 days from the final decision of the
EEOC or MSPB to do so. The courts are apt to enforce these
limits strictly by throwing suits that do not abide by them out
of court, so it is very important to get a lawyer and move quickly
upon deciding to sue.

Another set of time limits protects the worker's right to go
to court fast. Congress wrote some safeguards into the act, so
that if the employing agency or the EEOC or MSPB stalls, the
employee can get action by going to court. Once she files her
formal complaint with the agency, she may go directly to court
if the agency does not reach its final decision within a certain
time period. She may go to court after 180 days if the complaint
is one of "pure discrimination" (the kind of case that is appealable to the EEOC). She may go even sooner—after 120 days—
if the charge mixes discrimination and civil service violation
claims (the kind of case that is appealable to the MSPB). If
instead of going to court she appeals the employing agency's
final decision to the EEOC or the MSPB, the EEOC has 180
days to take action and the MSPB has 120 days before she again
has the right to go to court, whether they have acted or not.

**Can a court award attorneys' fees and court costs in a
successful suit against the federal government?**

Yes. Again, this important feature was designed to encourage
attorneys to take such cases.

**Can each federal agency discipline agency personnel re-
sponsible for discriminatory practices?**

Yes, and this remedy should be pressed, as it is likely to
have a salutary effect on other agency personnel inclined to
discriminate.

**Is there anything women can read to better understand
employment discrimination procedures for federal employees?**

Yes. For a more complete description of the procedures read
the EEOC regulations, set forth at 29 C.F.R. pt. 1613, the
MSPB regulations, set forth at 5 C.F.R. §§ 1200-2, and the
parts of Title VII dealing with federal employees, 42 U.S.C. §
2000e-16.

Do other laws besides Title VII make it illegal to discriminate against women workers?

Yes. They all cover some of the ground covered by Title VII, so the rest of the chapter will not discuss them in as much detail as Title VII. They include the Equal Pay Act, two executive orders, the Age Discrimination Act, and many state fair employment practice laws.

THE CIVIL RIGHTS ACT OF 1991

The new Civil Rights Act, which amends Title VII of the Civil Rights Act of 1964, was signed into law by President Bush on 21 November 1991. It is part of Title VII now and is, therefore enforced in the same way. It is the result of a series of compromises between the Democrats and Republicans and between relatively moderate and more conservative Republicans. As such, it is hardly ideal, but the bottom line is that people who suffer employment discrimination resulting from practices or policies that have a disproportionately adverse effect on groups identifiable by race, sex, national origin, or religion now have a better chance of redress in the courts, at least under Title VII.

What effect does the act have on the law of disparate impact?

Section 105 of the act, entitled "Burden of Proof in Disparate Impact Cases" effectively reverses *Wards Cove Packing Co. v. Atonio*,[57] with respect to two of its three major holdings, and mitigates somewhat the harshness of the third.

First, it returns to the defendant the burden of proving that a challenged employment practice (one which has disparate impact on the basis of race, sex, national origin, or religion) is "job related for the position in question and required by business necessity."

Second, although the terms "business necessity" and "job related" are not defined in this version, one of the stated purposes of the act is to "codify the[se] concepts . . . as enunciated by the Supreme Court in *Griggs* . . . and [its progeny] prior to *Wards Cove*."

Third, although the act does not completely reverse the third holding of *Wards Cove,* which required a claimant to identify a particular employment practice that is causing the disparate impact, it permits a claimant to show the disparate impact caused by an employer's decision making process as a whole where she or he can show that the various elements of the process are "not capable of separation for analysis."

Does the Act have any effect on the remedies available in cases of discrimination in testing?

Yes. The act prohibits the adjustment of scores or using different cut off scores on the basis of race, sex, national origin, or religion. Unfortunately, however, there is no concomitant requirement that an employment test must be both valid and fair.

Many tests, especially standardized tests, discriminate against women and minorities. For example, the Scholastic Aptitude Test (SAT) is supposed to predict a student's first year grades in college. Women, on the average, score lower than men, on the average, on the SAT. However, women as a group get higher grades the first year of college than men. This means that if a woman and a man have the same SAT score, the woman is likely to get higher grades. If the new Title VII rule were applied to education cases, the respective scores could not be adjusted or "normed" to account for this unfairness.

Does the act affect challenges to litigated or consent judgments and orders?

Yes. Section 108 of the act addresses the issue of white males' lawsuits (known as collateral attacks) against litigated or consent orders, i.e., court-approved settlements. Under certain circumstances, the provision prohibits such challenges to employment practices that implement the terms of a litigated or consent order resolving claims of discrimination by other employees.

Persons barred from bringing a new lawsuit to challenge an affirmative action plan would include (1) those who had notice that the outcome of the proceeding might affect their interests and who had a reasonable opportunity to present objections; (2) those whose interests were already adequately represented in the proceedings; and (3) those as to whom the court determines reasonable efforts were made, consistent with due process, to provide notice.

The idea was to provide a framework to achieve finality in employment discrimination cases that include hiring or promotion orders that may affect the rights of white men. It is unclear how well or poorly this provision will work in practice. This will emerge from its actual application to cases.

Does the act provide for damages in cases of intentional sex discrimination?

Yes. Punitive and compensatory damages, including those for pain and suffering, have long been available under 42 U.S.C. § 1981 to persons claiming intentional race discrimination in employment. Race discrimination in this context has been interpreted to include any classification that would have been regarded as racial in 1866 when that law was passed. As a practical matter, this includes virtually all nationalities and some religions (i.e., Jews were considered a race then). Sex and disability discrimination claimants were excluded. There was no federal cause of action allowing any remedies other than back pay and injunctive relief in these cases, in particular in cases of sexual harassment.

Section 102 of the act addresses this problem *up to a point*. It creates a new cause of action (to be codified as 42 U.S.C. § 1981A) for intentional discrimination in employment on the basis of sex and/or disability as defined in the Americans with Disabilities Act (ADA). This cause of action provides punitive and compensatory damages and a jury trial. Unfortunately, the compromise required agreeing to caps—or a maximum—on damages (though the caps do not apply to back pay and actual expenses). The caps are based on the number of covered employees in the employers workforce, as follows: 15 to 100 employees—$50,000 per employees maximum damages; 101 to 200—$100,000; 201 to 500—$200,000; over 500—$300,000. Legislation (the Equal Remedies Act) to repeal the caps has been introduced but has not yet passed.

What does the act do about impermissible consideration of race, sex, national origin, and religion if the plaintiff is unqualified for the job in question?

In *Price-Waterhouse v. Hopkins*,[38] the Supreme Court held that in so-called mixed motive cases, i.e., where the plaintiff could show that impermissible consideration of race, sex, national origin, or religion played a role in the decision-making process, the burden of proof shifted to the respondent to prove that the outcome would have been the same even in the absence of the discrimination. This was considered a victory. The problem was that if the respondent could make the required showing as to a particular plaintiff, there would be no relief at all—that is, no order that the discriminatory consideration of sex, etc. that the company did use must cease.

Section 107 of the act clarifies that a plaintiff who makes such a showing has won the case and is entitled to a court order against the discrimination and attorneys' fees. The plaintiff cannot recover any *monetary* damages, however if the respondent shows that it would have made the same decision as to *her,* anyway.

What does the act do about the statute of limitations on challenges to intentionally discriminatory seniority systems?

In *Lorance v. AT&T Technologies,*[59] the Supreme Court held that for the purposes of a challenge to an intentionally discriminatory seniority system, the Title VII statute of limitations starts to run when the plan goes into effect. That meant women had to start a lawsuit when a new system began, not when it first affected the women years later. In essence, the Court required the employees to anticipate the discriminatory effects of such a system and initiate suit to prevent future adverse applications of the system no matter how speculative or unlikely these applications might be.

Section 112 of the act provides that the cause of action arises when the seniority system is adopted, when a person is subject to it, or when an individual is actually injured by its application. Thus, women can now wait to see until they are actually affected by the new system.

What does the act do to protect American citizens working for American companies abroad?

The act reverses the case of *EEOC v. Arabian American Oil Co. (Aramco),*[60] which found no extraterritorial application of Title VII and the ADA to Americans working for United States companies abroad, but only where it would not violate foreign law to do so. In other words, if the law of the host country requires some form of discrimination (and several do) the practice will not be covered.

Does the act do anything to help Federal employees?

Yes. Section 114 extends the 30-day time limit for the initial filing of a discrimination charge to 90 days and allows for the accrual post-judgment interest in the same manner as for private employment.

Does the act make Title VII applicable to employees of Congress?

Yes. Employees of the Senate and the House of Representatives are now covered by Title VII but with different procedural rules for enforcement.

Does the act permit plaintiffs to collect expert witness fees?

In *West Virginia University Hospitals v. Casey*,[61] the Supreme Court ruled that the fees paid to expert witnesses could not be considered part of the attorneys' fees and costs to which a winning claimant was entitled. The act provides for the recovery of expert witness fees in some but not all types of discrimination cases. Expert fees are recoverable under Title VII, which prohibits discrimination in employment, the focus of the act. Expert fees are also recoverable in cases brought under § 1981, a law passed in 1866, which grants all people the same right to contract that is enjoyed by white people. This provision has been used by racial and national origin minorities to challenge employment practices.

THE EQUAL PAY ACT

What does the Equal Pay Act forbid?

The name of this law suggests the answer: companies may not pay women who are doing the same work as men less than they pay those men. However, "equal pay for equal work" is not as simple as it first appears. The law is mired by a lot of technical distinctions. The work of the men and women must be compared against certain standards before there can be a decision on whether it is equal work requiring equal pay.

First, both the men and the women must work in the same "establishment"—that is, a distinct physical place of business or location (such as a complex of buildings). The job of each must require equal skill, equal effort, and equal responsibility—each factor to be examined separately. The work must be performed under similar working conditions. Finally, the work itself must be "equal"—which means that the tasks involved in a woman's job are substantially equal even if not identical to those in a man's job. If any one of these standards is not fulfilled, a company does not violate the Equal Pay Act when it pays women less than men—which leaves companies with a lot of loopholes.

Can an employment practice be legal under the Equal Pay Act but illegal under Title VII?

Definitely. As the previous question indicated, the Equal Pay Act covers one very narrowly defined form of wage discrimination. In contrast, Title VII covers a panoply of discriminatory practices and can be used to force change in employment patterns where the Equal Pay Act cannot. For instance, a company that assigns all its assembly line work to men and all its clerical work to women, with the men receiving salaries double the amount of those of the women, does not violate the Equal Pay Act since the jobs are in no way equal. But this practice does violate Title VII because the company has assigned jobs on the basis of sex and denied women the chance to double their income. The women could sue under Title VII to force the company to integrate the two jobs and to recover the income lost in the past. Integration would be a major change in employment patterns, and it would probably lead to other changes as well. The men workers in the clerical jobs might well force the wage scale up—which would also benefit the women clerical workers. Viewed in this light, Title VII offers a far greater chance for meaningful change in employment practices than the Equal Pay Act.

May a company avoid complying with the Equal Pay Act by transferring all the men who receive higher wages into another job so that only women are left doing the first job at the lower rate?

No. Once the company establishes a higher rate for men, it

must pay women that rate even after the men are transferred out. Be aware, also, that it would violate Title VII to transfer workers out of a job on the basis of sex.

May a company comply with the Equal Pay Act by lowering the wages of the more highly paid men?

No. One of the provisions in the act says that companies must always raise the wages of the more lowly paid sex (almost always women) and not lower the wages of the other sex.

May a company avoid the Equal Pay Act by giving men extra weight-lifting tasks?

No, although several companies have tried to do this. When the Wheaton Glass Company was sued, it listed seventeen extra tasks its male selector-packers had to perform to try to justify higher wages for men, but the court found that the work of both men and women workers was "substantially equal" and warranted equal pay.[62] The amount of back wages the women won shows the importance of this concept. The women were underpaid by only twenty-one cents an hour, but this added up to almost a million dollars under the final court order.

May a company avoid responsibility for unequal wages when a union threatens to strike if the company pays equal wages?

No. It is just as illegal for the union to try—by any method—to force unequal wages on the company as it is for the company to pay them. In such a situation, both would be found guilty of violating the act.[63]

What kinds of jobs have been found to be equal under the Equal Pay Act, forcing companies to raise the wages of women workers?

Jobs found to be equal include nurse's aides and orderlies in hospitals; assembly line workers in factories, where some of the men do a little heavy lifting; janitors and maids in colleges; and salesclerks in department stores, no matter what kind of merchandise they sell. Other jobs in which women gained back wages are bank teller, laboratory technician, inspector, press operator, machine operator, and packer. The list could, of course, continue; so women who suspect they are being paid less than men for doing the same work should be sure to challenge the practice.

Which federal agency enforces the Equal Pay Act?

The Equal Employment Opportunity Commission administers this law. Responsibility for enforcing the law was transferred to the EEOC from the Wage and Hour Division of the Department of Labor on 1 July 1979 under President Carter's Civil Rights Reorganization Plan No. 1.

How can women enforce their rights under the Equal Pay Act?

They must first contact a local or area office of the EEOC and explain the circumstances in which they and/or other women are being paid less than men; they must then give their name and address in order to be contacted for further information. If they have a lawyer, a lawsuit can be brought against the company immediately without going to the EEOC at all.[64]

Will the EEOC keep women's names confidential on request?

Yes, in an equal pay investigation, the EEOC is supposed to go to great lengths to protect the anonymity of anyone who fears exposure. For example, if the only woman faculty member in the English department of a university files an Equal Pay Act charge and wants to remain anonymous, the EEOC should investigate a number of departments. This way the investigation will include a number of women faculty, not just the complainant, and the complainant can remain unidentified.

If the charge includes both an Equal Pay Act and a Title VII violation, it will be more difficult to protect women's anonymity.

May an organization report unequal wages to the EEOC?

Yes, and there is no requirement that the organization obtain the permission of any of the affected women.

What steps will the EEOC take to enforce your rights?

The EEOC investigative procedures for Equal Pay Act complaints are very similar to those used for Title VII cases.

Will the EEOC refer the Equal Pay Act charge to a state FEP agency for initial investigation?

No. There is no requirement that the EEOC give state agencies a chance to act first under the Equal Pay Act. If a charge claims a violation of Title VII in addition to a violation of the Equal Pay Act, the state agency gives up any right it may have to investigate first the Title VII part of the charge. This allows the EEOC to begin processing both parts of charge immediately, and for that reason it is often advantageous to add an Equal Pay violation whenever appropriate to any charge of discrimination.

How long will it take the EEOC to act on a complaint?

Because of the limited kind of charge brought under the Equal Pay Act, it will usually does not take as long to process as a Title VII charge.

Are all companies covered by the Equal Pay Act?

The official definition is that a company must be "engaged in commerce" or "engaged in the production of goods for commerce." This definition is not very helpful, but the courts have interpreted it broadly to reach many companies and even some public institutions, like schools and hospitals. When in doubt, it is wise to assume that an employer is covered until it is determined otherwise. If an employer must comply with the federal minimum wage and overtime pay law (the Fair Labor Standards Act), it must also obey the Equal Pay Act. In addition, executive, administrative, and professional employees, who are exempt from the minimum wage and overtime provisions of the Fair Labor Standards Act, are included under the Equal Pay Act. A local EEOC Office may be contacted for assistance in determining whether or not a situation is covered.

Are there any time limits under the Equal Pay Act?

Only one. The lawsuit must be brought within two years of the discrimination, or within three years if the company discriminated "willfully." Obviously, if the company is still underpaying its women workers, there is no problem. But if the company recently decided to comply with the law, the lawsuit must be filed within two years from the time the company stopped discriminating.

The two-year limit also affects the amount of back pay. Back pay can be collected only for the two years prior to the filing of the lawsuit; hence, the sooner one sues, the more money one collects. (Compare this to Title VII, where the date on which the charge is filed with the EEOC is the relevant date for computing back wages. Unlike that situation, filing a complaint with the EEOC under the Equal Pay Act will not increase your back wages; here the relevant date is that of starting the lawsuit, so it is important not to waste time in doing so.)

It is important to remember also that going to the EEOC is not the same as starting a lawsuit. One woman complained to the EEOC about wage discrimination immediately but did not start her lawsuit until more than three years later. She lost her case under the Equal Pay Act because of this delay.[65] So the two- (or three-) year deadline for starting an equal pay lawsuit must be kept in mind, even if a Title VII complaint is filed with the EEOC about the same incident.

What are women in a successful lawsuit under the Equal Pay Act entitled to recover?

They can win the wages they should have earned (back wages)—up to two years worth—plus the same amount as punishment for the company, plus attorneys' fees and court costs. Since Title VII does not provide for the recovery of "double" back wages, an Equal Pay Act charge should be added to every Title VII lawsuit when the facts support doing so. The provision for attorney's fees is supposed to help women locate a lawyer, just as the Title VII provision is. A court may also award back wages for three years, doubled as punishment for the company, if the lawyer can prove that the company discriminated "willfully." However, in a suit brought by a worker or workers, the judge cannot order the company to raise the salaries of the women to the legal level for the future (as he can in lawsuits brought by the EEOC).[66]

What can women read to better understand the Equal Pay Act?

The statute is found in 29 U.S.C. § 206(d). The EEOC has adopted Equal Pay Act regulations, published in 29 C.F.R. §§ 1620.1–.34. They are also found in the CCH *Employment*

Practices Guide and the BNA *Fair Employment Practice Manual*.

THE EXECUTIVE ORDER

What are executive orders?

Executive orders are directives issued by the President, telling the executive branch of the government to take certain action as set forth in the order. In most respects, an executive order has the force and effect of a law.

What executive order forbids employment discrimination against women workers?

Executive Order No. 11246, issued by President Lyndon Johnson, requires any employer that has a contract with the federal government not to discriminate. Initially, this forbade race discrimination only, but the President later issued Executive Order No. 11375, which amended the former order by adding sex discrimination to its prohibitions.

Which employers are covered by Executive Order No. 11246 (as amended by Executive Order No. 11375)?

The executive order applies to any company or institution that has a contract for more than $10,000 with the federal government, whether it is to sell typewriters to the government, to do scientific research, or to produce missiles. The order also applies to subcontractors of the contractor (both are referred to in this chapter as *contractors*) although the order is seldom enforced as to subcontractors. Finally, anyone applying for federal construction money (referred to here as an *applicant*) is also covered and must obtain promises of nondiscrimination from the contractors who will perform the construction work for the applicant.

The executive order applies to all branches of a company that has a contract with the government, even though only one branch may have the contract. It does not apply directly to any unions involved with the company although strong pressure is exerted on the unions indirectly.

What action must the executive branch take under the executive order?

Every agency or department in the executive branch must obtain a promise from any contractor with whom it has a contract that the company will not discriminate against its workers. The agency must also demand that applicants for federal construction money agree to put the same promise in their contract with the construction company doing the actual work. This promise is generally called the Equal Employment Opportunity (EEO) clause, and pertinent positions include the following.

During the performance of this contract, the contractor agrees as follows:

1) The contractor will not discriminate against any employee or applicant for employment because of race, color, religion, sex, or national origin. The contractor will take affirmative action to ensure that applicants are employed, and that employees are treated during employment without regard to their race, color, religion, sex, or national origin. Such action shall include, but not be limited to the following: employment, upgrading, demotion, or transfer, recruitment or recruitment advertising; layoff or termination; rates of pay or other forms of compensation; and selection for training, including is apprenticeship.

Unless the contractor or applicant agrees to this clause, she or he cannot get the contract or the federal money. For example, if Columbia University wants a federal contract to do research on guinea pigs, it will have to agree to these conditions before the government will give it the contract. And if Chicago wants federal money for a construction project, it will have to put this clause in its contract with the Big Bull Construction Company, which will actually do the work.

What practices by a contractor constitute discrimination against women workers in violation of the EEO contract clause?

Discrimination under the executive order is generally measured by the same standards as discrimination under Title VII; therefore, if something is illegal under Title VII, it is almost always a violation of the contract, too. (There are some variations, but they are not very important.) Given this fact, women workers should consider and use all the legal standards of what constitutes discrimination set forth above for Title VII when they want to bring charges against a contractor, including the charge of retaliation, which is illegal under both laws.

Does the EEO clause require the contractor to do anything other than refrain from discriminating?

Yes. Under the EEO clause, the contractor must also take "affirmative action" to ensure fair treatment to women workers. All contractors have this obligation if they want the federal contract, and therein lies the chief difference with Title VII. Whether or not anyone ever files a charge against a particular contractor, she or he will have to undertake affirmative action under the executive order.

Under Title VII, a company almost always has the same theoretical obligation because affirmative action is necessary to correct the effects of past discrimination and most companies have discriminated in the past. However, a company is not specifically required to take affirmative action under Title VII unless a court makes a finding of discrimination. Few companies have elected to comply with the spirit of Title VII to correct the effects of past discrimination and implement affirmative action unless there was such a finding. In fact the decision of one company to implement an affirmative action plan was challenged by a white man in 1979 on the theory that voluntary race-based affirmative action resulted in reverse discrimination and was forbidden by Title VII. The Supreme Court upheld the company's action as legal because it was within the objectives of Title VII.[67] This result was reaffirmed in 1987 in a challenge by a white man to a sex-based affirmative action plan by a county government.[68]

But as a practical matter, few companies, unless covered by Executive Order No. 11246, voluntarily undertake affirmative action. They gamble that women will not sue under Title VII and thereby avoid the trouble and expense of affirmative action. Of course if women do sue under Title VII, the company has to take action and recompense the women for its failure to do so earlier, but that is a gamble many companies are willing to take.

What exactly is an affirmative action plan?

An affirmative action plan is the formal plan the contractor (at least, those with fifty or more employees and a yearly aggregate of $50,000 or more in federal government contracts) must draw up to meet its affirmative action requirements. Generally the contractor must analyze those jobs in which it underutilizes women, set numerical goals and a specific timetable for increasing the utilization of women, and describe in detail the methods it will use to do so, specifying which company personnel will be responsible for the program. Setting goals and timetables constitutes the heart of the program. An example is an agreement by the company to increase women blue-collar workers to between 10 and 15 percent of its workforce during the first year of the contract and to between 12 and 17 percent during the second year.

The specific requirements for the affirmative action plan are too elaborate to discuss in detail here. However, readers interested in learning more should read the applicable government regulations, found at 41 C.F.R. pt. 60.

If the contractor fails to meet the numerical goals it sets on the specified time schedule, will the government penalize it?

Not necessarily. All the government requires is that the contractor make an effort in good faith to meet the goals. If the company fails but can demonstrate it took action in good faith, it will be home free.

What government agency enforces Executive Order No. 11246 (as amended by Executive Order No. 11375)?

It is enforced by a special office in the Department of Labor, the Office of Federal Contract Compliance Programs (OFCCP).

How does the OFCCP enforce the executive order?

There are two basic methods: compliance reviews and complaint procedures. In theory, the OFCCP conducts periodic reviews of contractors to see whether they discriminate or have fulfilled their duty to take affirmative action. In addition, OFCCP regulations require reviews of certain large contractors before they are awarded a contract. In actual practice though, even prior to the Reagan administration, compliance reviews (either before or after contracts were awarded) were not conducted regularly. Since the early 1980s, the situation improved somewhat. But the OFCCP is understaffed, making it very difficult for it to do its job. And the entire concept of affirmative action is under increasing political attack, which complicates matters further.

The OFCCP has also established a complaint procedure under which any employee of or job applicant with a contractor can accuse the contractor of discrimination by writing to the OFCCP. This is the second way of turning up evidence that a contractor is violating the terms of its EEO contract clause.

How can women file complaints of discrimination with the OFCCP?

They can send a letter to the Director of the OFCCP, Department of Labor, 200 Constitution Avenue, N.W., Washington, D.C. 20010, or to any OFCCP regional or area office, setting forth: (1) the complainant's name, address, and phone number; (2) the name and address of the contractor; (3) a description of the discrimination (using the Title VII standards set forth in the first half of this chapter and keeping in mind the advantages of describing a continuing policy of discrimination); and 4) any other pertinent information. Organizations may file on behalf of the person who is discriminated against. The regulations also require that the complaint be filed within 180 days of the discrimination unless the time limit is extended for a good reason.

What will the OFCCP do with such a complaint?

Individual complaints will be transferred to the EEOC where they will be processed under Title VII. Class and systemic complaints will be investigated by the OFCCP. Women should thus file only class and systemic complaints with the OFFCP and should make clear in the complaint that it concerns classwide discrimination.

What penalties can the OFCCP impose when it finds that a contractor discriminates against women or has not carried out its affirmative action plan?

The OFCCP may hold up funds on the contract until it gets compliance (including back pay for the class of affected women), cancel a contract or part of a contract, or order the contractor debarred from future contracts with the government. All of these penalties could have an enormous impact on companies that depend on government contracts for most of their business, for if they lose government work they will often go out of business.

An alternative penalty is to refer the company's case to the Justice Department. The Justice Department theoretically can sue the company to enforce the provisions of the contract in which the contractor agreed to provide equal employment opportunity.

Does the OFCCP usually impose these penalties?

Rarely. The OFCCP has often been criticized for its failure to utilize fully the very powerful sanctions it has available. To some extent, the inaction is due to understaffing, but it has also been due to political judgement. Whatever the reason, the OFCCP rarely imposes the penalties that the executive order requires.

Given the failure of full enforcement of the executive orders, should women bother to file complaints under the OFCCP?

It depends on what the women hope to accomplish. If their purpose is to force the company to stop discriminating, this is not the best avenue because there is no way they can force the OFCCP to take action against a company. On the other hand, the executive order complaint is an excellent way to put some pressure on the company, especially when this method is used in conjunction with other laws. But the courts do not have the political freedom to refuse to act on a Title VII or Equal Pay Act complaint; the OFCCP does in refusing to act on an executive order complaint. Courts may try to duck the issue, they may find the facts against the complainant, but they cannot refuse to act at all; and there is always the option to appeal to higher courts if the results are not favorable. Moreover, some courts have reached excellent decisions under Title VII and the Equal Pay Act, which have forced companies to take effective action to end discrimination. Given these factors, women should concentrate their main enforcement efforts on Title VII and use executive order complaints and negotiations as a backstop to the main action.

Some women have failed to understand this point and have used the executive order as their main weapon. This approach was once useful in the area of university discrimination against teachers, who were not protected by Title VII until the March 1972 amendments and therefore had no other way to protest sex discrimination. But executive order complaints should not be the prime route for women protected by Title VII, which now means most women workers. If possible, any woman covered by Title VII should use a lawsuit under that statute as her main enforcement method. It can't hurt, however, to file complaints with the OFCCP in addition to such a lawsuit because that will maximize the pressure on the company. Even if the OFCCP does nothing in the short run, action may be taken during a compliance review if the OFCCP finds that women have lodged a number of complaints against a company.

May women bring a lawsuit under the executive order against a federal contractor if the OFCCP refuses to take action?
No. Several persons have tried this, and to date the courts have always said that there is no right to sue under the executive order.

What can women read to understand the executive order better?
Read Executive Order No. 11246 (as amended by Executive Order No. 11375) and the OFCCP regulations. The first is found at 3 C.F.R. 1966–1970 Comp., p. 685; the second at 41 C.F.R. pts. 60-1, -2, -4, and -20. Both are also found in the CCH and BNA books. Part 60-1 of the OFCCP regulations deals with compliance reviews and complaint procedures. Part 60-2 discusses the affirmative action program for nonconstruction contractors and is the part generally referred to as revised Order No. 4. Part 60-4 discusses affirmative action for women in construction.

What steps can women take besides filing complaints to protect their rights under the executive order?
One possibility is to get involved in helping the company develop its affirmative action plan. Women workers who hesitate to start a lawsuit might still make a significant impact on

company policy by insisting on a voice in these plans. Women at all levels in the company should be involved—not just the professionals. Many women caught in dead-end, low-paying jobs, like that of telephone operator, clerk, salesperson, or assembly-line worker, will have strong ideas about how to improve their job situation.

Another step is to ask to see the company plan in order to monitor the company's compliance with it. In general, the OFCCP encourages companies to reveal these plans although the regulations do not explicitly require this, and many companies are reluctant to do so. But the company could be pressured about its good faith if it is unwilling to let women employees see what it has promised the government it would do. The OFCCP has published a compliance manual, and women should seek copies of it. Comparing the program to the requirements of the manual is another way to monitor the company's progress.

Finally, women's groups can and should start pressuring the OFCCP to enforce the executive order. Pressure from women has already forced the OFCCP to amend its regulations. Federal agencies are vulnerable to pressure, and much more needs to be applied to this one.

STATE ANTIDISCRIMINATION LAWS

What are state fair employment practice laws?

Most states have passed one or more laws forbidding employment discrimination, often using language or concepts parallel or identical to the federal laws discussed in this chapter. States have their own equal pay acts, fair employment practice acts modeled on Title VII, public works laws modeled on Executive Order No. 11246, and public employee laws modeled on Executive Order No. 11478. The federal and state laws cover much the same practices, although state laws are often interpreted more conservatively. State laws may, however, provide that victims of discrimination are entitled to full damages for pain and suffering or punitive damages, in which case they are worth pursuing because damages for women are limited under Title VII. For further details, see the above section on The Civil

Rights Acts of 1991. It may beneficial to check state law before filing a complaint with the EEOC.

It is particularly important in the 1990's to consider using the state laws, because Republican administrations in the 1980's and early 1990's appointed avowedly conservative judges to the federal courts. Those judges are often very hostile to women and minorities who bring employment discrimination suits. In some states, there may be strong state laws and state judges who are willing to enforce them. In those states, then, women may wish to consider proceeding under state law in state court, rather than under federal law in federal court.

AGE DISCRIMINATION LAWS

What laws forbid discrimination on the basis of age?
A federal law, the Age Discrimination in Employment Act of 1967, forbids discrimination against workers aged at least forty years old. The act is found at 29 U.S.C. § 621 *et seq.*; the regulations, at 29 C.F.R. pt. 1625. Several states have passed age discrimination laws, some with different age limits. Both the federal and the state laws provide another avenue of redress for older women, who often face virulent discrimination, especially if they are entering the labor market for the first time. Women should be aware of the potential of these laws although this book will not discuss them in detail.

Which federal agency enforces the Age Discrimination Act?
It is enforced by the EEOC under a transfer of authority from the Wage and Hour Department of the Department of Labor on 1 July 1979.

GENERAL CONSIDERATIONS

Why is it important to understand the differences among all these laws?
Different laws prohibit different practices and help different workers. For instance, Title VII forbids segregating jobs by sex; the Equal Pay Act does not. On the other hand, Title VII

does not protect workers in companies with fewer than fifteen employees, but many state fair employment laws do.

If a woman turns to the wrong law, she will not succeed in changing her situation, even though another law may offer her protection; thus it is crucial that women and their advisors know the range of laws available and the details of their application. Sometimes, too, there is overlap among the various laws. When more than one prohibits the same practice, women can maximize the pressure on their employer or union by resorting to all the applicable laws to stop the discrimination.

What are the chief differences between each of these laws?
First, each differs drastically in the number of discriminatory practices covered. Title VII is the broadest law of all, covering almost all forms of discrimination; the Equal Pay Act goes to the opposite extreme, prohibiting only a very narrowly defined kind of wage discrimination; Executive Order No. 11246 (as amended by Executive Order No. 11375) lies somewhere in between, primarily because the agency that enforces it is oriented more toward setting up affirmative action plans than toward compensating particular women for past discrimination. The number of practices prohibited by state laws generally parallel these three federal laws but often with significant differences. For example, many state fair-employment-practice laws forbid newspapers to carry segregated help-wanted advertising columns while Title VII reaches only the advertiser.

A second difference is found in the kinds of entities covered by each law. Title VII covers employers, unions, and employment agencies; the Equal Pay Act is limited to employers and unions; Executive Order No. 11246 reaches only employers; and there are wide variations among the state laws. Within each covered group, there are other differences, with Title VII reaching employers of fifteen or more, the Equal Pay Act directed at producers of goods for interstate commerce, and the executive order limited to contractors with the federal government. Many state fair-employment-practice laws reach employers with fewer than fifteen employees.

Other important differences concern the nature and extent of the relief available under each law; whether there is a practical necessity for getting a lawyer; the degree to which an agency will enforce rights; and the number of procedural obstacles, such as strict time limits, to bringing successful lawsuits.

As emphasized throughout this chapter, women should try to use Title VII whenever possible. It reaches the most discrimination and holds out the best hope of getting an effective remedy. But if getting a lawyer is a problem or the preservation of total anonymity is a concern, the Equal Pay Act should be considered, even though it is much narrower than Title VII. The executive order may provide an effective organizing and negotiating tool in some instances, but it provides little or no guarantee of any effective relief. State laws can be useful to a small company not covered by any of the federal laws, to get faster action than might be available in a federal forum, or to get back pay for a longer period of time, or to get other forms of monetary relief such as damages rather than the limited damages available under Title VII. In the past, state agencies were more conservative than the EEOC and did not offer effective relief. But as the federal government became more hostile to women's rights and civil rights generally in the 1980s the state agencies, at least in some progressive states, became more appealing forums. Women should consult with experienced employment discrimination attorneys or local women's or civil rights groups about whether this is true in their states.

What concrete proof must a person have of discrimination before she can file a charge?

Absolutely none. Women often believe that they must have some conclusive evidence that their employer or union discriminates before they can walk into a federal or state agency and ask for help. They hope to discover the incriminating memorandum from the company president vowing never, in a thousand years, to hire a woman salesman. In fact, it is the agency's job to uncover evidence of discrimination, not the complainant's. Women who have nothing stronger than their own suspicions can walk into the right agency and fill out a complaint. It might read, for instance, the Company X refuses to promote women into management positions because of their sex. That will be enough to require the agency to look into the matter.

There is a significant practical caveat to the statutory requirement that an agency investigate such a complaint. Most agencies are overworked and understaffed. The more specific information women can point to, the better the job the agency can do for the women. Therefore, they should analyze their work situation in light of all the concepts in this chapter, as well as their own gut feelings of fairness, in order to identify specific discriminatory practices and point them out to the agency in charge. For instance: are all the secretaries women and all the managers men? What are the comparative pay scales and fringe benefits of "male" and "female" jobs? Are sex distinctions built into the collective-bargaining agreement? Some companies and unions have so clearly conceived of particular jobs as either male or female that the contract will describe some jobs using female pronouns and other jobs using male pronouns. What does the contract say about fringe benefits? Are pregnancy-related conditions excluded from the sick-pay and medical insurance provisions? Are women allowed to retire earlier than men or are they forced to retire earlier? In considering these and other questions, women should remember that they know their own job situation better than anyone else, and their analysis of its discriminatory nature is therefore potentially better than that of anyone else, no matter how expert that other person may be.

How do lawyers and agencies prove that someone has been discriminated against on the basis of sex?

There are many different ways. One of the most important is the use of statistics. Courts have said that under certain circumstances statistics may be highly indicative of discrimination. The ramifications of this point have been enormous. For instance, a company hires a lot of women, but a closer look at the statistics reveals that women hold only 0 to 1 percent of the managerial or highly paid blue-collar jobs and 95 percent of the low-paid secretarial jobs. Those statistics alone will not establish a prima facie case of discrimination. In order to have a court presume discrimination, it may have to be shown that women are present in the labor pool of blue-collar or managerial workers but are not hired for those jobs in proportion to their availability. Or there may need to be a specific non-job-related requirement that proportionately keeps women out of the higher-paying jobs. Another example is a company that hires very few women in particular jobs compared to other companies; here the statistics show discrimination in the hiring process rather than in the assignment of particular jobs. Lawyers then must generally use statistics to show not only a disproportionate distribution of men and women but also to find out at what point in the employment process the distribution takes place.

Another way to prove discrimination is through company documents, which often set forth blatantly discriminatory practices. The pension plan booklet, when read carefully, may reveal that men and women must or may retire at different ages, solely because of their sex. The health plan may show that pregnancy is not covered or is covered only minimally, although full coverage is provided for all other medical conditions. The collective bargaining agreement may use female pronouns for certain jobs, male pronouns for others—clearly indicating that the company reserves some jobs for men, others for women. The company may place help-wanted ads in segregated newspaper columns or use sex-typed language in the ad copy. All these documents can be introduced at trial to prove discrimination.

Still another way to prove discrimination is through the testimony of various workers and officials. In some situations coworkers may be willing to testify that the manager told them he would never hire a woman for a particular job because it's not suitable for women, or that they knew of the existence of a discriminatory job practice, or that the company's claim that women do different work from men is untrue.

What can women workers do to help their lawyers prove discrimination or to convince the EEOC or other agencies that they have been discriminated against?

The workers are the people who best know their job situation. They also have friends in the company or union who have access to important documents proving discrimination. If women study the concepts of what constitutes job discrimination set forth in this chapter and analyze their job situations in light of those concepts, they can help their lawyers enormously. For, unfortunately, many lawyers and agencies do not understand all these concepts, nor do they have the time and energy to go after the necessary evidence, nor do they always care about sex discrimination. The more kinds of discrimination women workers analyze, therefore, and the more statistics, documents, and testimony or affidavits of friends and sympathizers they produce, the more likely they are to win their case. In other words, trying to end discrimination must be a joint venture between the women on one hand and the governmental agency personnel and lawyers on the other hand.

If a woman wins a lawsuit, what can the judge order the company to do?

First, the judge can order the company to pay any wages lost by women because of the discrimination. The amount of back wages available depends on the statute in question. (See discussions above of how back wages are computed under Title VII and the Equal Pay Act.) The judge can also award money to cover the costs of bringing the lawsuit, the lawyers' fees, and interest for the company's use of your back wages. Even more important, under the new Civil Rights Act of 1991, the judge can award compensatory and punitive damages in cases of intentional discrimination. For further details, see the section above on the Civil Rights Act of 1991.

Second, under Title VII the judge can order a company to change its employment practices in the future. This applies to any discrimination and is a way of forcing the company to recruit and hire more women, to transfer them to better jobs, to train them for different positions, to change discriminatory health plans, to increase women's wages, and so on. (Under the Equal Pay Act, only the wages can be increased.) It is this power to change employment practices that makes Title VII such a powerful weapon.

Can women get back wages, damages, and changes in company practices through negotiations with the company?

Yes. Under both Title VII and many of the state fair-employment-practice laws, the company will be asked by the appropriate agency to negotiate a settlement of the case. Women should be wary of accepting settlements, though, that do not effectively provide the relief they want. Some agencies are often more responsive to business interests than to women workers, and the settlements they propose are at times so vague as to be meaningless. Since a court may later refuse to award the relief a woman is entitled to because she signed such a settlement, it is important not to enter into one lightly. Thus, if a proposed settlement is inadequate, it should be rejected and other legal remedies should be pursued—including suing the company, if necessary.

What role can women's paralegal groups play in the field of employment discrimination law?

First, they might establish a counseling service to help women who call in with complaints of job discrimination. After studying employment discrimination law and procedures, the paralegal groups can direct these women to the proper agency or agencies and make sure that they comply with all the necessary procedural steps. More important, these groups can help women analyze the discrimination at their company, question them to find forms of discrimination that the women may have overlooked, and make sure they fill out the charge or complaint forms with all the discriminatory practices that can be identified. The women worker who calls or walks in the door may have seized on a single form of discrimination because it is particularly onerous at that point in time; the chances are she faces a myriad of other discriminatory practices in her job, all of which should be attacked at once in order to maximize results.

Counseling can continue even after the charge is filed with the appropriate agency. Paralegal advisors can help women locate evidence of discrimination by telling them what to look for and can refer these women to lawyers. They can also try to convince other women workers to join in the lawsuit by alleviating fears and explaining what the lawsuit is about and the advantages of joining in.

Besides individual counseling, paralegal groups can also take on a very important educational function. Most women simply do not understand the full extent of their rights. Speeches can be made, radio and television programs developed, printed materials distributed—all with the aim of helping women understand their rights and how to assert them.

A third paralegal project could be to start organizing women workers. Women need to push their labor unions to help them with sex discrimination problems, and new unions should be formed where the workers are unorganized. A labor union lawyer, with the force of a union behind her, can accomplish broad institutional changes—often without having to bring a lawsuit.

The workers themselves can also do much by organizing other women in the process of bringing employment discrimination lawsuits. It is difficult for one woman, acting on her own, to bring about much change. She must enlist the help of others, including sympathetic men. Concerted effort can force an employer to make some major changes in its policies; just as important, it can heighten the consciousness of many women workers who are too frightened initially even to discuss the subject of discrimination. Women must take that kind of action to achieve real change.

NOTES

1. 42 U.S.C. 2000e *et seq.* (Effective July 1965.)
2. S. Rep. No. 1137, 91st Cong., 2d Sess. 15 (1970).
3. *The American Woman, 1990–1991: A Status Report*, edited by Sara E. Rix for the Women's Research and Education Institute (W. W. Norton & Co., New York, 1990), table 19. Source: U.S. Bureau of Labor Statistics, January 1976, table 2 and January 1989, table 22.
4. 401 U.S. 424 (1971). See also *Dothard v. Rawlinson*, 433 U.S. 321 (1977). In that case, height and weight standards for correctional counselors in the Alabama state penitentiary system—which appeared on the surface to be neutral job requirements because they applied to both men and women—were found to exclude more women than men from the job; thus they were held to be sexually discriminatory and illegal under Title VII.
5. 490 U.S. 642 (1989).
6. See chapter 8 for general information on Title IX. In 1982 the Supreme Court ruled that Title IX prohibits sex-based discrimination not only against students but also against employees in federally funded education programs. *North Haven Board of Education v. Bell*, 456 U.S. 519.
7. 433 U.S. 321 (1977).
8. *See, e.g., Gunther v. Iowa State Men's Reformatory*, 612 F.2d 1079, (8th Cir.), *cert. denied*, 446 U.S. 966 (1980); *Griffin v. Michigan Dept. of Corrections*, 654 F. Supp. 690 (E.D. Mich. 1982); *Hardin v. Stynchcomb*, 691 F.2d. 1364 (11th Cir.1982), *reh'g denied*, 696 F.2d 1007 (11th Cir. 1983).
9. *See Brooks v. ACF Industries*, 537 F. Supp. 1122 (S.D. W. Va. 1982);

Fesel v. Masonic Home of Del. Inc., 447 F. Supp. 1346 (D. Del. 1978), *aff'd*, 591 F.2d 1334 (3d Cir. 1979); *Backus v. Baptist Medical Center*, 510 F. Supp. 1191 (E.D. Ark. 1981) *vacated on other grounds*, 671 F.2d 1100 (8th Cir. 1981). For a discussion of the competing rights of privacy and equal employment opportunity see Caloway, *Equal Opportunity and Third Party Privacy Interests: An Analytical Framework for Reconciling Competing Rights*, 54 Fordham L. Rev. 327 (1985).

10. *Torres v. Wisconsin Dept. of Health & Social Services*, 859 F.2d 1523 (7th Cir. 1988) (*en banc*), *cert. denied*, 109 S. Ct. 1133 and 1537 (1989). This case illustrates the difficulty of this issue. While this result seems advantageous to the women inmates, it sets a precedent that may someday be used against women seeking jobs where men's privacy interests are at stake.

11. *Rosenfeld v. Southern Pacific Railroad Company*, 444 F.2d 1219 (9th Cir. 1971).

12. 452 U.S. 161 (1981). For other cases on the issue, see *IUE v. Westinghouse Electric Corp.*, 631 F.2d 1094 (3d Cir.) *cert. denied*, 449 U.S. 888 (1980); *Christensen v. State of Iowa*, 563 F.2d 353 (8th Cir. 1977); *Lemons v. City and County of Denver*, 620 F.2d 228 (10th Cir.) *cert. denied*, 449 U.S. 888 (1980).

13. 770 F.2d 1401 (9th Cir. 1985), *rev'g*, 578 F. Supp. 846 (W.D. Wash. 1983).

14. 770 F.2d at 1405.

15. *See, e.g., American Nurses Association v. Illinois*, 783 F.2d 716 (7th Cir. 1986). Several years earlier, just before the *Gunther* decision was issued, a federal judge in Pennsylvania did rely in part on a job evaluation plan in ruling that an employer who paid men more than women violated Title VII. *Taylor v. Charley Brothers Company*, 25 FEP Cases 602 (W.D. Pa. 1981), shows the kinds of proof that one court thought would be helpful in proving wage discrimination cases.

16. 478 U.S. 385 (1986).

17. *Sobel v. Yeshiva University*, 839 F.2d 18 (2d Cir. 1988), *cert. denied*, 490 U.S. 1105 (1989).

18. 20 U. Mich. J.L. Ref. 7 (1986).

19. Safran, *What Men Do to Women on the Job: A Shocking Look at Sexual Harassment*, 148 Redbook 149 (1976).

20. *See, e.g.*, U.S. Merit Systems Protection Board Office of Policy and Evaluation; Sexual Harassment in the Federal Government: An Update (1988). *See also Thomas Battle Spotlights Harassment*, Wall Street Journal, Oct. 9, 1991 (sexual harassment complaints filed with the EEOC rose 25% between 1986 and 1990; *Evaluating Sexual Harassment in the Workplace*, Wash. Post, July 4, 1988; *Two Out of*

Three Women in Military Study Report Sexual Harassment Incidents, N.Y. Times, Sept. 12, 1990.

21. 477 U.S. 57 (1986).

22. 29 C.F.R. § 1604.11. The Supreme Court in *Meritor Savings Bank,* referred approvingly to these guidelines, 477 U.S. at 65.

23. *Hall v. Gus Construction Co., Inc.,* 842 F. 2d 1010 (8th Cir. 1988)

24. *Resse v. Hayden,* No 85-0827 (D.D.C. Oct. 4, 1986)

25. *Kyriazi v. Western Electric Co.,* 461 F. Supp. 894 (D.N.J. 1978).

26. *Bowe v. Colgate-Palmolive Co.,* 416 F.2d 711 (7th Cir. 1969).

27. *Weeks v. Southern Bell Tel.,* 408 F.2d 288 (5th Cir. 1969).

28. 29 C.F.R. § 1604.2.

29. 444 F.2d 1219 (9th Cir. 1971).

30. 29 C.F.R. § 1604.2(b)(3)–(5).

31. *Bastardo v. Warren,* 332 F. Supp. 501 (W.D. Wis. 1970).

32. *Burns v. Rohr Corporation,* 346 F. Supp. 994 (S.D. Cal. 1972).

33. *Hays v. Potlatch Forests, Inc.,* 465 F.2d 1081 (8th Cir. 1972). *But see State v. Fairfield Communities Land Co.,* 538 S.W.2d 698 (Ark. 1976), *cert. denied,* 429 U.S. 1004 (1976).

34. *Homemakers, Inc. v. Division of Industrial Welfare,* 509 F.2d 20 (9th Cir. 1974), *cert. denied,* 423 U.S. 1063 (1976).

35. Another possibility is to provide for voluntary overtime on the basis of seniority. That is, the most senior employees—male and female—may decline overtime, while the most junior employees must accept it (if there are not enough volunteers).

36. *American Tobacco Co. v. Patterson,* 456 U.S. 63 (1982).

37. 490 U.S. 900 (1989).

38. 433 U.S. 321 (1977).

39. *Brush v. San Francisco Newspaper Printing Co.,* 315 F. Supp. 577 (N.D. Cal. 1970) *aff'd,* 469 F.2d 89 (9th Cir. 1972), *cert. denied,* 410 U.S. 943 (1973). *Greenfield v. Field Enterprises, Inc.,* 4 FEP Cases 548 (N.D. Ill. 1972); *Morrow v. Mississippi Publishers Corp.,* 5 FEP Cases 287 (S.D. Miss. 1972), *reh'g denied,* 414 U.S. 881 (1973).

40. *Pittsburgh Press Co. v. Pittsburgh Commission on Human Relations,* 413 U.S. 376 (1973). Such laws have an added clause covering anyone who "aids or abets" someone else in discriminating. At the very least, the newspaper aids and abets discriminatory companies when it gives them the sex-segregated column that enables them to discriminate. States with such laws include Alaska, Arizona, California, Colorado, Connecticut, Hawaii, Illinois, Indiana, Iowa, Kansas, Kentucky, Maine, Massachusetts, Michigan, Minnesota, Missouri, New Hampshire, New Jersey, New Mexico, New York, Ohio, Oklahoma, Oregon, Pennsylvania, Rhode Island, South Dakota, Utah, and West Virginia.

41. 401 U.S. 424 (1971).

42.   Uniform Guidelines on Employee Selection Procedures (1978), 48
      Fed. Reg. 34766 (Aug. 1, 1983); 29 C.F.R. pt. 1607, § 6A.

43.   *Brunet v. City of Columbus*, 642 F. Supp. 1214 (S.D. Ohio, 1986)
      appeal dismissed 826 F.2d 1062 (6th Cir.. 1987) *cert. denied*, 485 U.S.
      1034. *See also Sontag v. Bronstein*, 306 N.E.2d 405 (N.Y. 1973).

44.   *E.g., Berkman v. New York Fire Department*, 812 F.2d 52, (2d Cir.
      1987), *cert. denied*, 484 U.S. 848 (1987).

45.   *See* Bem and Bem, "Case Study of a Nonconscious Ideology: Training
      the Women to Know Her Place," in Bem, *Beliefs, Attitudes and
      Human Affairs* (1970) (citing Goldberg, *Are Women Prejudiced
      Against Women?* Transaction (April 1968)). On the problem of sex
      stereotyping generally see Taub, *Keeping Women in Their Place:
      Stereotyping Per se as a Form of Employment Discrimination*, 21
      B.C.L. Rev. 345, 352–57 (1980).

46.   Guidelines on Affirmative Action, 49 Fed. Reg. 31411 (Aug. 7, 1984),
      29 C.F.R. pt. 1608.

47.   *Steelworkers v. Weber*, 443 U.S. 193 (1979), *reh'g. denied*, 444 U.S.
      889 (1979).

48.   *Ruhe v. Philadelphia Inquirer*, 14 FEP Cases 1304 (E.D. Pa. 1975).

49.   *Advocates for Women v. Marshall*, No. 76-0862 (E.D. Pa. 1975)

50.   *Arizona Governing Committee v. Norris*, 463 U.S. 1073 (1983); *Los
      Angeles Dept. of Water & Power v. Manhart*, 435 U.S. 702 (1978);
      Bartmess v. Drewry's U.S.A. Inc. 444 F.2d 1186 (7th Cir.), *cert.
      denied*, 404 U.S. 939 (1971); and *Rosen v. Public Services Electric and
      Gas Company*, 409 F.2d 775 (3d Cir. 1969), followed by 477 F.2d 90
      (3d Cir. 1973).

51.   29 C.F.R. § 1604.9(f).

52.   *Arizona Governing Committee v. Norris*, 463 U.S. 1073 (1983). *See
      also* the cases cited therein at 1081 n.9.

53.   *Wambhein v. J.C. Penney Co.*, 642 F.2d 362 (9th Cir. 1981) *cert.
      denied*, 467 U.S. 1255 (1984). *EEOC v. J.C. Penney & Co.*, 843 F.2d
      249 (6th Cir. 1988).

54.   *Los Angeles Dept. of Water & Power v. Manhart*, 435 U.S. 702 (1978);
      29 C.F.R. § 1604.9(e).

55.   This might occur, for example, if the employer has fewer than 15
      employees or if charges are not filed within the time allowed.

56.   For possible limits on this concept, see *United Airlines, v. Evans*, 431
      U.S. 553 (1977) and *Lorance v. AT&T Technologies*, 490 U.S. 900
      (1989).

57.   490 U.S. 642 (1989).

58.   490 U.S. 228 (1989).

59.   490 U.S. 900 (1989).

60.   _____ U.S. _____, 111 S. Ct. 1227 (1991).

61. _____ U.S. _____, 111 S. Ct. 1138 (1991).

62. *Schultz v. Wheaton Glass Company*, 421 F. 2d 259 (3d Cir. 1970), *cert. denied, Wheaton Glass Co. v. Schultz*, 398 U.S. 905 (1970).

63. *Hodgson v. Sagner, Inc.*, 462 F.2d 180 (4th Cir. 1972).

64. The EEOC and the Department of Labor have signed an agreement that Wage and Hour Division offices of the Department of Labor will continue to take complaints under the Equal Pay Act. After taking the complaint the Wage and Hour Division office will transfer the complaint to the EEOC. This arrangement was made because there are many more Wage and Hour offices than EEOC offices around the country and because workers are familiar with filing Equal Pay Act complaints at Wage and Hour offices. Although the arrangement is to continue indefinitely, complainants should file directly with the EEOC whenever possible because most Wage and Hour employees who used to handle equal pay complaints have been transferred and soon very few Wage and Hour employees will be familiar with the Equal Pay Act.

65. *Wells v. Pioneer Wear, Inc.*, 19 EPD ¶ 9244 (10th Cir. 1979).

66. This problem can be remedied by bringing the lawsuit under both Title VII and the Equal Pay Act because the court can order the company to raise salaries under Title VII.

67. *Steelworkers v. Weber*, 443 U.S. 193 (1979), *reh'g denied*, 444 U.S. 889 (1979).

68. *Johnson v. Transportation Agency, Santa Clara County*, 480 U.S. 616 (1987).

III

Parenting and Work

In 1978 Congress amended Title VII to make it clear that employment discrimination based on pregnancy, childbirth, and related medical conditions is illegal sex discrimination.[1] This amendment was designed to override a famous 1976 Supreme Court decision, *General Electric Co. v. Gilbert*.[2] The Court ruled in that case that it was not discriminatory to deny pregnant workers fringe benefits (pay while disabled from working) given to other workers for all other disabilities. The Court's logic is perhaps best summed up by saying that discrimination based on sex occurs only when you have a group of men to compare to a group of women. Since there are no pregnant men, GE's denial of disability benefits to pregnant women was not sex discrimination. This logic had frightening potential for women workers—almost any discriminatory policy could be justified on the theory that women have been, are, or could become pregnant.

The 1978 Pregnancy Discrimination Act (PDA) firmly rejected this logic. Instead, the act spelled out that pregnant women who are able to work must be treated like other able workers, and likewise that women disabled by pregnancy, childbirth, or related medical conditions must be treated like other disabled workers. The ramifications of this general theory are set forth more fully in answer to the next questions.

Two related problems also deserve special attention: the exclusion of fertile women from workplaces (traditionally male-dominated) where they may be exposed to hazardous chemicals; and the difficulties facing workers in need of childcare. This chapter first discusses women's general rights under the PDA and then considers the specific problems.

THE PREGNANCY DISCRIMINATION ACT

How does the PDA protect women workers?

The PDA has helped many women to secure pregnancy-related benefits, including leaves of absence with job security, medical insurance coverage for childbirth, and paid leave while they are in the hospital or recuperating from childbirth, as well as at least some relief from the pervasive employer hostility to pregnant workers and new mothers.[3] However, *the PDA does not require employers to provide any special benefits* to pregnant workers, on the theory that laws treating pregnant women differently than other workers will eventually be used against women, as they have been in the past.[4]

May a woman be fired or forced to take unpaid maternity leave just because she is pregnant?

No. The reason is fairly simple. Pregnancy is like other medical conditions; if a woman is physically incapable of working, just as a person with a broken leg may be incapable of working, she does not have to be kept on the job. But if she is physically able to work, the employer has no right to get rid of her, whether the motivation is Victorian paternalistic concern for her welfare or prudish embarrassment because she is pregnant. Moreover, even if she is temporarily unable to do part of her job (for example, because her doctor says she should not do heavy lifting), she may have a right to transfer to another job—if that is how the employer treats other employees who are temporarily disabled from doing part of their job.

In short, pregnant workers may not be fired or forced to take maternity leave while they are willing and able to work, unless the same policy applies to all workers expecting to have temporary disabilities in the immediate future. Similarly, an employer may not limit the number of days of "maternity" leave while the woman is disabled (e.g., when she is recuperating from childbirth), if the employer permits unlimited leave for other incapacitating physical conditions.

May an employer refuse to hire a woman because she is pregnant?

Generally, no. As an initial matter, employers may not question a woman applicant about her prior pregnancies, childcare arrangements, marital status, and other such concerns if they do not make similar inquiries of male applicants.[5] Even more important, employers may not refuse to hire a woman because she is pregnant, unless they inquire about and refuse to hire other applicants with other medical conditions that will similarly require sick leave in the future.

Can employers have a formal policy of never hiring pregnant women or of firing all pregnant women upon learning of their pregnancy?

Almost never. In an important decision in 1991 (see the section below on reproductive hazards), the Supreme Court announced a very tough standard for judging the legality of formal employer rules barring all pregnant women from the workplace.[6] The Court said that employers with such rules would have to show that "substantially all" pregnant workers were incapable of performing their jobs. Moreover, the job duties at stake would have to be those involving "the core of the employee's job performance" and the "central purpose" of the business. Virtually no employer rules barring pregnant workers will survive this kind of probing scrutiny.

Even if employers don't admit to a formal policy of refusing to hire pregnant women, or of firing or demoting women while they are pregnant, can women who suspect discrimination take their employers to court?

Yes, and they can win if they can prove the employer was motivated by the woman's pregnancy and not by valid reasons. But an employer may refuse to hire a pregnant woman if it has a legitimate, nondiscriminatory reason for doing so. One court, for example, allowed a county court to withdraw an offer of a position as staff attorney to a woman who disclosed her pregnancy after she had been offered the position. The court reasoned that it would be a bad business practice to hire a worker who would need to take a leave of absence during on-the-job training.[7]

Sorting out when employers have a legitimate reason and when they are really discriminating against pregnant workers can be difficult. Employers may try to get away with discriminating by coming up with an excuse to alter the woman's conditions of employment after learning of her pregnancy. In such cases, the employer typically claims that the woman is not performing her job at an acceptable level. Courts usually decide these cases by examining evidence as to whether or not the employer's proffered explanation is "pretextual," which means that an employer is using a false reason as a coverup for its real desire to terminate, demote, or otherwise discriminate against a pregnant woman because of her pregnancy. Courts allow women to show that the asserted reason is merely pretextual "either directly by persuading the court that a discriminatory reason more likely motivated the employer or indirectly by showing that the employer's proffered explanation is unworthy of credence."[8]

Evidence of pretext may be demonstrated by showing, for example, that the employer never complained about poor performance and gave the employee consistently high performance ratings until her pregnancy became apparent, or that employees engaging in the same behavior (e.g., frequent absences) were not similarly treated. In one case,[9] an employer fired a pregnant woman—allegedly for absenteeism, failure to follow company procedure for taking leave, and a disrespectful attitude toward her supervisor. The woman won by showing that she did follow company procedure, she had apologized for her heated remarks, and other employees had received prior written warnings for poor conduct while she had not. She also successfully challenged the company action of removing her from a management training program three days after learning she was pregnant, by showing that she was qualified to remain in the training program and that her supervisors considered her pregnancy to be a problem. In other typical cases, a woman's less desirable reassignment upon return from pregnancy-related leave was attributed to sex discrimination,[10] and a pregnant woman who was fired allegedly because she refused to wear makeup proved successfully that her pregnancy, not the makeup, was the real reason for her termination.[11] Thus, women who try to show that the employer's asserted reasons were pretextual—a coverup for discriminatory motive—do have a strong chance of winning their cases.

How do women challenge pregnancy discrimination in court?

By using their rights under Title VII of the 1964 Civil Rights Act. See chapter 2, Employment Discrimination, for a discussion of the procedures and time frames that must be followed in these cases.

Do single women have any protection against pregnancy-based discrimination?

Yes, although single pregnant women may sometimes have a hard time protecting their rights. Several courts and the Equal Employment Opportunity Commission (EEOC) have ruled that the discharge of a single pregnant woman constitutes a violation of Title VII's ban on sex discrimination[12] or the equal protection clause of the Fourteenth Amendment.[13] Some cases have not succeeded, however, where courts have agreed with employers' contentions that the women were not good "role models."[14]

Is a woman who is physically disabled by pregnancy, childbirth, or related conditions entitled to the same fringe benefits given to other disabled employees?

Yes. The EEOC guidelines state:

Disabilities caused or contributed to by pregnancy, childbirth, or related medical conditions, for all job-related purposes, shall be treated the same as disabilities caused or contributed to by other medical conditions, under any health or temporary disability insurance or sick leave plan available in connection with employment. Written or unwritten employment policies and practices involving matters such as the commencement and duration of leave, the availability of extensions, the accrual of seniority and other benefits and privileges, reinstatement, and payment under any health or temporary disability insurance or sick leave plan, formal or informal, shall be applied to disability due to pregnancy, childbirth, or related medical conditions on the same terms and conditions as they are applied to other disabilities.[15]

This guideline means that women disabled by pregnancy-related conditions (e.g., childbirth and the typical six-week recuperation period after birth) are entitled to the same sick leave and sick-leave pay and benefits that a man might get for a broken leg, to the same health insurance payments, and to the same amount of time off. In short, disabled pregnant women must be treated just like all other sick or disabled employees in every employment policy relating to sickness or disability.

On the other hand, a pregnant woman who is *not* disabled from working is not entitled to sick benefits. The distinction is important because most people fail to realize that, depending on the job and the woman, there will be various periods of physical disability in any pregnancy. Some women will not be disabled until labor starts; others will hemorrhage in early pregnancy and be sent to bed for several months. The EEOC guidelines apply only to "disabilities *caused or contributed to by*" pregnancy and childbirth—not to the entire period of pregnancy (unless a woman is disabled from doing her job during the entire pregnancy).

Many employers now treat pregnancy and childbirth less favorably than all other medical conditions. Some do not give pregnant women any sick-leave pay; others exempt childbirth from health insurance plans; still others require a woman to pay a large deductible for pregnancy but not for other conditions under the health insurance plan. There are numerous other variations on the basic scheme of treating women disabled by pregnancy and childbirth differently from employees disabled by other conditions. All these variations are illegal.

May an employer treat pregnancy less favorably than other conditions in medical insurance coverage, if it only affects the wives of male workers?

No. In 1983 the Supreme Court decisively ruled that such differential treatment was illegal in the context of an employer's health insurance plan covering the dependents of employees.[16] The Newport News Shipbuilding and Dry Dock Company provided comprehensive medical insurance to the spouses of company employees but imposed a $500 limit on pregnancy-related hospitalization costs for the wives of male workers. The Court threw out this restriction, stating it discriminated against male workers, since female workers got comprehensive spousal coverage but the men did not.

Are women who have had abortions protected against employment discrimination in the same way as pregnant workers?

Generally, yes. Employers may not fire or refuse to hire women who have had abortions. Similarly, employers must give such women the same paid sick leave, temporary disability payments, or other fringe benefits that others workers receive. However, Congress wrote one exception into the law: employers are not required to pay for health insurance benefits for abortion unless the woman's life would be endangered if the pregnancy were continued until term or unless there are complications. The National Conference of Catholic Bishops successfully fought for this exception (although Congress did reject the bishops' attempt to allow employers to fire women who have had abortions). Some women believe that the exception constitutes a violation of the First Amendment guarantee of church-state separation. Any woman whose employer has denied her health benefits for an abortion might consider starting a law suit under the First Amendment to challenge the provision.

To how long a period of sick leave is a pregnant woman entitled?

She is entitled to the same length of time as are employees on sick leave for similar physical conditions. Moreover, employers who guarantee their employees that their jobs will be available upon return from sick or unpaid leave must provide the same guarantee to workers who are on sick or unpaid leave for pregnancy-related disabilities such as childbirth.

Is a pregnant woman entitled to extensions of time if the sick-leave period is too short?

If employees can get extensions for other physical conditions, she can too. Even if extensions are not available, the EEOC has said that she may be able to get a longer leave if she can show that more women than men lose their jobs because leave periods are too short. If that is true, the company may have to allow longer leave time for everyone.

Can employers treat pregnant women more favorably than other employees with temporary illnesses?

Yes, under a few state laws. In *California Federal Savings and Loan Association v. Guerra*,[17] the Supreme Court upheld a California law which required employers to provide women disabled by pregnancy, childbirth, or related medical conditions with up to four months unpaid disability leave for the length of their disability. They then had the right to return to the same or a similar job.[18] The Supreme Court ruled that in enacting the PDA, Congress provided "'a floor beneath which pregnancy disability benefits may not drop—not a ceiling above which they may not rise.'"[19]

Thus, despite the PDA's seemingly unequivocal mandate that employees disabled by pregnancy and childbirth shall be treated the same as employees disabled by other temporary disabilities, the Court allowed pregnancy to be treated as "special." It qualified this ruling, though. Special treatment may not be based on archaic or stereotypical generalizations about the abilities of pregnant workers.[20] And special treatment is limited to the period of time the woman is actually disabled.[21]

The decision, however, is of limited practical significance. It does not require employers to initiate new benefit programs where none had existed, but merely to comply with special state laws.[22] Only a few states—including California, Connecticut, Massachusetts, and Montana—and the Commonwealth of Puerto Rico in fact have such laws.[23] Employers in states without such laws cannot treat pregnant women preferentially. Nor did the Court suggest that states could legislate more extensively. Any legislation that did not apply solely and specifically to periods of physical disability associated with pregnancy would be impermissible unless it provided the nondisability leave to workers of both sexes. For example, states cannot require childcare leave for adoptive mothers while denying it to adoptive fathers.[24] Nor can biological fathers be denied childcare leave, if biological mothers get such leave after they have fully recuperated from childbirth.

May an employer refuse to hire or promote mothers because of their childcare responsibilities, if it hires or promotes fathers?

No. In *Phillips v. Martin Marietta Corporation*[25] the Supreme Court rejected the employer's decision not to hire Ms. Phillips as an assembly trainee because she had preschool children, even though it would hire fathers who had such young children. The Court said that it is illegal to have "one hiring policy for women and another for men—each having preschool-age children."[26] Ms. Phillips thus won a big battle and helped make it clear that Title VII means what it says: women and men must be treated equally on the job.

Reproductive Hazards in the Workplace[27]
In 1991 the Supreme Court decided one of the most important sex discrimination cases ever to come before it: *International Union, UAW v. Johnson Controls.*[28] The Court threw out a company policy that excluded *all fertile women* from jobs in which they would be exposed to lead, regardless of their childbearing intentions. The Court ruled that the policy was illegal sex-based discrimination because the company disregarded the risks of lead to male workers and chose instead to "protect" women by denying them jobs, rather than improving workplace conditions for all workers.[29]

The company policy restricted opportunities for women who were willing and able to work because of the remote chance that they might become pregnant and that a workplace hazard might harm the fetus. In a variety of forms, these policies were already pervasive; they were most pronounced in industries and jobs historically closed to women, where high wages and good benefits made the jobs at stake particularly attractive to unskilled workers with few other options.[30] The Court's decision ensured that companies could not limit women's access to as many as twenty million industrial jobs.

Under the *Johnson Controls* decision, is an employer allowed to exclude women who are already pregnant from jobs because of fetal risk?
No. The Court ruled that the PDA allows employers to exclude pregnant women from jobs *only* if "pregnancy actually interferes with the employee's ability to perform the job."[31] In most jobs, pregnancy rarely prevents women from carrying out their normal job duties. Only in unusual situations—for example, when complications of pregnancy send a woman to bed—does pregnancy prevent the woman from performing her job.

Does the Court's decision mean that employers will be unable to prevent fetal risk?
Not at all. Employers can take measures to protect against

fetal risk, but the measures must apply across gender lines, to both male and female workers. Johnson Controls' failure to do so points up the fatal scientific flaw in its policy. It ignored the risks created to male workers by their exposure to chemicals. Johnson Controls said it feared the effects of lead, but the Court found it turned a blind eye to unconceived children of male employees, by ignoring the "debilitating effect of lead exposure on the male reproductive system."[32] Indeed, there are studies linking lead exposure in male workers with a high death rate among offspring in the first years of life. The Supreme Court decision ensures that children of male workers will be just as protected as the children of female workers.

It also ensures that employers will not be able to cause fetal injury by depriving pregnant women of jobs. When Congress passed the PDA, it relied on medical testimony showing that women deprived of income had a higher rate of premature delivery, which is associated with central nervous system disabilities such as mental retardation and learning defects. The Court acknowledged the importance of the pregnant worker's economic support for her family when it concluded:

> It is no more appropriate for the courts than it is for individual employers to decide whether a woman's reproductive role is more important to herself and her family than her economic role. Congress has left this choice to the woman as hers to make.[33]

Why did the ACLU oppose the exclusion of women from jobs in which there may be fetal risk?

The most important reasons are that these policies keep poor women poor and fail to promote the health of women, men, and their families.

Policies that deny women employment fail to recognize that many women cannot forego employment without serious consequences. In dual wage-earner families, for example, full-time working wives contribute an average of 37.6% of family income. The poorer the family, the more critical the wife's contribution. In families in which the total annual income is less than $15,000, her contribution averages more than half the family income.[34] And in 1984, poverty was 35% lower than it would have been had wives not worked.[35]

Moreover, in many families women are the primary or sole wage earners. An estimated 45% of women in the labor force are single, separated, divorced, or widowed.[36] Many of these women have families, and many are poor.[37] Another 15% of women in the labor force are married to men earning less than $15,000 a year.[38]

Access to traditionally male jobs, like those at issue in *Johnson Controls*, is especially important to unskilled women if they are to escape from poverty. Statistics on the extent of the wage disparity due to occupational segregation reflect the pervasiveness of practices that limit women's access to lucrative employment. The data reveal that the problem is particularly acute for unskilled women who are concentrated in low-paying, female-intensive industries[39] and minimum wage jobs.[40]

Title VII and other civil rights measures brought these women the promise of more lucrative employment,[41] but policies like those of Johnson Controls would have closed the workplace doors once again. Moreover, sex-based fetal "protection" policies take their most extreme and oppressive form in occupations characterized by high wages, good benefits, and entrenched gender-based segregation. The *Johnson Controls* policy, effectively excluding women from all employment in its battery plants, was typical of the restrictions in such male-dominated industries.

Testimony before Congress during the hearings on the PDA also documented the link between all types of discriminatory employment practices and the health and well being of women and their families. Congress recognized that when women are denied access to good jobs and adequate benefits, their families—especially the children—suffer the consequences. This is because income is inversely related to nutritional deficiency in children,[42] and both are linked with a host of negative health effects including delayed growth, weakened resistance to infection, and increased vulnerability to environmental toxins.[43] Ironically, children from poor families are at particular risk of lead exposure, and black children face the greatest risk.[44]

In general, there is a higher frequency of health problems among poor children. They receive less medical care than wealthier children; they are more likely to suffer from medical illnesses and more likely to experience adverse consequences from illness.[45] The developmental hazards associated with poverty and malnutrition may be exacerbated by school absences or by health-related curtailments of normal childhood activities.[46]

Full access to traditionally male employment opportunities is also significant to the health of women and their families because critical benefits such as medical insurance are most commonly available in larger firms and in unionized, male-dominated occupations.[47] It is not surprising, therefore, that among women of childbearing age, those most likely to be uninsured, are either unemployed or working in low-wage jobs.[48]

Moreover, lack of adequate insurance has specific negative health consequences. The uninsured are more likely to delay seeking medical care.[49] Many uninsured children are treated only in response to an immediate crisis and seldom receive essential preventative pediatric services. This is also true in insured but low-income families, since many policies require significant employee contributions, have high deductibles, and/or exclude the cost of preventative care.

Also, pregnant women's income and insurance benefits bear directly on the likelihood of healthy pregnancy and birth outcomes. Congress specifically acknowledged the "concrete connection between loss of income during pregnancy and a deterioration of the health of the pregnant woman and her child which results from impaired access to a healthful life situation."[50] Lack of prenatal care and inadequate maternal nutrition, both of which are correlated with poverty,[51] are also strongly associated with low birth weight and prematurity, the causes of most infant morbidity and mortality in the United States.[52]

Finally, exclusionary policies allow companies to avoid cleaning up the workplace for all employees. By subjecting men to continued exposure, the policies continue to place future generations at risk since they will accumulate significant body lead levels at the same time they are having families. Lead exposure can have a variety of negative reproductive health effects in men.

For all of these reasons, Johnson Controls' policy was as unwise as a public health matter as it was contrary to the law. Indeed, over forty health, medical, and advocacy organizations joined in an *amici* (friend of the court) brief, organized by the ACLU's Women's Rights Project in opposition to Johnson Controls' policy.

CHILDCARE

Can an employee take off time to care for a newborn?

It depends on the policy of each state because there is no national parental leave policy to protect the jobs of all parents who must take time off to be with newborn children. The PDA protects the jobs of new mothers for the six- to eight-week recuperation period after childbirth whenever the employer has a sick leave policy for other workers. Generally, government support for other childcare is indirect, through AFDC (Aid to Families with Dependent Children) and other programs contributing to the welfare of children whose mothers are *not* in the labor force. Among Western nations, the United States stands out for its lack of a coordinated national policy for working parents and its scarcity of childcare facilities and resources. The absence of federal standards of childcare quality has left the states with their own varying regulations in the area.[53]

In particular, the structure of the PDA—which operates only to prohibit discrimination and not to secure a minimum benefit level if the employer does not provide benefits to other workers—makes it difficult for many women to take leaves and for men to assume greater childcare responsibilities. Even if an employer provides childbirth leave, a working woman may have to rush back to work before she has fully recuperated because her company does not provide paid leave. The National Commission on Working Women, for example, estimates that only 40% of all women in the workplace have paid pregnancy disability leave. Nor does the PDA require employers to provide any *childcare* leave for workers. In contrast, many European countries provide leave benefits both for recuperation from childbirth and for subsequent childcare needs—sometimes to parents of both sexes, sometimes even including paid leave.

In 1985 many groups, including the American Civil Liberties Union, worked with Congress to introduce the first Family and Medical Leave Act (FMLA),[54] in order to insure leave benefits both for childbirth recovery (medical leave) and subsequent childcare time (family leave). The bill did not pass. Three years later, the act was reintroduced in the 101st Congress by Representatives William L. Clay, Patricia Schroeder, and Marge Roukema and Senators Christopher Dodd, Edward

Kennedy, and Robert Packwood. The House bill had 130 co-sponsors and the Senate Bill 20 cosponsors. Over one hundred organizations, including the Women's Legal Defense Fund and the National Women's Law Center, actively lobbied for passage of the legislation. By 1990 the bill passed both Houses, but President Bush vetoed it and Congress was unable to override the veto.

The FMLA would have required companies with fifty or more employees to provide up to twelve weeks of unpaid medical leave for a mother's recuperation from childbirth. After recuperation, she could also take the rest of her twelve weeks as childcare family leave, while fathers and adoptive parents would have twelve weeks of family leave for care of a newly born or adopted child. Family leave could also be used for the care of a seriously ill child or parent, and medical leave could be used for any of an employee's own serious medical conditions. The employer would have been required to continue health insurance benefits throughout a leave and guarantee the same job, or the equivalent, upon the employee's return.

Passage of the FMLA would have helped to rationalize the patchwork system that currently exists in the states. The major benefit of federal legislation would (probably) be to create a uniform floor establishing a minimum acceptable benefit level. Also, the inclusion of family leave to care for a sick parent as well as a child is long overdue and would help people to keep their elderly parents with the family.

The legislation was far from perfect, however. First, the leaves were unpaid, making family leave unavailable to many poor workers as a practical matter. (Another problematic provision of the House bill allowed employers to deny benefits to their five highest paid employees, or those in the top ten percentile of their salary bracket. This provision allowed employers to fire mothers at the top for giving birth, and it implied that taking time from work to care for a child is incompatible with holding an important position in a company. One potential consequence is that women with families would be kept in second-string jobs.) Another problem with both bills was that they did not provide family leave to care for a sick spouse. Nor did the FMLA provisions match the leave benefit packages of other industrialized countries. On balance, though, the FMLA would have been an important step toward meeting the needs of workers who must weigh both work and family responsibilities.

Opponents of the bill argued that its cost would be excessive, although the General Accounting Office (GAO) has disagreed. In testimony before Congress, GAO officials predicted that "there will be little if any measurable net cost to companies" and that the primary costs would be those associated with maintaining insurance benefits.[55] In addition, workers who are disabled have no choice about being absent from work, and this disruption would occur regardless of the benefits provided by the FMLA. Finally, the costs of not having a bill are enormous. The Institute for Women's Policy Research estimates that the total cost to society for the lack of leave for childbearing and parenting is $715 million annually.[56]

Do any state laws require employers to provide medical and family care leave?

Yes. An increasing number of states—including Connecticut, Maine, Wisconsin, and the District of Columbia—have adopted comprehensive laws giving both forms of leave.[57] For a discussion of the different state approaches to this issue, see the chapter on "Legal Aspects of Parental Leave: At the Crossroads" by Susan Deller Ross in *Parental Leave and Childcare: Setting a Research and Policy Agenda* (eds. J. S. Hyde and M. J. Essex, Temple University Press, 1991).

Are employers required to provide childcare programs?

No. Yet some employers are responding to the changing character of the workforce by providing childcare facilities on the job or by improving employee access to them. Three thousand corporations provided some form of childcare assistance in 1986.[58] Employers, such as AT&T, IBM, Procter and Gamble, and Time Warner, have also begun to provide family leave voluntarily. Childcare facilities have also been incorporated as an amenity in newly constructed industrial and commercial parks. Such facilities are typically funded by a consortium of companies whose employees participate in childcare programs in order to offset the large initial expense involved.

Research has shown that companies benefit from policies that accommodate the life needs of their employees. The majority of employers who support childcare report benefits in such crucial job-related areas as employee turnover, productivity, morale, and, most significantly, ability to recruit new employees. For many, corporate support for childcare is the factor which will "tip the balance" in favor of deciding whether to work with a particular company, particularly where children can be kept in close physical proximity to their parents during work hours. In fact, several major pharmaceutical companies, such as Hoffman-LaRoche and Merck, have such centers as a standard feature of their facilities.

Companies that operate on-site childcare centers are still in the minority. More common arrangements focus on support for existing childcare facilities. Proctor and Gamble, for example, supports outside childcare by allocating portions of an employee's salary to a workers' account for childcare. Yet on-site centers do exist: Wang Laboratories and Campbell Soup are two of the best known examples.

Many more companies provide flexible benefit policies that facilitate home childcare for working women and men through such vehicles as timesharing, flexible work hours, sick-child allowances, and parental leave. Some corporations allow employees to take leaves to care for sick parents, family members, or adopted children. Others make it easier for parents to acquire quality childcare by operating extensive childcare referral services for employees.

In some instances the private sector and local governments have worked together to address the problem on a community-wide level. A 1975 San Francisco ordinance, for example, requires developers of new projects to provide childcare centers or contribute to the maintenance of existing ones. The state of Massachusetts offers low-interest loans of up to $250,000 to corporations that are willing to set up their own centers.[59] Some labor unions have actively worked for wider corporate sponsorship of childcare. The International Ladies Garment Workers Union (ILGWU), for example, founded a childcare center in New York's Chinatown.

Those interested in knowing what options a company provides should check with the personnel office. The major obstacle, however, to all of these options is that the state and federal governments do not provide any funds to help parents take advantage of the childcare facilities in their area. Nor do most corporations provide paid leave, thus making the option available only for those who can afford to take off several months without pay. It is therefore important to find out from an employer: how long and for what purpose an employee is entitled to take off; whether she or he will be guaranteed the same job upon return; whether she or he is entitled to paid leave; and whether he or she will receive benefits for the duration of the leave.

For more information about childcare:

Child Care Action Campaign
330 7th Avenue
New York, New York 10001
(212) 239-0138

National Association of Child Care Resource and Referral
  Agencies
2116 Campus Dr., S.E.
Rochester, MN 55904
(507) 287-2220

NOTES

1. Pub. L. No. 95-555, referred to as the Pregnancy Discrimination Act; its principal provision is found in § 701(k) of Title VII, 42 U.S.C. § 2000(e)–(k).
2. *General Electric Co. v. Gilbert*, 429 U.S. 125 (1976), *reh'g denied*, 429 U.S. 1079 (1977).
3. *See infra* and Wendy Webster Williams, *Equality's Riddle: Pregnancy and the Equal Treatment/Special Treatment Debate*, 13 N.Y.U. Rev. L. & Soc. Change 325, 349, 356 (1984–85).
4. Committee on Labor and Human Resources, U.S. Senate, 96th Cong., 2d Sess., Legislative History of the Pregnancy Discrimination Act of 1978, at 41, 63, 67, 68, 133, 135 (1979).
5. *King v. Trans World Airlines Inc.*, 738 F.2d 255 (8th Cir. 1984).
6. *UAW v. Johnson Controls, Inc.*, 499 U.S. 1196, 113 L. Ed.2d 158, 111 S. Ct. 1196 (1991).
7. *Marafino v. St. Louis County Circuit Court*, 707 F.2d 1005 (8th Cir. 1983).
8. *Texas Department of Community Affairs v. Burdine*, 450 U.S. 248, 256 (1981).

9. *Beck v. QuikTrip Corp.*, 708 F.2d 532 (10th Cir. 1983).

10. *Garner v. Wal-Mart Stores, Inc.*, 807 F.2d 1536 (11th Cir. 1987).

11. *Tamimi v. Howard Johnson Co. Inc.*, 807 F.2d 1550 (11th Cir. 1987). *But see Beatty v. Chesapeake Center*, 835 F.2d 71 (4th Cir. 1987)(en banc).

12. *See, e.g., Jacobs v. Martin Sweets Co.*, 550 F.2d 364 (6th Cir. 1977) *cert. denied*, 431 U.S. 917 (1977); *Ponton v. Newport News School Board*, 632 F. Supp. 1056 (E.D. Va. 1986).

13. *Avery v. Homewood City Bd. of Education*, 674 F.2d 337 (5th Cir. 1982), *cert. denied*, 461 U.S. 943 (1983); *Andrews v. Drew Municipal Separate School District*, 507 F.2d 611 (5th Cir. 1975), *cert. dismissed as improvidently granted*, 425 U.S. 559 (1976).

14. In one case, *Harvey v. Young Women's Christian Association*, 533 F. Supp. 949 (W.D.N.C. 1982), the court upheld the discharge of an African-American single pregnant woman because of her alleged intention to present herself as a role model for an "alternative lifestyle." The court refused to require the YWCA, an organization "rooted in Christian faith," to employ a person whose philosophy and actions were incompatible with the principles and goals of the organization. In a second case, the court upheld the discharge of a pregnant worker by the Omaha Girls Club on the theory that she provided a "bad role model" to teenage girls served by the program. *Chambers v. Omaha Girls Clubs, Inc.*, 834 F.2d 697 (8th Cir. 1987), *reh'g denied*, 890 F.2d 883 (8th Cir. 1988)(en banc).

15. 29 C.F.R. § 1604.10(b).

16. *Newport News Shipbuilding and Dry Dock Co. v. EEOC*, 462 U.S. 669 (1983).

17. 479 U.S. 272 (1987).

18. The case was brought by a bank receptionist who tried to return to her job but was told that she could not because the position had been filled. She filed a complaint with the California Department of Fair Employment and Housing (because she was seeking protection under state law), which then served a complaint on the bank. The bank then challenged the state law, which the Supreme Court upheld.

19. 479 U.S. at 285.

20. *Id.* at 285 n.17, 290.

21. *Id.* at 290.

22. *Id.* at 287 (quoting H.R. Rep. No. 948, 95th Cong. 2d Sess. 4, reprinted in 1978 U.S.C.C. A. N. 4749, 4752).

23. Cal. Gov't Code § 12945 (West 1980)(permitting pregnancy leave of up to four months); Conn. Gen. Stat. Ann. §§ 46a–60 (West Supp. 1986)(requiring reasonable effort to transfer pregnant employee who believes present position may cause injury to self or fetus); Mass. Gen.

Laws Ann. ch. 151B, § 4; ch. 149, 105D (West 1982) (providing up to eight-week maternity leave); Mont. Code Ann. §§ 49-2-310 to -311 (1985)(guaranteeing reinstatement to original job with full benefits).

24. The Massachusetts law does this in violation of the Supreme Court's guidelines.
25. 400 U.S. 542 (1971).
26. *Id.* at 544.
27. Joan E. Bertin and Elizabeth Werby are coauthors of this section and were the principal authors of several *amici* briefs in *UAW v. Johnson Controls*.
28. 499 U.S. 1196, 113 L. Ed. 2d 158, 111 S. Ct. 1196 (1991).
29. Johnson Controls asserted that hazardous conditions could not be improved. This was palpably untrue, as federal regulators and public health experts have found. *See* Brief *amici curiae* of the American Public Health Ass'n, et al. ("APHA Brief"). If Johnson Controls could not comply with occupational health standards, it would be required to apply to the Secretary of Labor for a variance. 29 U.S.C. § 655(6)(A). *See also General Electric Co. v. Secretary of Labor*, 576 F.2d 558 (3d Cir. 1978).
30. *See* Paul, et al., *Corporate Response to Reproductive Hazards in the Workplace: Results of the Family, Work and Health Survey*, 16 Am. J. Occ. Med. 267 (1989), reporting a higher incidence of discriminatory policies in male-intensive industries. *See generally* Committee on Education and Labor, A Report on the EEOC, Title VII and Workplace Fetal Protection Policies in the 1980s, 101st Cong., 2d Sess. (Comm. Print 1990).
31. 113 L. Ed. 2d at 176.
32. *Id.* at 173.
33. *Id.* at 181.
34. *Supporting a Family: Providing the Basics: Hearing Before the House Comm. on Children, Youth, and Families*, 98th Cong. 1st Sess., 39–40 (1983) (Statement of Diana Pearce). Among black couples, the median family income of those families with a wife in the paid labor force was nearly double that of families where the wife did not go out to work, and among Hispanics, it was nearly 75 percent higher. Appendix, "Median Annual Income of Families by Family Type, Race and Hispanic Origin, 1987," in *The American Woman 1990–91, A Status Report* 362 (S. Rix, ed. 1990).
35. *Work in America: Implications for Families: Hearing Before the House Select Comm. on Children, Youth, and Families*, 99th Cong., 2d Sess. 4 (1986) (Opening statement of George Miller)(hereinafter *Work in America*).
36. Women's Bureau, Office of the Secretary, U.S. Dept. of Labor, Fact

Sheet No. 88-2, *Facts on Women Workers*, ¶ 9 (1988) (hereinafter *Facts on Women Workers*).

37. Nearly half of all female-headed households (including both working and nonworking mothers) lived in poverty in 1987, and most of these were households with children. *U.S. Children and Their Families: Current Conditions and Recent Trends, 1989,* H.R. Rep. No. 356, 101st Cong., 1st Sess. 110–11 (1989) (hereinafter *Children and Their Families*). Female-headed households represent an increasing share of all families in poverty (51.4% in 1986 as compared to 45.7% in 1982). *Children and Families in Poverty: The Struggle to Survive: Hearing Before the House Select Comm. on Children, Youth, and Families,* 100th Cong., 2d Sess. 11 (1988).

38. *Facts on Women Workers, supra* note 36 at ¶ 19.

39. There is a clear inverse correlation between wages and the proportion of female employees in jobs. *Work in America, supra* note 35, at 29, table 4 (Statement of Janet Norwood). In 1981 the expected median wage in occupations filled exclusively by women was less than half that of the median in exclusively male occupations. National Academy of Sciences, National Research Council, *Women's Work: Men's Work, Sex Segregation on the Job* (B. Reskin, H. Hartmann, eds.) 1, 10 (1986).

40. Smith, *The Paradox of Women's Poverty: Wage Earning Women and Economic Transformation,* in *Women and Poverty* 122, 137 (C. Gelpi, et al., eds., 1986). Minimum wage now equals only about three-quarters of federal poverty guidelines for a family of three. Children's Defense Fund, *The Unmasking of Decent Family Income,* in *A Vision for America's Future* 18 (1989).

41. *See, e.g.,* Becker, M., *From Muller v. Oregon to Fetal Vulnerability Policies,* 53 U. Chi. L. Rev. 1219, 1239 (1986).

42. Physician Task Force on Hunger in America, *Malnutrition, Ill Health and Hunger,* in *Hunger in America* (1985) at 115 (hereinafter *Hunger in America*).

43. *Id.* at 99, 116, 118–22; Ebuonu and Starfield, *Child Health and Social Statutes,* 69 Pediatrics 550 (1982).

44. Mahaffey, *et al., National Estimates of Blood Lead Levels: United States, 1976–1980,* 307 New Eng. J. of Med. 573, 577 (1982).

45. Starfield, *Family Income, Ill Health, and Medical Care of U.S. Children,* 3 J. of Public Health Policy 245, 247 (1982). At every age level and for every cause of death, poor children die at a higher rate than nonpoor. Department of Human Services, State of Maine, *Children's Deaths in Maine, 1976–1980 (Final Report)* (1983).

46. *Hunger in America, supra* note 42, at 101.

47. Kamerman and Kahn, "Employers' Response to Their Employees,"

in *The Responsive Workplace: Employers and a Changing Labor Force* 60–61 (1987).

48. *Adolescent Pregnancy Prevention: Prenatal Care Campaign, Children's Defense Fund*, in *The Health of America's Children: Maternal and Child Health Date Book* 48 (1989) (hereinafter *Health of America's Children*). Black women are more likely to be uninsured than their white counterparts. *Id.*

49. Gold, *et al.*, *Health Insurance Loss Among the Unemployed: Extent of the Problem and Policy Options*, 8 J. of Public Health Policy 44, 54 (1987).

50. *Comm. on Labor and Human Resources, Legislative History of the Pregnancy Discrimination Act of 1978*, 96th Cong., 2d Sess. 65 (Comm. Print 1979).

51. It has been demonstrated repeatedly that financial constraints are the most significant obstacle to attaining adequate prenatal care, *Health of America's Children, supra* note 48, at 52, and poverty is, of course, linked with nutritional deficiencies.

52. *See,* Binsacca, *et al.*, *Factors Associated with Low Birth Weight in an Inner City Population: The Role of Financial Problems*, 77 Am. J. Pub. Health 505 (1987). *See also Children and Their Families, supra* note 37, at 139.

53. *See* Zigler, Edward E. & Gordon, Edmund W., *Day Care: Scientific and Social Policy Issues*, Auburn House, Boston (1982), Zigler, Edward D. & Goodman, Jody, "Battle for Day Care in America: A View from the Trenches," ch. 17, 354–58.

54. The bills pending in 1991 were S.5, 102d Cong., 1st Sess. (1991), and H.R.2, 102d Cong., 1st Sess. (1991).

55. Summary of GAO Testimony by William J. Gainor on GAO's Cost Estimate of S.249, the "Parental & Medical Leave Act of 1987," United States General Accounting Office, Oct. 29, 1987, at 5.

56. Spaeter-Roth, R., Hartmann, H., *Unnecessary Losses: Costs to America of the Lack of Family and Medical Leave* (1988), available from 1400 20th St., N.W., Suite 104, Washington, D.C. 20036, (202) 785-5100.

57. The medical leave provisions included: Conn. Gen. Stat. Ann. § 5-248a(a)(2) (West Supp. 1989) (state employees entitled to "a maximum of twenty-four weeks of medical leave of absence within any two-year period upon the serious illness of such employee"); D.C. Law 8-181 § 4(a)(1) (LEXIS, Codes Library, D.C. Code file) ("any employee who becomes unable to perform the functions of the employee's position because of a serious health condition shall be entitled to medical leave for as long as the employee is unable to perform the functions" but no more than "16 workweeks during any 24-month period"); Me. Rev.

Stat. Ann. tit. 26, §§ 843(4), 844(l) (West 1988) (employees entitled to "up to 8-consecutive work weeks of family medical leave in any 2 years," for, among other purposes, the "[s]erious illness of the employee"); Wis. Stat. Ann. § 103.10(4) (West Supp. 1988) ("employee who has a serious health condition which makes the employee unable to perform his or her employment duties" entitled to no more than "2 weeks of medical leave during a 12-month period" for "the period during which he or she is unable to perform those duties").

The family leave provisions included: Conn. Gen. Stat. Ann. § 5-248a(a)(l) (West Supp. 1989) (state employees entitled to "[a] maximum of twenty-four weeks of family leave of absence within any two-year period upon the birth or adoption of a child of such employee, or upon the serious illness of a child, spouse or parent of such employee"); D.C. Law 8-181 §§ 3(a)(1)–3(a)(4) (LEXIS, Codes library, D.C. Code file) (total of 16 workweeks of family leave during any 24-month period for (1) birth of child; (2) "placement of a child with the employee for adoption or foster care"; (3) "placement of a child with the employee for whom the employee permanently assumes and discharges parental responsibility"; (4) "care for family member of the employee who has a serious health condition"); Me. Rev. Stat. Ann. tit. 26, §§ 843(4), 844(l) (West Supp. 1988) (the 8-week family medical leave may also be used for "[t]he birth of the employee's child; . . . [t]he placement of a child 16 years of age or less with the employee in connection with the adoption of the child by the employee; or . . . [a] child, parent or spouse with a serious illness"); Wis. Stat. Ann. § 103.10(3) (West Supp. 1988) (in a 12-month period, employees entitled to : (1) a maximum of 6 weeks leave for birth or adoption, "if the leave begins within sixteen weeks of the child's birth" or placement; (2) a maximum of 2 weeks "[t]o care for the employee's child, spouse or parent, if the child, spouse or parent has a serious health condition"; and (3) a combined maximum of 8 weeks for leave taken for any combination of the above reasons).

58. Clark, C., *Corporate Employee Child Care and Encouraging Business to Respond to a Crisis*, 15 Fla. St. U.L. Rev. 839 (1987).

59. Newsweek, Mar. 31, 1986, at 57, 1Y *id.*

IV

Family Law

LEARNING ABOUT FAMILY LAW *BEFORE* ENTERING A NEW RELATIONSHIP

New couples—those who are about to marry or to live together—seldom think about the consequences of a possible future separation because they are in the rosy glow of a new relationship that they hope will succeed.[1] But the hard reality is that many couples do separate eventually, and that they face difficult issues when they do. By then, they may have children, they may have accumulated property together, and one of them may have sacrificed job and career prospects in order to care for the couple's children or home. They will therefore have to decide at a very difficult time, how to divide the property, whether one person will support the other, and how the children will be cared for. One way to help make such transitions easier is for couples to learn about the family law principles applying to these problems—and to plan in advance on how to resolve them—before they enter into the new relationship.

This chapter is designed to give couples the tools to plan in this way. It explains the law about divorce, custody, property division, alimony, and child support. Section G explains the law concerning premarital and marital agreements for those who would like to reach agreements on such issues as property division before they marry. For unmarried couples—whether heterosexual or homosexual—section H explains the legal protections they can achieve in such areas as property and custody rights. Of course legal issues can arise in relationships, in which the parties want to remain together rather that split up. Domestic violence is an example. Some who experience it would like to end the violence but maintain the relationship; some do not wish to maintain the relationship. For either situation, section J, on domestic violence, explains the legal options for getting protection.

Yet another issue concerns names. People entering a new relationship may want to decide what surnames they will use, either as individuals or as a couple. When the family unit has children, new name issues arise: will the children have a surname reflecting that of one parent, of both parents, or of neither? At divorce or separation, the issues of what names the ex-partners will now use surface. The law concerning all these issues, as well as the procedure for changing one's name if one desires to do so, are discussed in section K.

THE DIVORCE PROCESS AND FINDING A LAWYER

For many women (and men), the most difficult legal issue they ever face is getting a divorce. Emotional and legal problems mingle, exacerbating each other. The husband may threaten to harm the wife or take the children away; he may remove all the money from the joint savings account. The wife may feel lonely and scared, yet find that this is the time when she is most under pressure to cope, to find a lawyer, to protect herself.

In addition, divorce often causes a severe decline in the standard of living for women. A study in California revealed that one year after legal divorce, men experience a 42% improvement in their postdivorce standard of living, while women experience a 73% decline.[2]

This section is not designed to enable women to get their own divorces or to learn the legal grounds for divorce. Rather, it is designed to show women the kinds of issues they should be concerned with in divorce and to convince them that they can and should protect their own interests.

What is an annulment?

An annulment declares that a marriage was invalid when it took place. There are several possible grounds for annulment that are narrowly defined, such as one party was under the age of consent; one party had an incurable physical incapacity at the time of marriage that would prevent the couple from having sexual relations; or one party had a severe mental incapacity at the time of the marriage that prevented an understanding of the nature of the marriage relationship.

What is a legal separation?

A legal separation is usually a preliminary step to divorce but some people—for religious, economic, or personal reasons—prefer to have a legal separation and perhaps not ever seek a divorce. Generally, the marital partners must file papers in court asking to become legally separated. They may want to enter into a separation agreement that addresses issues such as maintenance of the dependent spouse, custody and support of children, visitation rights, and responsibility for paying debts. Or you can ask the court to order maintenance for the dependent spouse and child support.

What are grounds for divorce?

Grounds for divorce vary from state to state. There has been a widespread adoption of "no-fault" grounds for divorce; that is, a couple is allowed to get divorced without a showing that one party is at fault. No-fault grounds for divorce include irretrievable breakdown of the marriage, irreconcilable differences, incompatibility, and separation (that is living separately and apart for a certain length of time, at least more than six months and in many states two or three years). Some states allow one spouse to seek and obtain a no-fault divorce without the other spouse's agreement; other states require the court to grant a divorce if both spouses seek it; still others require the court to make its own determination in each case of whether a divorce is warranted.

Depending on the state, it may also be possible to obtain a divorce based on traditional fault grounds such as adultery, desertion, extreme cruelty, drug or alcohol addiction, imprisonment, and deviant sexual conduct.

If a woman has a common-law marriage, does she have to get a divorce to end it?

Yes, and it is important to do so. There is no such thing as a common-law divorce, and if she does not get a regular court divorce, any later marriage, including a ceremonial one, will be invalid. Several states still recognize common-law marriage and women should find out if their state does, particularly if they have agreed with their partner to be married or if they have been holding themselves out to others as married—e.g., by taking a lease as husband and wife, or by introducing oneself as "Mrs. Brown."

Is a full-scale trial necessary to get the best property settlement, alimony, and child support payments?

No. Nationally, less than ten percent of divorces result in a full-scale trial.[3] In those few cases, each side presents evidence, and the judge makes the final decisions on whether to grant a divorce, who gets custody of the children, the amount of alimony and child support that should be awarded, and who is entitled to the couple's property. In most cases, however, the couple's lawyers—or the husband and wife themselves, if they each lack lawyers—negotiate their own decisions about these details, and the judge merely gives formal approval. The parties then make only a pro forma courtroom appearance to finalize the breakup.

Generally, it is wise to reach an acceptable agreement without a full-scale trial. A trial sends attorneys' fees skyrocketing because preparation for trial and a trial itself are very time consuming. In addition, a trial may bring a private controversy out into the open. It makes both people anxious to show the world that the other side was at fault, and it usually ends with bitterness and hostility. For these reasons, most people find it better to negotiate the details of a divorce themselves and then go through a pro forma court hearing.

This said, it must still be emphasized that there will be some divorces that women will want to litigate. If a husband will not negotiate or will not agree to terms acceptable to the wife, a trial may be the only way the wife can secure the financial arrangements that are her due. In this situation the wife may decide, in consultation with her lawyer, that a full-scale court hearing is the best way to achieve her goals.

What is mediation?

Divorce mediation is a relatively new concept. It is generally a voluntary process in which a neutral third party, a mediator, helps the couple reach a mutually acceptable agreement about their respective rights and responsibilities after divorce. It is less formal than court proceedings, and even if the people are represented by lawyers, the lawyers usually do not actively participate in the mediation process itself. The goal of mediation is to help reach an agreement, and the mediator does not have authority to impose a decision on the parties, although some mediators do pressure parties to agree to a settlement.

Is mediation ever mandatory?

Yes, mediation is mandatory in some states, such as California. In some states mediation is required on certain issues, such as custody. In some other states it is strongly encouraged but not required.

What are the advantages and disadvantages of mediation in the divorce process?

Many women's advocates believe that the disadvantages of mediation outweigh the advantages. Others disagree. Mediation is sometimes less costly and less time consuming than the litigation process. However, it can be more costly if each party retains an attorney in addition to paying the mediator (which is definitely advisable). And it is usually more time consuming if the mediation is not successful, since then the parties have to begin or reenter the court process. It is also generally more informal and can be less acrimonious than a judge-decided divorce, but informality may sometimes work to the woman's disadvantage.

The chief disadvantage of mediation is that because it does not operate under any specific legal standards, it works best between parties of equal bargaining power, and there is still pervasive inequality between men and women in our society. Also, in most states neither the mediators nor the mediation process is regulated. Moreover, mediation privatizes family disputes at a time when women's advocates have made great progress in improving laws to give women more rights in divorce. Despite these considerations, for strong women who take the time to understand their rights, it may be an effective tool.

Finally, in assessing mediation, it should be remembered that most divorces are only lawyer-assisted negotiations because the couples usually resolve the issues without a full-scale trial. Against that backdrop, mediation may not be cheaper or faster than the regular divorce process and may result in a less favorable result for women.

**Are there any situations where mediation should definitely
not be used?**

Yes. Generally, victims of domestic violence or of physical,
sexual, or emotional abuse should not use mediation. This is
because the mediation process relies on good-faith bargaining
between parties who possess equal bargaining power, which
usually does not exist in an abuser/victim situation. For example, despite a woman's expectations, she may be too fearful of
retaliation to speak up forcefully for her own interests.

Is it necessary to hire a lawyer for divorce proceedings?

If there are no children and property, marital couples may
be able to handle their own divorce without lawyers. This is
called appearing *pro se* ("for oneself"). In some areas, the clerk's
office in the court may have forms or otherwise be willing to
help in handling the paperwork. Although this alternative is
much less costly than hiring a lawyer, it can be confusing and
time consuming. Anyone who has children, property, or other
complex issues should seek the advice of a lawyer.

**Does a woman need her own lawyer for divorce proceedings
even when she and her husband have made a friendly agreement to negotiate the details?**

Yes. No matter how amicable the relationship with the husband, once a woman is seriously considering a divorce she has
interests separate from his and should be represented separately. *This is vital.* Even if she decides eventually not to retain
a lawyer to represent her, she should consult with a lawyer of
her own at least once to get impartial advice on her situation.

**Should a woman retain a lawyer to whom she is referred
by her husband's lawyer?**

Definitely not. This will be a tempting course to follow for
any woman who has had little or no prior exposure to lawyers,
has no idea of how to get one, and feels bewildered and frightened by the whole process. However, the temptation should
be avoided. The person the husband's lawyer recommends may
be a fine attorney, but if he or she is brought into the case in
this way, the attorney may be more sympathetic toward the
husband's interests than is desirable. This may happen for
several reasons. The recommended lawyer may need business

and may find that the husband's lawyer ceases to refer business if he or she represents the wife's interests too firmly; therefore, the wife's lawyer may make certain compromises in advocating her interests, perhaps only at a subconscious level. Another possibility is that the two lawyers may simply be good friends, and the recommended lawyer may be swayed too much by the arguments of a good friend who is closer to the situation.

The fact that these things can happen does not mean that in any particular case they will happen. However, there is no reason to tempt fate by accepting a referral arrangement that can lead to problems. Most husbands and wives have at least some conflicting interests. Each party considering a divorce should get a lawyer who will represent those interests fully, without any possibility of a conflict in loyalties. As indicated below, this is so even if you have no resources to hire a lawyer.

How should a woman go about finding a divorce lawyer?

There are a number of ways. Probably the best is to ask other friends or acquaintances who have obtained divorces whether they were satisfied with their lawyers' services. If they were, this may be a good recommendation.

A woman with little or no income or assets should check with the Legal Aid Society or a legal services program; they often do divorce work and should be listed in the telephone directory. A woman can check with them even if she is not sure whether she would qualify for free help; they might be able to refer her to a lawyer even if they cannot provide free services.

Another way to find a lawyer is through the local bar association. Such groups usually maintain a lawyer referral service, which will give out a list of names to anyone who needs a lawyer. In the past few years, women's bar associations have increased in number and size, and some of them may have their own referral services. A person should use any of these services with caution, however, since the bar association does not guarantee the lawyers are competent; it simply gives the names of all lawyers who ask to be placed on the list.

Finally, a women's organization may have a referral list of recommended lawyers. The best way to locate such a group is to look in the telephone book for a women's center, a local child support or divorce support group, or a local chapter of NOW (the National Organization for Women).

A woman should shop around before finally choosing a lawyer. She should arrange a short interview before making her decision in order to find out whether the lawyer operates a well-organized office, can work effectively with her, and charges a fee she can afford. There is usually no fee or only a modest one for such a preliminary interview, but this should be confirmed before the meeting.

How much does a divorce cost?

Paying for a divorce involves paying mainly for the lawyer's time, plus out-of-pocket expenses incurred by the lawyer in the course of representing the case. Lawyers' fees tend to vary widely, with different fees charged in different parts of the country. Therefore it is advisable to shop around to determine the range of fees usually charged in a particular area.

Generally a divorce that is uncontested—that is, one that both partners husband agree to and in which all the details are negotiated before going to court—costs less than a contested divorce. A fairly standard range is $750 to $1500 for an uncomplicated, uncontested divorce; this fee covers simple negotiations, drafting of a simple settlement agreement, and standard courtroom procedures. For a contested divorce or for an uncomplicated, uncontested one requiring further negotiations over children or over real estate or other property, the lawyer may charge an hourly fee of $85 to $120 (or $200 or more for a high-priced lawyer). Some costs will also be charged by the court, usually in the range of $50 to $100. There may be further costs for publication of newspaper notices or for paying a process server to serve court papers on a spouse.

Who pays the attorney's fees for a woman's lawyer?

It depends on the situation. If a woman seeking divorce qualifies for Legal Aid or a legal services program, there is no charge. If not, she must hire a private attorney. If a wife has fewer financial resources than her husband, her lawyer may be able to bargain for some reimbursement from him. In addition, in cases where the husband earns more than the wife, he may be ordered by the court to pay for her attorney. In some states, the lawyer can collect a part of this fee early in the case, when he or she arranges for temporary alimony and/or child support. However, in many places, court-awarded fees are awarded at the very end of the divorce case, if at all, and are far lower than those generally charged by divorce lawyers. Many lawyers will refuse to rely on the possibility of eventual payment of fees by a husband and will look to the wife to pay some or all of the fee in advance and to be ultimately responsible for any part of the fee not paid by the husband. Thus, unless a woman qualifies for free legal services, she probably should expect to pay at least a portion of the fee herself, in advance, and make arrangements to borrow or save funds for this purpose.

Is it necessary to have a written fee agreement with a lawyer?

It is not absolutely necessary, but it is advisable. (Some states, such as New Jersey, require a written fee agreement in all divorce cases.) The agreement should specify the amount paid as an initial retainer (a sum as an advance payment made for services the lawyer will render), what services this payment covers, and whether and under what circumstances it is refundable. The agreement should also spell out the basis for further charges—i.e., will there be an hourly charge in *addition* to the initial payment or *out of* the initial payment? Will a higher fee be charged if the divorce becomes contested? When and how will further payments be required? Who is responsible for payments, the husband or the wife? What extra services or costs will be charged? These may include court costs, photocopying, transcripts, and other similar items. It is also advisable to ask for a monthly itemized bill.

If a woman is unhappy with her lawyer and believes that he or she is not representing her adequately, what can she do?

She can fire the lawyer. Many people fail to keep in mind that the relationship between a lawyer and a client is that of employee and employer. The client is the employer and has a perfect right to fire his or her employee at any time.

Firing a lawyer may present tricky financial problems though. First, if the lawyer required a retainer ahead of time, he or she may try to keep it, whether or not any work has been done. The lawyer is entitled to payment only for work actually done and must refund unearned portions of the fee. A client should ask for an itemized bill, setting forth hours worked and the nature of work done during that time. If the charges seem unjustified, a client can ask for a refund. A new lawyer may be able to help collect a refund if the first lawyer proves recalcitrant.

Second, some lawyers will try to keep any original papers given them for the divorce, under what is called a lawyer's lien, unless they are paid the agreed-upon fee. Since the client needs the papers to get the divorce, the lawyer has the client over a barrel until the fees are paid. A new lawyer can also help negotiate this matter, but the situation can be avoided altogether by giving lawyers only copies of original documents. In that way, the client always has the papers he or she needs, and the papers can never be withheld as a way to force payment of an unearned fee. If the lawyer does need the originals for the courtroom proceedings, the client can provide them at that stage, being sure to make and keep copies.

A less drastic method than firing an attorney may be to tell him or her clearly and calmly what the problems are and see whether this produces any changes.

If a woman believes her lawyer has acted unethically or has failed to represent her fully, this should be reported to the organization or person that referred her to the lawyer and to the bar association or other attorney disciplinary body in her state. A lawyer who behaves unethically can lose the license to practice law. Before doing this, it is wise to consult another lawyer or an experienced friend.

How does one determine if a lawyer is providing adequate representation?

There are no hard-and-fast rules, but there are a few things to look out for. The lawyer should send itemized bills for services, detailed by the hour (unless a flat fee was agreed upon for the entire case), and should be willing to explain any item under question. He or she should send copies of all papers and letters prepared for the case. The lawyer should be willing to explain what is happening on the case in terms that make sense to the client and should inform the client promptly of any significant developments in the case, such as the scheduling of an upcoming court hearing. The lawyer should insist on fair financial and custody arrangements on the client's behalf (there will be some discussion of these concepts later in this chapter), and the client should be able to feel totally confident about the lawyer's representation. Also, a lawyer should interview his or her client in depth initially in order to determine the unique needs, desires, and family situation of the individual. For instance, a lawyer should not assume a woman wants custody of the children or does not need alimony to cover expenses for additional training or education. Above all a lawyer should always recognize that any decision regarding how to proceed in the divorce is entirely up to the client, although the client should of course weigh the lawyer's advice carefully. Finally, a lawyer should have or make time to talk with the client (although the client should also remember that lawyers charge for their time and that the "meter is running" during their conversation) and should return phone calls within a reasonably prompt period of time. If it seems a lawyer does not have sufficient time for a case, it is better to find one who does have time. A woman should use the occasion of a divorce to prepare for her future and therefore needs a lawyer who is willing and able to help her do this.

CUSTODY

Is a woman automatically entitled to custody of her children if she is a fit mother?

No. Indeed, under old common-law principles, courts deemed custody of children in a divorce to be a sort of property right of the husband; if he wanted to keep the children he could do so automatically. This, of course, was a major deterrent to women seeking divorces. Then, for many years, courts followed a legal rule called the *tender years doctrine* under which the mother was presumed to be the better custodian for children of "tender years" (usually under age seven). Children over the "tender years," particularly boys, were deemed to be better off with their fathers. The corollary principle was that a husband could obtain custody of young children only if he could show that his wife was "unfit." This led to nasty courtroom battles in which the husband would try to drag in as many negative factors as possible against the wife. It also led to a double standard; any deviation from the "good wife" role—such as an affair—might result in the wife being found "unfit" while similar conduct would ordinarily not prevent the husband from getting custody. This doctrine is probably unconstitutional today under the Equal Protection Clause; it allows an important legal right to be determined solely on the basis of the sex of the parent because of stereotyped notions about the relationships of male and female parents with their children.

In most states, custody decisions are now at least ostensibly based on "the best interests of the child," without regard to a presumption about which parent is best suited. This standard is good in theory but not always in practice. For example, some judges take into account the relative economic position of the parents. This usually puts women, who are more often poorer, at a disadvantage. It is also not unheard of for judges to award custody to a father who has remarried on the ground that he is able to provide a two-parent household or a "stay at home mom" while the mother is a single parent who must work. While women still get custody in a majority of cases, this is at least in part because men do not usually request it. One study showed that when men do request custody they prevail over half of the time.[4]

Several state supreme courts have begun to develop a new way of analyzing custody cases; they presume that custody should be awarded to the parent who has been the child's primary caretaker.[5] In most families this standard results in the wife getting custody, but in families in which the husband has played a larger role in childrearing, he has a correspondingly greater chance of convincing a judge in a contested case that he should have custody.

Is there a way to avoid either parent having sole custody?
There is a growing recognition of *joint custody*—in which the parents continue to be jointly responsible for the child, making decisions and arrangements for the child on a day-to-day basis—and *split custody*—in which the parents alternate having sole custody of the child (with the other parent allowed visitation rights). Theoretically, these arrangements mean that the children spend approximately equal amounts of time in the care of each parent. In practice, however, it may be little different than sole custody, except when it comes to decision making. In several states joint or split custody can be done only by agreement of the parties; in several states it cannot be done

at all. In other states there is a legal presumption in favor of joint custody. It is not clear whether it is generally better for children to have a single, continuous primary caretaker able to make a final decision on important questions such as medical treatment and schools or whether it is more important for children to have equal access to and nurturing from both parents. It is certainly not clear what will be best in any particular situation.

Parents considering joint or split custody may need to consider whether it is desirable for their child to move repeatedly or whether equal access to both parents is more important. An important issue in joint custody is whether the parents will want to continue to deal with each other on a day-to-day basis to make decisions about the children after divorce, considering their ability to discuss and solve problems together or their lack thereof. Futhermore, a woman should not simply give in and accept joint custody to avoid a fight with her husband if she really believes it is preferable for her children for her to have sole custody. In fact, if a woman agrees to joint custody knowing something about her husband that would make him a bad caretaker, she may be in a poor position to bring it up later if the agreement breaks down and she wants to obtain sole custody. Finally, the amount of child support payments must be very carefully negotiated in joint or split custody arrangements. Fathers sometimes argue they should not pay support if they have the children half of the time—although usually they have far more than half of the income, and often, after initial interest wears off, keep the children little more than they might in traditional sole custody by the mother with visitation arrangements.

If a woman wants custody of the children, are there any special steps she should take?

Yes. She should be discreet about any sexual relationship with another person. The legal system still tends to impose a double standard, and a mother is often judged much more harshly for extramarital affairs than is a father. If a husband is trying to get custody of his children and the wife wants to retain custody, it would be wise for her to avoid any sexual relationships for the interim period. Some women may choose to fight the issue openly in order to establish precedents to help other women in the same predicament; the risk they take is losing custody of their children. Before deciding to fight the issue, the risks should be considered carefully.

Several states require that persons seeking divorce see a social worker, a friend of the court, or a marriage counselor before the divorce is granted. Women are advised to be as discreet as possible with any of them. This includes being careful about what is displayed in the home as well as what is said in their presence. A woman should talk to her lawyer about these matters before engaging in any interviews or visits. As a practical matter, these people are powerful. Judges rarely overturn their recommendations on child custody, so if a woman seeking custody offends them on matters related to sexual behavior, it is likely to have serious consequences.

Is it important for a woman to maintain custody of her children in the period preceding the actual divorce?

Definitely. Women often want to leave their children with their husbands for a much-needed break or to return to school themselves when they first separate. However, this choice has its risks. Just as the amount of temporary alimony received sets a precedent for the award of permanent alimony, the party having temporary custody of the children following separation is usually granted permanent custody.

Does a woman need a court order for temporary custody before the actual divorce if her husband agrees to leave the children with her?

Until there is a court order, husband and wife are equally entitled to custody of their children. Therefore, until there is an order it is perfectly legal for the husband to take the children even if he has signed a written agreement to leave them with the wife. The police will not intervene in this case, and the wife will have to start the court process from the beginning to regain custody. If there is the slightest suspicion that the father may take the children, it is best to obtain a temporary custody order prior to the actual divorce. This may be critical if the father has threatened to take the children out of state.

If the ex-husband's visits upset the children, can these visits be prevented after the divorce is final?

Sometimes. The question of visitation rights can theoretically be reopened and new arrangements made if the old arrangements prove unsatisfactory. However, judges are loathe to deprive fathers of all access to their children, and the mother may have to answer to the accusation that she has influenced the children against their father. This may be a particular problem in cases involving the highly charged area of alleged sexual abuse of a child by the father.

PROPERTY DIVISION AT DIVORCE

What is property division and how does it differ alimony?
Alimony (also called maintenance or spousal support) and property division are separate concepts; both should be fully negotiated and settled in a separation agreement or court order. Alimony is discussed in more detail in the next section.

Property includes all physical and financial possessions that have been acquired in the family after marriage up to the time of divorce: cash, house, furnishings, car, boat, land, stocks, bonds, businesses, or business interests, and so on. Pension rights are usually included, as is the value of a professional education or professional practice in some states.

At the time of divorce, property is divided between the husband and wife by separation agreement or property settlement agreement or by court order. The principles used and the resulting divisions vary widely from state to state, as discussed below. However, the division of property is a onetime event and the arrangements are settled at the close of the divorce case—even if some property is still to be transferred or some payments are still to be made under the plan. It is not possible to return to court some time later and ask that the question of property division be reopened (unless there has been fraud or coercion or a misrepresentation of assets).

The basic rule is that jointly owned property may be evenly divided by the husband and wife without either paying federal income tax on the transferred property. Tax problems sometimes arise when the property that is transferred has increased in value since it was purchased. The tax aspects of the property division should be fully explored with one's lawyer.

What right does a woman have to property acquired during the marriage?

The answer depends on whether she lives in what is regarded as a *community-property* or *common-law* state. Each of the two systems classifies property by different names even though the definitions are getting to be more and more similar.

How is property divided at divorce in a community-property state?

In the eight community-property states—Arizona, California, Idaho, Louisiana, Nevada, New Mexico, Texas, and Washington—property is classified as *separate* or *community*. Separate property generally includes property that a spouse owned prior to the marriage, the property a spouse acquired during the marriage by gift or inheritance, and property acquired during the marriage that can be traced back to property included in one of those two categories. Community property consists of all other property acquired during the marriage; each spouse owns an undivided one-half interest in all community property from the time of its acquisition.

At the time of divorce, community property is usually divided in two equal shares. However, the rules vary from state to state. For example, in a few of the states, "equitable" principles are applied to vary this rule. One such principle awards the family home to whichever parent has custody of the children.[6]

How is property divided at divorce in a common-law state?

In the remaining states and the District of Columbia, property is now classified similarly to community-property states as either *separate* or *marital* property.[7] As with community property, marital property generally includes all the property acquired during the marriage except inheritances and gifts. However, the common-law states differ in that marital property is not assumed to belong to both parties at the time of acquisition. In most common-law states, marital property must be "equitably divided" at the time of divorce. (Indiana applies a presumption of equal division.)[8]

The "equitable division" can work differently depending on the state. Basically there are two methods: (1) division of only marital property and (2) division of both marital and separate property. The majority of states automatically exclude gifts and inheritances from consideration for either of these methods, but some do not.[9]

Most equitable distribution laws provide a list of factors the divorce court should weigh in deciding on a fair division of property. These often include length of marriage; age, health, and earning ability of husband and wife; contribution of each to homemaking and care of the children and, in money or work, to acquiring the property; and who will have custody of the children. Because these laws specify a whole list of factors, marital "fault," such as adultery, desertion, or cruelty, is often eliminated or diminished in importance in dividing the marital property, although sometimes it is used covertly.

Does a woman have a right to a share of her former husband's pension and other work benefits?

Yes. Pensions are now recognized as part of the joint property acquired during marriage and as part of the assets to be divided during divorce. As a result of the Retirement Equity Act of 1984, state courts can treat private pensions as joint property in divorce proceedings. Military, civil service, and foreign service pensions are also subject to division under federal law. Pension and retirement benefits that are earned during marriage are potentially of great value and, particularly in a longer marriage, they may be the most valuable asset a couple owns. For more extensive information about this subject, readers may want to order the two-hundred-page book *Your Pension Rights at Divorce: What Women Need to Know*. It is available for $14.50 (book rate mailing; $16.00 first class) by writing to the Pension Rights Center, 918 16th Street, N.W., Suite 704, Washington D.C. 20006.

ALIMONY

What is alimony?

Alimony, also called *maintenance* or *spousal support*, consists of periodic support payments to the husband or wife after the marriage has ended.[10] There is an obligation under an agreement or court order to make support payments of a certain amount on a periodic basis (weekly, monthly, annually), usually until the spouse receiving alimony remarries or until the husband or the wife dies. Because it is uncertain when these events may occur, the total amount of alimony that will be received is unknown. It is possible for a wife to return to court later to ask for increased alimony if circumstances change or for the husband to ask for decreased payments if his income decreases. Alimony payments are taxable to the one who receives them and are deducted from the income of the one who makes them.

One state, Texas, does not allow court-ordered alimony at divorce, although it does permit it by agreement of the parties.[11] Other states sharply limit the availability of alimony depending on the length of the marriage, the wife's ability to earn income, and other factors.

Throughout the following discussion of alimony and child support, usage of the terms "man," "woman," "husband," and "wife" reflects traditional roles and the most frequently encountered situations. The reader should keep in mind that in theory, if not often in practice, either spouse may be awarded alimony or child support depending on financial need.

What kinds of expenses does alimony cover?
Alimony is designed to provide financial support for the economically dependent former spouse.

What are the factors used in deciding whether to award alimony?
Usually courts use a variety of factors that are set out either in the laws or cases of that state. These factors are used not only in deciding whether to award alimony but also in deciding how much and for how long.

The Uniform Marriage and Divorce Act of 1974 suggests that the following factors be considered: the financial resources of the party requesting alimony; the time necessary for that person to acquire education or training for employment; the standard of living during the marriage; the length of the marriage; the age, physical fitness, and emotional condition of the party requesting support; and the ability of the other partner to meet his or her own needs and still contribute to the former spouse's support.

Can marital fault be considered in alimony awards?

Despite the widespread adoption of no-fault grounds for divorce, many states continue to use the fault principle in awarding alimony. Marital fault has been excluded as a factor in awarding alimony in twenty-nine states, may be considered as a factor in eleven states and the District of Columbia, and is a bar to alimony in eight states.[12]

Can a woman be required to pay alimony?

Yes, in some instances. The Supreme Court ruled in 1979 that an Alabama law under which husbands could be required to support their ex-wives, but under which wives could never be required to support their ex-husbands, violated the Equal Protection Clause of the United States Constitution.[13]

Under current alimony laws, whichever spouse has the greater income or wage-earning capacity may usually be ordered to pay alimony if the other spouse is in financial need. Ideally, the need for the parent with custody of the children to spend time caring for them will be taken into account. Because men generally have greater income and wage-earning opportunities than their wives (as a result of low pay for women and inequitable distribution of homemaking responsibilities during marriage) and because few husbands have custody of the children, few wives will be required to pay alimony. But in those cases where the husband has suffered a loss of wage-earning capacity as a result of marriage and is unemployed, chronically ill, or otherwise unable to support himself adequately it is fair to ask a financially able wife to help support him.

Should a woman ask for alimony?

Probably—if she is in the circumstances of most wives. Many women have begun to feel guilty about asking for alimony and traditionally, contrary to popular perception, very few women have received alimony. According to a 1986 Census Bureau survey, fewer than 15% of all women who had ever been divorced or were currently separated had obtained an agreement or court order to receive alimony.[14]

Although the situation is slowly improving, marriage still places all but a few women at a tremendous financial disadvantage. Many women do not get enough training or education before marriage to maximize their wage-earning capacity; they are conditioned to believe that their husbands will take care of them and that they need not plan for a career. Then society encourages women to bear and rear children. This further decreases a woman's wage-earning capacity, for even when she has somehow managed to acquire education or training, she loses work experience during the years of childrearing. Nor are women paid for their years of work in the home even though this work has economic value. Thus, they often have no way to acquire property unless the husband "gives" it to them. Some women work to put their husbands through law or medical school or other kinds of extended education without ever receiving comparable training themselves or even a repayment of the money. Finally, society encourages most women to take custody of dependent children upon divorce, usually without adequate child support. With these factors combined, alimony is often necessary to compensate women for those financial disabilities caused or aggravated by marriage.

Thus, women should not be reluctant to ask for alimony. Women have earned alimony and will continue to earn it. And they should receive it. It is a different story, of course, for women who have been married only briefly and have suffered no change in earning capacity or for those few women who have equal or greater wage-earning capacity and whose husbands have shared equally in the responsibilities of home life and will continue to carry an equal burden for the children after the divorce. But until other women achieve that status, they deserve alimony.

Is alimony always permanent or does it give a woman help only for a year or two to get on her feet or to receive further education?

Historically, alimony has been permanent, at least until the husband died or the wife remarried. (Of course, it has always been possible to agree in a separation agreement to payments over a shorter time.) Recently, however, in what has been a mixed blessing for women, a number of states have passed laws allowing courts to award *rehabilitative alimony* or *short-term alimony*. In theory, these are available to aid a woman who may not require long-term assistance but who does need help in establishing herself in a job or in furthering her education. In practice, many feminist lawyers believe that unsympathetic judges have awarded short-term, rehabilitative alimony instead of permanent alimony in situations in which there is little hope the wife will ever be able to support herself adequately.

At least half the states permit or require awards of rehabilitative alimony.[15] Delaware, Indiana, and Kansas place mandatory time limits on alimony awards.[16] Fortunately, the tide seems to be turning, and more and more judges are recognizing the need for permanent alimony, particularly in cases of older women who have been full-time homemakers in long marriages.

If the husband has a small income at the time of the divorce, resulting in a small alimony, is there any way to assure an increase in alimony in the future?

In some states to assure this, an escalation clause can be requested for inclusion in the divorce agreement and will provide for a stated increase in alimony for every stated increase in the husband's income.

How can an alimony award be enforced?

First, it is important to point out that only 73% of women who were supposed to receive alimony payments in 1985 received all or part of the amount due.[17]

As a practical matter, the first step a woman should take is to write a letter to her spouse, outlining the violations of the divorce judgment. A copy of this letter should be kept as a record of this action. If the letter does not result in voluntary payment, it will be a useful document to attach to a later court action. Then, a lawyer has several options available as enforcement techniques, including contempt, execution, garnishment, wage or income assignment, attachment, liens, and requiring security.[18] In order to take any action to enforce an alimony award, however, it is vital that accurate records of payments received are kept.

In addition to returning to the lawyer who originally handled her divorce, a woman may also be able to use the services of the state or local child support enforcement agency. The next section, on child support, discusses how those agencies work. But this service can only be used if the woman is also owed child support payments by the same man.

CHILD SUPPORT

Is a spouse entitled to child support payments?

Yes, if she has custody of the children. Again, women should not hesitate to ask that the husband contribute his fair share to the support of their children. The traditional insufficiency of child support awards and the difficulty of collecting payments has been one of the primary causes of the feminization of poverty. For example, Census Bureau statistics indicate that in about two-thirds of female-headed single-parent families, the father contributes no support at all. And only half the mothers in this country due child support received full payment in 1987.[19] Contrary to popular belief, there is little relationship between the father's ability to pay child support and the extent of compliance with the order. The result of this national disgrace is that the majority of Americans living below the poverty line are in households headed solely by a woman. Moreover, the lack of child support awards, awards that are too low, and inadequate enforcement have had a particularly devastating effect on poor women, particularly African-American women and never-married teen mothers.

What has been done to improve child support?

In the 1980s Congress passed two major laws to deal with this crisis. The first was in 1984, followed by the Family Support Act in 1988.[20] Basically the laws require that the states, as a condition of receiving welfare payments from the federal government, implement procedures for establishing and enforcing child support orders. The requirements of these laws are discussed in more detail below.

What should be included in child support?

The basic child support award, usually established according to a formula set out in a guideline (see below), is theoretically considered to be sufficient to cover the essentials of childrearing, such as food, clothing, and shelter. In reality, the amounts are often far too low. Therefore, it is essential to consider ways to obtain an award that is higher than the basic amount dictated by the guidelines. For example, it is important to negotiate for continued health insurance coverage and for additional support when there are high medical expenses not covered by insurance. These often include bills for eyeglasses, dentistry, and psychiatry. Extras such as summer camp and music lessons should be included. If it is financially feasible, one should also negotiate for the costs of a college education and even the cost of graduate school (although the latter is hard to get). The separation agreement or court order should also specify who pays for travel and long-distance calls to an out-of-town parent who does not have custody.

Have guidelines been established to determine the proper amounts of child support?

Yes. Federal legislation in 1984 mandated that all states set guidelines for support orders, and all states have now done so. Guidelines often lead judges and hearing officers to order a somewhat greater amount of support than might have been ordered prior to the guidelines. Also, guidelines establish consistency among orders so that people in similar situations do not have widely differing awards. The 1988 Family Support Act requires states to follow the support guidelines in all cases. The only exception allowed is when the court explicitly finds that applying the guidelines would be unjust or inappropriate. In addition, the Family Support Act requires states to review their guidelines every four years.

Can child support be increased to keep up with inflation?

Yes. In fact, the Family Support Act requires periodic review and adjustment of the support guidelines, as well as the individual support awards.

In addition, if possible, a separation agreement or court order should provide for both an automatic cost-of-living adjustment and increased payments as children grow older and have higher expenses. (Electric guitars and stereos are far more expensive than teddy bears and overalls.) If an agreement does not cover this or if the payments are based on a court order, it is often possible to return to court to ask for higher payments to keep up with inflation or increased expenses.

What are the tax differences between alimony and child support?

The husband can deduct alimony from his income for federal income tax purposes; he cannot deduct child support. So then the wife must pay federal income tax on alimony and does not have to pay tax on child support.

What are the practical consequences of the tax difference?

The tax difference induces husbands to try to disguise child support payments as alimony. However, accepting a large alimony payment in lieu of adequate child support can lead to real financial hardship for the wife and children. First, as already noted, the wife must pay taxes on alimony. This means that while an alimony settlement is a tax advantage for the man, it is a decided disadvantage for the woman. Second, alimony ceases upon remarriage, but child support ceases only when the children reach the age of majority (18 to 21, depending on the state). If a woman agrees to call some child support money alimony, she will lose it if she remarries, even though her children may still need the money. Her new husband may not be able to support her children and in most states he is not legally obligated to do so unless he adopts them. In fact, a lack of adequate child support from the ex-husband might even discourage a man from marrying a woman. Furthermore, it is important to bargain for enough alimony to meet one's own personal needs. Failing to do this and relying instead on child support may render a woman destitute when the children grow up and the child support ceases. A study by the Rand Corporation in California showed that some former wives of wealthy doctors and lawyers were living on welfare[21]—a sad commentary on how well their lawyers negotiated for them.

The general rule, then, in bargaining for alimony and child support, is to remember that they serve different purposes. Getting the right amount of money for each category ensures that the children will have the money they need as long as they need it and the woman will have the personal income she needs as long as she needs it. Of course, if it is possible to get more money by departing from this rule (for example, by splitting the amount of the former husband's tax advantage with him or by asking for larger child support when a woman knows she will remarry soon) provided the woman has planned for her financial needs once either alimony or child support ceases.

Once a child support order is obtained, what can be done to enforce it?

Traditionally it has been very difficult to enforce child support orders but the 1984 and 1988 federal laws, in combination with individual state laws, have somewhat improved the situation. Lack of child support enforcement has been probably the single most important cause of the feminization of poverty.

What are the enforcement options available?

Probably the best option is a preventive one. The 1988 federal law requires automatic wage withholding for all child support awards, rather than waiting to initiate withholding in response to a failure to pay. Automatic withholding applies unless both parties agree in writing to an alternative arrangement or the judge finds that there is a good reason for establishing another arrangement (such as the establishment and maintenance of an escrow account for child support).[22]

Automatic wage withholding is probably the most effective enforcement technique because child support is simply deducted from a paycheck, like the withholding tax for Social Security. It is of limited use, however, if a man is self-employed or is paid "under the table."

Where can a woman go for assistance if her husband has fallen behind on child support payments?

There are a variety of options. Of course, she can return to the lawyer who originally represented her and request that he or she bring an enforcement action. This may be very costly. Or she can go to her local or state child support enforcement agency (sometimes referred to as *support collection units* or *IV-D agencies*); they are usually part of a social service department, family court, probation office, or the state attorney general's office. Such agencies are publicly funded under the Social Security Act and serve both welfare and nonwelfare clients (they are permitted to charge certain fees and costs to nonwelfare clients). Remedies that these agencies use include liens, intercepting tax refunds, and reporting support arrearages to credit bureaus. (If the spouse is also behind in alimony payments, the agency can collect those in addition to the child support award.)

The Family Support Act (FSA) mandated that as of 1 October 1990 the states must follow certain time frames in pursuing each stage of child support cases. Prior to the new law, cases often languished for many months at each stage of the process.

The FSA established specific time limits that apply to taking applications for assistance, locating the father, establishing paternity, and obtaining and enforcing support orders.

What can be done if the nonpaying spouse lives out of state?

The usual difficulties of collecting child support are exacerbated when the spouse lives out of state. Initially, the Uniform Reciprocal Enforcement of Support Act (URESA) may be used to obtain a support order. This act is available in some form in all states.

If the dependent spouse has already obtained a support order, either before the delinquent spouse left the state or through a lawsuit under URESA, the most effective way to enforce it is through interstate income withholding, where the state in which the delinquent spouse lives withholds income from wages or other sources in order to collect the child support and then sends it to the dependent spouse. Again, a lawyer or child support enforcement agency can take the necessary steps.

Can a woman obtain child support payments if she has never been married to the father of the child?

Yes. The new federal laws require child support enforcement agencies to provide services to establish paternity to both welfare and nonwelfare mothers. In addition, federal law requires states to have procedures to permit the establishment of paternity at any time prior to a child's eighteenth birthday (in the past, establishing paternity was sometimes difficult because the actions had to be brought within a short span of time). Establishing paternity not only opens the door to receiving paternal child support payments but is also often critical to establishing eligibility for Social Security (if the father dies or becomes disabled or retires), worker's compensation, and inheritance.

PREMARITAL AND MARITAL AGREEMENTS

What are premarital and marital agreements?

A premarital agreement (also called a prenuptial or antenuptial agreement) is a contract entered into by both parties prior to marriage that sets out their respective rights and obligations under certain circumstances such as separation, divorce, or death. Traditionally, premarital agreements were used by wealthy people to clarify financial arrangements, usually to protect property rights for their children or other relatives in the event of a divorce or the spouse's death. Now they are increasingly used by middle-class people, who recognize the possibility of divorce and wish to plan for the economic future in a manner that is tailored to individual circumstances.

A marital agreement (also called a postnuptial agreement) is a similar contract entered into during marriage.

When should couples have a premarital agreement?

Any couple may choose to draw up a premarital agreement. The wealthy partner in a couple where there is a large disparity in wealth between the partners may often insist on such an agreement. They are sometimes used if one partner has children from a previous marriage. A woman who plans to support her husband by being a full-time homemaker could also use them to contract for an appropriate value of her services because courts may not protect her by providing for income based on an equal partnership model at the time of divorce.[23] Premarital agreements can either harm or help women. A wealthy man can use one to attempt to ensure that a wife without assets will not get her fair share in a divorce. Conversely, the same wife could use one to attempt to ensure that she *does* get her fair share in a divorce. As these circumstances suggest, it is obviously important to consider premarital agreements very closely before signing them.

Is it necessary to have a lawyer to make a premarital agreement?

A lawyer is technically not unnecessary, but it is advisable to consult a lawyer, particularly if the agreement is detailed or complicated. Form agreements are available from books in libraries or bookstores.

Should each partner secure his or her own lawyer?

Yes. If you use a lawyer, as in the case of divorce, it is preferable that each person have independent, separately paid counsel. If both people are represented by the same lawyer, the lawyer may have an automatic conflict of interest and a court will be less likely to enforce the agreement.

What issues should be included in a premarital agreement?

Some of the common issues that such agreements address are division of property, including property inherited during the marriage; division of insurance and pension benefits; support of spouse at separation or divorce; provisions in a will (in that case wills must be made to conform to the premarital agreement); and child support for children from a previous marriage.

It is against public policy to waive child support payments for children born of the marriage. The right to child support belongs to the child, not the parents, and courts refuse to enforce provisions that waive such support.

Do courts recognize and enforce premarital agreements?

Until recently, courts were reluctant to recognize and enforce premarital agreements on the ground that such agreements encourage divorce. However, courts in a majority of states now enforce premarital agreements. For example, in late 1990 the Kentucky Supreme Court overturned its long-held prohibition of such agreements. Rejecting the view that premarital agreements encourage divorce, the court noted changes in the state's divorce laws and the prevalence of divorce since the rule against premarital agreements was established in 1916.[24] Courts seem to be realizing that such agreements can actually promote marital harmony by forcing people to think in advance of marriage about monetary issues and that premarital agreements can reduce court involvement in private property disputes. In deciding to enforce premarital agreements, courts have set forth certain requirements and standards for enforcement.[25]

What are the prerequisites and standards for enforcement of a premarital agreement?

One of the most important prerequisites for enforcing a premarital agreement is that both people must disclose all their financial information to each other. Incomplete disclosure can be grounds for not enforcing the agreement, on the theory that the agreement is then fraudulent. One way to ensure complete disclosure is to attach a list of each person's assets and liabilities to the agreement.

Some courts have also required that each person be informed prior to the agreement of his or her rights without the agreement, particularly those rights that are guaranteed by state law. For example, if a woman agrees to give up her right to alimony without being aware that she would be entitled to it under state law, courts have been reluctant to enforce the agreement.

A certain degree of formality is also important. While a premarital agreement does not need to be written in "legalese," courtship letters do not have enough formality to constitute a premarital agreement.[26]

Finally, courts scrutinize the treatment of alimony very closely. Some courts will not enforce *any* agreement in which a spouse forfeits all rights to alimony, finding such an agreement to be against public policy. The rationale for this rule is that the state does not want a spouse to become a public charge.

The majority of courts, however, decide on a case-by-case basis whether to enforce an agreement that waives alimony and use some kind of fairness standard.[27] A 1990 case from Arizona said the court must decide "whether the agreement between the parties was fairly reached and whether it adequately provides for support of the spouse consistent with the needs and resources of both spouses at the time of dissolution."[28]

Even if an agreement does not forfeit all right to alimony, some courts evaluate premarital agreements to determine whether they are reasonable at the time of their execution and/or at the time enforcement is sought, even though other contracts between adults are not evaluated for fairness.[29] For example, in a case from the District of Columbia, the court said that it would uphold a premarital contract in a marriage of short duration as fair if it allowed each spouse to live as well as he or she did before the marriage.[30] For a marriage of long duration, however, the court suggested a different criterion of fairness: maintaining the living standard of the parties *during* marriage. The court also considered it important to examine whether the agreement was really voluntary and whether there was full disclosure of each other's assets. Using the "reasonableness" standard, some courts also inquire whether the terms of the agreement provide an incentive for divorce or separation.[31]

Other courts have decided that premarital agreements should be treated like any other contract.[32] In a 1990 Pennsylvania case, for example, the Pennsylvania Supreme Court rejected prior case authority that said premarital contracts should be evaluated for reasonableness. In this case the woman was presented with a premarital contract on the eve of the wedding. She was an unemployed nurse and her husband a neurosurgeon with an income of $90,000 per year and assets of $300,000. The agreement provided for support payments of $200 monthly, limited to a total of $25,000. The only lawyer involved was the man's lawyer, who had written the agreement but who did advise the woman of the legal rights she gave up with the agreement. The court upheld the agreement on the grounds that although earlier decisions had required that parties to premarital contracts be aware of the statutory rights they were relinquishing, the court believed such an approach reflected paternalistic thinking about women and that in the future premarital contracts should be binding and judged like any other contract, without regard to whether the terms were fully understood by both parties.[33]

Feminists disagree about whether a premarital agreement should be interpreted like any other contract or whether it should be subject to stricter judicial scrutiny because the parties are not dealing at arms length. Some feminists argue that premarital agreements should not be judged like ordinary contracts, under which people are bound to their agreement even if it is a bad deal, but instead should be judged under a standard of fairness or reasonableness. Other feminists assert that such a rule only reinforces traditional ways of thinking about women, i.e., that they need greater protection because they are too emotional or unsophisticated to bargain for themselves.

Are contracts made during the marriage enforceable?

While some states, such as New York,[34] explicitly recognize agreements made during marriage, many states have not yet addressed the issue. They thus may not be enforceable in such states. One can always sign such agreements on the assumption that they may be enforceable, and of course they should be written and considered with the same care as a premarital contract.

ESTABLISHING LEGAL PROTECTION
FOR THOSE IN SAME SEX RELATIONSHIPS
AND FOR UNMARRIED PARTNERS

The issues pertaining to lesbian women are more thoroughly discussed in the recently issued third edition of *The Rights of Lesbians and Gay Men* (1992), another book in the ACLU handbook series. The rights of unmarried heterosexual women are also discussed in *The Rights of Single People* (1985).

Do unmarried couples, whether heterosexual or lesbian, need to make legal arrangements to protect themselves?

Yes. Ideally, an unmarried couple should do several things. The partners should explore the various types of co-ownership of property in order to choose the one that best suits their needs and keep good records of the financial contributions each makes for the property in question. They should enter into a written relationship agreement to settle questions of property ownership, support, and division if they break up. They should prepare will and trust instruments if they want property to go to each other at the time of death because under state inheritance laws no property will be given to an unmarried surviving partner without a will. Finally, they should anticipate crises by executing a power of attorney, a medical consent form, and a form nominating their partner as guardian of any children. A power of attorney is a legal document in which one person authorizes another to make decisions and take certain actions on his or her behalf. Powers of attorney can be special—that is, limited to one type of act, such as selling a home or general or durable—in which case it continues in force even after the person making it becomes incompetent. These forms give each partner the rights that usually go to the next of kin in a crisis (except that a guardianship form cannot defeat the rights of a living parent).

If an unmarried couple separates, what rights does each partner have to a property settlement or monetary award?

Traditionally, courts have refused to protect property interests in such situations because such agreements were considered to be based on "immoral consideration"—i.e., illicit sex.

This rule was rejected, however, in a famous 1976 case. Michelle Triola Marvin sued actor Lee Marvin for one-half of his earnings during the seven years they lived together. She claimed they had orally agreed to pool their earnings and property. The California Supreme Court made history by agreeing that express and implied contracts between unmarried partners were enforceable by the courts. The trial judge later ruled, however, that Ms. Marvin had failed to prove they had actually agreed to pool the resources, so she lost her claim to half of his earnings. Instead, she won a much smaller amount ($104,000) for rehabilitation.[35] This decision, establishing a right in California to what the popular press has dubbed "palimony," has since been followed by courts in many other states in determining the rights of unmarried heterosexual couples.

The reasoning of the court in the *Marvin* case seems just as applicable to lesbian couples, and some courts have issued opinions that appear to apply the ruling to lesbian or gay couples.[36] But many courts seem less willing to require palimony for lesbian couples and go out of their way to find the provision of sexual services an inseparable part of financial agreements between lesbian and gay couples.

Women in similar situations should take precautions to protect their property interests. Partners who have an agreement to share earnings and property need to put it in writing, perhaps as part of a contract dealing with other domestic issues, and they should be sure the title to any property is in both names.

Do unmarried couples have the right to inherit from each other if they do not have wills?

No. If a person dies without a will, her property is distributed according to the laws of the state in which she lived at the time of her death. These laws, called the *laws of intestate succession*, generally specify the estate will be distributed in specified percentages among various defined survivors, such as spouses, children, parents, brothers, and sisters.

What are some of the ways in which courts have recognized the family relationships of lesbian couples?

A landmark case argued by the ACLU and decided by the Court of Appeals, the highest court in New York, interpreted the statutory definition of family, in the context of New York's rent-control laws, to include "two adult lifetime partners whose relationship is long-term and characterized by an emotional and financial commitment and interdependence."[37] Specifically, the court set forth a number of factors to be used in defining a family, including "the exclusivity and longevity of the relationship, the level of emotional and financial commitment, the manner in which the parties have conducted their everyday lives and held themselves out to society, and the reliance placed upon one another for daily family services."[38]

Similarly, the California Workers' Compensation Appeals Board found, several years earlier, that a gay man was entitled to benefits after the job-related suicide of his lover. The board reasoned that "the inability to enter a recognized marriage should not control the issue of a good faith member of a household."[39]

Can lesbian couples and unmarried partners obtain any financial benefits through government or employment?

Because no state recognizes marriage between people of the same sex, lesbian couples are deprived of many of the financial benefits that the government confers on married people, such as Social Security benefits. Some cities and some companies, however, are beginning to provide domestic-partner benefits, particularly for health insurance and leave policies. These benefits usually are provided to unmarried heterosexual couples as well as to lesbian and gay couples.

What should an unwed mother do to be assured of custody?

Although unwed mothers are often automatically entitled to custody, it is not safe to rely on this assumption. The Supreme Court has recognized that unwed fathers have some rights, too, such as right to notice and a hearing before his child can be placed for adoption. Unwed fathers may also have the right to take, kidnap, and even keep their children if the mother does not have a legal custody order.

Thus, in order to protect herself, an unwed mother should go to court for a custody order. However, going to court requires naming the father in the court papers and notifying him of the case, which could cause him to ask for visitation rights or custody, something he may not have considered previously.

Have courts upheld the rights of lesbian women to be granted custody of their children when they are divorced?

Although many courts still discriminate against lesbian and gay parents in custody disputes, in recent years there has been a growing trend toward acceptance of custody rights for lesbian parents. One author has suggested that much of the resistance to lesbian and gay parental rights is now concentrated in the central and southern regions of the United States, while the courts on the east and west coasts have grown more accepting of lesbian and gay parents.[40] A lesbian parent whose custody rights are challenged should obtain the help of a lawyer who is sympathetic to the rights of lesbian and gay parents to have custody of their children.

Can second-parent adoption be used to create legal rights for lesbian mothers?

Sometimes. In some cases, where the decision to have a child was a joint decision and the couple has acted as co-equal parents for at least a few years, courts have allowed the nonbiological mother to adopt the child without loss of rights by the biological mother. This kind of adoption is called *second-parent adoption*. In the case of an adopted child, some courts have allowed both women to adopt.[41]

Can a same-sex partner obtain custody or visitation rights with respect to a child of her partner that she has helped to raise?

The law is mixed. One of the first questions is whether the child has a second legal parent. If the child already has a second legal parent, it is unlikely that courts will enforce the coparent's right with respect to the child. However, in situations where a lesbian woman is the sole legal parent, documents can be drafted to try to protect the relationship between the partner and the child. But there are no guarantees that such private arrangements will be enforced by the courts. For example, in one of the first cases to test this issue, the New York Court of Appeals refused to award visitation rights to a lesbian copartner, on the ground that she was not a "parent" within the meaning of the New York custody/visitation statute.[42]

Another approach to obtaining custody and visitation rights for lesbian mothers is to use legal theories developed in other contexts. For example, some judges have used a doctrine called *in loco parentis* to give stepparents custody and visitation rights, when the stepparents proved they acted in loco parentis—that is, in the place of the parent. A lesbian who actively parented a child but who is not the biological mother of the child can try to convince judges to extend the reasoning of the stepparent cases to her situation. For a discussion of this theory and other similar theories that could be used to achieve the same result, see Polikoff, *This Child Does Have Two Mothers*, 78 Georgetown Law Journal 459, 491–527 (1990).

In addition to using existing legal theories in a new way, legal scholars have also suggested redefining parenthood and family. Professor Katherine Bartlett has written an article entitled *Rethinking Parenthood as an Exclusive Status: The Need for Legal Alternatives When the Promise of the Nuclear Family Has Failed*, 70 Virginia Law Review 879 (1984). She argues that psychological parents should be entitled to seek custody or visitation rights and defines such parents as "adults who provide for the physical, emotional and social needs of the child." She also sets some limits on this definition, including only adults who have had "physical custody of the child for at least six months," who can show that their motive in seeking parental status is "genuine care and concern for the child," and who can prove the child's legal parent consented to the relationship or that it began under court order.[43]

Professor Polikoff has suggested that courts and legislatures looking for guidance in developing a new definition of parenthood should focus on "two criteria: the legally unrelated adult's performance of parenting functions and the child's view of that adult as a parent."[44] For example, an Oregon statute enacted in 1985 permits anyone to seek custody or visitation who "has established emotional ties creating a child-parent relationship with a child."[45] She also suggests protecting the "interests of *legal* parents in parental autonomy by focusing on the actions and intent of those parents in creating additional parental relationships." (Emphasis added.)[46]

Where can women obtain more information about lesbian custody issues?

The National Center for Lesbian Rights has an extensive publications list, including *A Lesbian and Gay Parents' Legal*

Guide to Child Custody, which may be ordered for $10.00 from NCLR at 1663 Mission Street, 5th Floor, San Francisco, CA 94103.

In 1991 the Lambda Legal Defense and Education Fund, Inc. published *Custody Visitation Packet: Issues and Court Briefs* and plans to publish future materials on parenting issues, adoption, and the rights of coparents. Materials may be obtained from Lambda at 666 Broadway, New York, NY 10012.

GENERAL INFORMATION ABOUT DIVORCE

Does one spouse have the right to force the other to leave the house?

No, generally not before a divorce hearing, especially if the other spouse wants the marriage to continue. If the husband wants to end the marriage and the wife does not agree to leave the home, he cannot insist that she move out. If the husband tries to force her to leave, she can probably obtain a court order, with a lawyer's help, allowing her to stay. If the wife wants the marriage to end and the husband does not, she may have to leave the home if she wants to live in separate households. She should talk to a lawyer at once if this situation arises. Regardless of who leaves, at the time of divorce the court may award the family home to either the husband or wife or order that the house be sold and the proceeds split, depending on state law on division of property.

Is it all right for a woman to have sexual relations with her husband once they have decided to get a divorce?

No. First, in many states, having sexual relations with each other may prevent a married couple from getting the divorce at all. If a woman is claiming her husband's adultery as "fault" grounds for divorce, having sex with him after the adultery occurred is legally construed as forgiving him for his actions. Thus, she loses her right to divorce him.

Second, even if the divorce is "no-fault" or uncontested (so that she does not need to prove adultery or any other grounds for divorce in court), the fact that a woman has a strong showing of "fault" against her husband can in some states put her in a better bargaining position in negotiations over important details of the divorce. Her husband may even have been advised to have sex with her for just this reason: to destroy her legal grounds for divorce or to weaken her claim for alimony or property, and thereby weaken her position in the negotiations.

Finally, the so-called no-fault grounds for divorce often require no "cohabitation" for a certain period of time, such as sixty days or one year. In many of these states, having sex or sharing a bed even once will be considered "cohabiting" for legal purposes and the couple will have to start counting the time period all over again.

Will it help the lawyer increase the amount of alimony and child support if a woman documents her past budget needs and the family assets?

Yes, in fact it cannot be done without this type of help. All expenses that need to be covered must be itemized and documented with past bills wherever possible. The lawyer must have this information in order to make a convincing case of the need for alimony and to a lesser extent, child support (specific information is less needed for child support because of the guidelines that are now in effect). Standard budget items include rent or mortgage payments; repair bills; utility and phone bills; household supplies; furniture replacements; transportation (including car and public transportation); insurance premiums (for health and life insurance); psychiatric, medical, and dental care expenses; food; clothing; children's tuition; recreation, including vacations; such work-related expenses as lunches, extra clothes, day care, and cleaning and laundry services; education and training costs; and taxes.

Work and education-related expenses should be emphasized because they are the kind of expenses most lawyers tend to overlook for a woman. Both are important for the woman's well-being since going to school or being employed will make it easier to adjust to the change and because the vast majority of women will never receive enough property, alimony, or child support to live comfortably. Moreover, few men keep the payments up. It is best to face these facts from the start. Thus a woman has a real need to improve and continue her education or training. Additional training will increase her wage-earning capacity and ability to support herself. Education, however, does not eliminate the need for alimony.

How should this documentation be prepared?

In addition to a solid budget, a list of the family assets and liabilities should be prepared. Originals or copies of all legal documents showing property of any kind owned by either or both partners and tax returns showing the husband's income should be obtained. These things should be done as soon as there is any indication of trouble in the marriage because some husbands hide these documents or change real estate, stocks, bonds, cash, and other property owned jointly to their names alone. Also, a woman should make sure she knows her husband's social security number.

What should be done about life insurance?

Upon divorcing, special arrangements should be made for the insurance on the husband's life so that there will be a viable policy to cover alimony and child support if the husband should die. One arrangement is for the husband to give his ex-wife the ownership of the policy so that he cannot use the policy as security for a loan or change the named beneficiaries; the court can order him to keep up the payments. Another approach is to have the woman request alimony money to make the premium payments herself; this ensures that the husband will not let the policy lapse.

What other legal documents will the lawyer need?

He or she will need the marriage certificate and documentation of any former marriages and divorces.

Is there any reason to collect budget, property, and income information quickly?

Yes. First, as mentioned above, the husband may be acting to hide the information in order to reduce his payments; the wife should get copies before he can do so. (She should have her own copies of this information anyway, or at least know where they are kept, since this information is also essential in case of sudden death.) Second, this information is needed for any temporary alimony and child support payments the lawyer will arrange for the interval before the divorce takes place.

Is it important to get good alimony and child support arrangements in the interim before the final divorce is secured?

Definitely. The amount of temporary alimony usually sets

the standard for the amount of permanent alimony. This holds true for child support payments as well. Thus, securing temporary payments is just as important as the final divorce proceeding itself. A woman who is unsure of the exact amount for any particular item and has no documentation does best to err on the generous side since the judge will almost always cut back on the figures.

Should the marital partners negotiate about alimony, child support, property, or other matters before seeing their lawyers?

Definitely not. They should know their rights before making any agreement—financial or otherwise. A woman may be entitled to much more than she realizes, or she might not have fully analyzed her future needs—and it is always best to have the facts before making a decision.

Should a woman leave her money or securities in a joint account if she is thinking about a divorce or suspects her husband wants a divorce?

Men are often advised to take all the money out of a joint account as a way of preventing their wives from getting any of it. A woman should withdraw the money she thinks is her own if she has even the slightest suspicion her husband would do such a thing. If she needs the money, it is best to take precautionary measures.

If the husband has cleaned out the joint savings or checking account or sold joint property is there anything the wife can do?

Yes. Her lawyer can get a court order forcing her husband to reimburse her in a property settlement. If he has not taken property or funds, but she suspects he plans to do so, her lawyer can also get an order forbidding any such action. This would prevent the husband from removing or selling any assets before the divorce.

What can a woman do if both she and her husband are so poor they cannot afford to live apart?

Many families have such a small income they cannot afford to set up two separate households. In this situation, the woman should think about obtaining welfare; another book in this series, *The Rights of the Poor* (the second edition is planned for 1993), explains in detail what one's rights to welfare are and how to go about asserting them. Another alternative is for the spouses to continue to live in the same household while pursuing their divorce or legal separation. If the couple wants to live apart and cannot afford to do so on the present income, the wife may decide to work for pay if she is not yet doing so. This might increase the family income enough so the couple can afford to live apart; it could also, however, diminish her chance of receiving alimony.

DOMESTIC VIOLENCE

In the United States, home is often not the safe, nurturing place pictured in the popular media.[47] Domestic violence pervades all classes and races at shocking rates; it is estimated a woman is battered every fifteen seconds in the United States. Domestic violence is the largest cause of injury to women in the United States; 20% of emergency room visits by women are for injuries caused by battering.[48] One-half of all wives experience some form of spouse-inflicted abuse,[49] and 31% of all female homicide victims in 1988 were killed by their husbands or boyfriends. Women are especially vulnerable during pregnancy; one study found that 37% of obstetric patients interviewed were physically abused during pregnancy.[50]

Although the law no longer explicitly condones domestic violence, its prevalence may in part be due to the historical fact that the British common law that was adopted by the United States colonies and states recognized the husband as ruler of the home. As part of the husband's authority, the common law authorized his use of violence against his wife, as long as he used a switch no bigger than his thumb.[51] This early common law still has ramifications today in the outright refusal or reluctance of police and other agencies to intervene in the "private" home to give women the protection and assistance they need.[52]

Nevertheless, the women's movement gained important legal protection for battered women in the 1980s. There are thus many steps that battered women can now take to get help.

What practical steps can a woman take to protect herself if her husband (or ex-husband or lover) beats, harasses, or threatens to harm her?

She should call the police immediately after an assault if she wants the attacker arrested or if she needs protection to leave her home safely. If emergency shelter is needed, she should secure refuge with relatives, friends, or a shelter for battered women. In any case, she should contact a shelter or battered women's advocacy group for personal support, legal information and referral, and practical advice. An increasing number of communities now have shelters where abused women and their children can live temporarily until they can begin to put their lives back in order. These shelters can provide help in getting welfare assistance, job training, jobs, and new homes, in addition to the other forms of help listed above.

What legal steps can a woman take to protect herself if her husband (or ex-husband or lover) beats, harasses, or threatens to harm her?

In most states, a woman has a choice of three traditional legal strategies in dealing with abuse or threats: (1) divorce or legal separation from the abusive husband, plus any needed "stay-away" order; (2) a protection order that requires him to stop abusing, threatening, or harassing her, either while they continue to live together or while they live apart; and (3) criminal prosecution of the abuser. In appropriate situations a woman may be able to get both criminal enforcement and protection orders.

Advocates for battered women have also developed new strategies, such as rehabilitative alimony, actions for civil damages to compensate for the effects of battering, and actions against police who are slow to enforce the law against abusers.

How does divorce or separation work as a remedy for domestic violence?

To use this remedy, a woman has her attorney file for a divorce or legal separation (which can usually be based on the physical abuse). The attorney then asks the judge to issue temporary orders giving the woman the protection she needs and providing for custody, visitation, and child support. The temporary orders stay in effect until the divorce or legal separation is granted, when they should be made part of the final court order.

The time of initial separation is often the most dangerous for battered women, and women should take extra care to keep their location and that of their children from becoming known to the abuser, where this is appropriate.

What is a protection order and how does it work?

A protection order is an order issued by a civil court judge commanding the husband (or ex-husband or lover) to stop abusing, harassing, or threatening the victim and to stay away from the victim. The order can also provide for custody, supervised or unsupervised visitation, and child and spousal support; the abuser's eviction from the family home (even if it is in his name); a prohibition from entering or from telephoning the victim at her residence, school, business, or place of employment; payment for the wife's moving, medical, and legal expenses; and a requirment that the batterer get counseling or participate in a drug or alcohol abuse or batterer's treatment program.

In some states, a woman may ask the court for such an order herself, without the aid of a lawyer (this is called appearing *pro se*). In others, an attorney must be present, whether her own private attorney, a free legal services lawyer or representative from a law school clinic, or a government attorney. Sometimes the woman may be able to get an immediate short-term protection order, without the abuser being present, on the basis of her own testimony or sworn statements, or even by talking on the phone with the police and judge. (However, this temporary order must then be served on the husband and followed by a full court hearing at which he has an opportunity to appear, before it can be extended for a longer period.) In other cases, it may take up to two months to find and serve the husband, hold a court hearing, and issue a longer-term protection order, which can be in effect for six months to two years.

As many women have learned, it takes further action to enforce the order if the man refuses to comply. In theory, the abuser will be found in contempt of court if he violates the order and could be fined or jailed. But the police frequently will not arrest him unless the state makes it a special crime to violate the order, a crime that subjects the violator to arrest on the basis of the victim's report. (In other places, police operate under mandatory arrest policies that require them to arrest whenever there is probable cause to believe the batterer has committed a crime such as assault.) In addition, the woman usually has to initiate contempt of court proceedings herself (or through her attorney or the government attorney); and many courts will not order the man to jail, although some will. Enforcement can also be effective if the court orders a jail sentence but suspends it on the condition that the man complies with the order in the future.

When women do obtain these orders, they should carry them in their pocketbooks and leave a certified copy at the local police precincts where they live or work, where the abusers live, or where any children go to school or are cared for; in other words, the women should make sure that wherever they are likely to be victimized by their abusers, the police in that area have been notifed that there is an order in effect. While the police often do not respond well to domestic violence situations, their performance improves—i.e., they may at least investigate the situation—if they know a woman has a protection order.

Is it possible to have the abuser ordered out of the house?
In some states, yes, even if the title or lease is in his name. A woman should definitely ask for this in the court order or ask for moving expenses and rent for herself and her children if she must leave.

Are there special considerations when children are involved?
If at all possible, a victim of abuse should not leave her children at home with the abuser, even if they are not in danger, since this may weaken her custody case later. Fortyone states have provided in their laws that judges may award temporary custody of children to the victim in civil protection order cases.[50] Accordingly, a victim should seek temporary custody of her children immediately as part of the legal proceedings for getting the civil protection order.

With regard to visitation, a victim should ask her lawyer to arrange to have the court order provide that she will not have to be alone with the children's father when he picks them up to visit—e.g., arrange pickups at a relative's home, a church, or a public place. Whenever possible, a third party should also be involved in making arrangements and transferring the children for visits, and if necessary, in supervising visits. If the abuser has a drinking or drug problem, the victim may want to ask the judge to allow her to refuse visitation if the abuser is impaired when he comes to pick up the children. In some states, interference with visitation is a crime, and if the judge's permission to refuse the visitation has not been secured, the victim may be charged with a crime or with contempt of court for doing what she believes is in the childrens' best interests.

Is wife abuse a crime? Will the abuser be put into jail?

Yes, it is a crime. No, he will probably not be put into jail, although it happens more frequently than it used to. Although the police are often reluctant to respond to "domestic" calls, assaulting or threatening a partner is a crime and the victim is entitled to a police response whether or not she intends to follow through with full criminal prosecution. If the victim wants the abuser arrested, she must say so. The police may refuse to arrest him on the spot because of their interpretation of the arrest rules. But their presence can give the victim a chance to get herself and the children out of the house. If the police do arrest the abuser, the victim should be sure to ask how long it is likely to be before he is released. (Often it is only hours.) If the victim decides to file criminal charges with the prosecutor and the case goes forward, her abuser may be fined, jailed, or put on probation, assuming he is found guilty or pleads guilty. Probation is the most common result. In this case, the victim should be sure to tell the prosecutor if she needs special conditions for her protection so that they can be made part of the probation order.

What is rehabilitative maintenance?

Even when a court is reluctant to order permanent alimony, temporary alimony or so-called rehabilitative maintenance (payments of support for a definite length of time after separation) can be used to enable a woman to gain the ability to support herself financially through education, training, and therapy. It can also be used to prevent financial hardship for the woman during the training period and can be enforced, like child support, through the courts and through a state or county administrative process.

Can a woman sue her abuser for damages?

Yes. Women have sued for damages either under civil suits for torts or under the domestic abuse prevention act in their state. Forty-nine states and the District of Columbia have family violence or spouse abuse prevention laws, although not every law allows women to collect damages. The only state that does not have a domestic violence statute is Delaware, and there the powers of the family courts have been interpreted to allow judges to protect family members from abuse under the theory that violence by a family member "imperils the family relationship." Under some of those domestic abuse prevention acts, a woman can sue for such items as loss of earnings, out-of-pocket expenses, and the costs and attorneys' fees needed to seek a protection order.

In a civil tort action, a woman can sue for medical bills, lost wages, loss of earning capacity, damage to property, pain and suffering, physical and psychological injury, permanent injuries, humiliation and shame, and punitive damages.[54] The civil action can also include a cause of action for rape in some states. If the woman is married to her assailant, however, she may be precluded from this action because only sixteen states (Alabama, Alaska, Arkansas, Colorado, Florida, Georgia, Indiana, Maine, Massachusetts, Nebraska, New Jersey, New York, North Dakota, Oregon, Vermont and Wisconsin)[55] have totally abolished the marital rape exemption (see chapter 7).[56] In the remaining states, the marital rape exemption could be challenged as a violation of the federal or state equal protection or due process clauses, or a state ERA, but if the challenge is unsuccessful, wives in that state might lose a suit for damages based on spousal rape.

What can be done against police or prosecutors who refuse to help?

Women have sometimes successfully sued police departments that have failed to arrest batterers.[57] In a Connecticut case, the plaintiff won a $2.3 million judgment, based in part on her claim that the department's differential treatment of criminal wife-battering cases violated her right to equal protection of the laws. That case has motivated police in other cities to change their policies in domestic abuse cases.

What steps can a woman take to build her case?

Whichever legal route a woman chooses, she will need to collect evidence to prove in court that she was subjected to abuse. She will also need personal support, both for the court action and in putting her life back together. Police logs, medical records, photographs, and the testimony of those who heard a fight or saw the woman's physical condition afterward can provide good courtroom evidence. To establish the evidence she should call the police and ask her neighbors to call, too; go for medical treatment and tell the doctor the full story; ask that photographs of her physical condition be taken immediately or take them herself. Torn or bloody clothing and anything used or threatened to be used as a weapon should be kept with the photographs in a secure place until they are turned over to a lawyer or prosecutor.

Are there legal procedures victims should be wary of?

Yes. Two in particular are forced mediation for domestic violence complainants and mutual protection orders imposed on both parties in a domestic abuse situation.

Where there is domestic violence, the power structure of the relationship is not in equilibrium. The abuser has a lot more power in the relationship than the victim. Therefore, most professional mediators will not mediate the issue of violence between these two people. The National Council of Juvenile and Family Court Judges has recommended that no judge should mandate mediation of violence in a case where family violence has occurred.[58] Nevertheless, mediation is often suggested as a way to avoid "wasting" court time and resources on these matters. Women should protest this, and explain why, if the court tries to order it.

Mutual protection orders have been discouraged by law in several states. Usually, mutual restraints are issued by a judge with the consent of the parties and include language such as

"Both parties will refrain from harassing or assaulting the other." It sounds harmless enough until the woman is abused again, and calls the police for help. They may refuse to help, or they may even arrest her, because they cannot tell who the likely aggressor is given that both parties have been ordered not to assault the other. The mutual civil protection order keeps the police, the court, and the abuser from acknowledging that a criminal act has occurred and sustains the illusion that domestic violence is just a type of marital dispute. Any such restraints on a victim's behavior should be rigorously avoided.

What is the "battered woman" syndrome and how is it used in court?

Battered woman syndrome is a description of the psychological impact of repeated battering on the victim. Expert testimony concerning the battered woman syndrome was developed to help juries understand the behavior of battered women who say they were acting in self-defense but are accused of murdering their batterers.

Can lesbians use any of the remedies for domestic violence?

Yes, although many domestic violence programs are designed only for straight women and police may be even more reluctant to intervene in a lesbian relationship. In about thirty states, the domestic abuse laws cover unrelated adults of the same sex, so lesbians can use these laws. In all states, criminal law prohibits physical assaults and threats, and lesbians interested in this approach can seek arrest and prosecution of abusers. Minnesota has become the first state to fund a full-time staff person to address lesbian battering, and shelters are beginning to address lesbian battering.[59]

Are there any special avenues of help for elderly women?

Many states acknowledge the problem when it exists in an institutional setting or when the abuse occurs at the hands of a child or spouse, and victims of elder abuse/domestic violence can generally get help through the state or local office on aging. Another approach is simply to use the domestic violence statutes that are available to all victims of domestic violence.

What else is being done to address systemic problems of domestic violence?

Some states and the District of Columbia have passed laws mandating that police make arrests in domestic violence situations where there is probable cause to believe that a crime has occurred. Typically, that standard means that if there is some corroboration of the violence—such as visible injuries, weapons, or a witness—police will arrest. In addition, many cities, counties, and states have decided that it should be the policy of their police departments to require arrests in all cases that meet certain criteria. The criteria vary from one jurisdiction to another, but it is generally accepted that arrest is one of the best ways to stop abuse and that police tend to under-arrest unless required to act.

Partly as a result of the media portraying women from all walks of life who have been battered, there is a greater awareness among teachers, clergy, child protection workers, and community mental health personnel that battering is a common phenomenon. Also, police departments often provide training on issues of domestic violence for new recruits, and hospitals train emergency room personnel to recognize signs that abuse is the cause of an injury. Those interested in helping to prevent domestic violence locally can seek to obtain similar arrest and training programs in their communities.

Has any federal legislation been proposed to address these problems?

Yes. A sweeping bill, the Violence Against Women Act, S. 15/H.R. 1502, was introduced in Congress in 1990 and reintroduced in 1991 and 1992. The bill would create a civil rights remedy for victims of sexual assault; provide money in grants to the states to improve safety for women in streets and parks and on public transit; would aid interstate enforcement of domestic violence orders; and would encourage states to adopt pro-arrest policies and improve tracking of cases involving domestic abuse. Congress also passed Resolution 172 in 1990; the measure expressed "the sense of the Congress that, for purposes of determining child custody, credible evidence of physical abuse of one's spouse should create a statutory presumption that it is detrimental to the child to be placed in the custody of the abusive spouse."

Where can women get further information on domestic violence or referrals to local battered women's support groups?

The phone book lists numbers for local women's shelters (look in the yellow pages under "women") and the state domestic violence hotline. Some national sources of information are listed below.

National Coalition Against Domestic Violence
(202) 638-6388
National Coalition Against Sexual Assault
(202) 483-7165
National Organization for Victim Assistance
(202) 232-NOVA
National Victim Center
(817) 877-3355
Center for Women and Family Law
(212) 674-8200
National Clearinghouse for the Defense of Battered Women
(215) 351-0010

NAMES AND NAME CHANGE

Names symbolize a person's identity, so it is not surprising that the subject of names has been important to many feminists.[60] Moreover, the system for naming people reflects women's status. Under the current system, almost every woman in this country uses the name of a man, whether father or husband, as her last name. Symbolically, then, most women's identity is still tied to a man.

Many women have searched for ways around this male-oriented system. A few refuse to use either their father's or their husband's name, and instead take a surname derived from another source. Other women choose to use their father's name, both before and after marriage. Still others prefer a husband's name to the father's or combine and hyphenate the two. Some decide with their husbands that both should take a new name—whether a combination of their fathers' names or an unrelated third name. Some women may even convince their husbands to adopt the woman's father's name. Others of course, do not feel it important to depart from the traditional pattern of naming women.

Each solution has advantages and disadvantages. Choosing a name different from either the father's or husband's allows one to express the greatest disagreement with the male orientation of the present system, but it takes time and effort to reeducate a woman's friends and relatives and officials to call her by a name that social custom has not sanctioned. Using the father's name allows a woman to retain the identity she grew up with and symbolizes equality upon marriage since the man also retains his father's name. Every woman who chooses to do this, however, still carries a symbolic tie to her father only—but none to her mother—and if she has children and gives them, in turn, the surname of their father, they will have the same problem. Some women prefer to use their husband's name because they like it better or feel they have some choice in taking it, even though the choice is between identification with one male and identification with another male. Married couples who hyphenate their fathers' names or take a third name also opt for a symbol of equality, and each partner contributes to the children's surname, but it sets off the family unit in a way some do not wish to perpetuate.

Ideally, we need a new, egalitarian system for naming children. Children could be given surnames that either reflect the names of both parents or possibly the names of neither. When these children marry in turn, both men and women could keep their surnames, combine them, or choose a third name. None of these choices would carry patriarchal connotations since none would favor a male's name over a female's name.

People are already experimenting with new approaches along these lines. Many couples with different last names now give their children a surname consisting of the parents' hyphenated surnames. Or such couples may give their children one parent's surname as a middle name and the other parent's surname as a last name. Others give children the mother's surname. Another alternative is labeled "bilineal," for it passes both parents' names through the generations, by naming boys for their father and girls for their mother. Or this might be done in reverse, with boys named after their mother and girls after their father. But as parents give children nonpatrilineal names or disagree about what names the children should use, new legal issues have arisen, for the legal system still tends to favor the father's right over the mother's right to name children where there is a dispute.

As far as adults are concerned, those women—and men—who want to deviate from tradition by taking names that reflect a more egalitarian view of the relationship between the sexes are free to do so. While there may be occasional mild difficulties in asserting their rights, this will not usually be the case, and there are easy remedies for those who face problems.

What are the historical reasons for women taking their husband's name?

Until the middle of the nineteenth century, a married couple was regarded as one person—the husband—under a legal doctrine called *coverture*. Under coverture, a married woman had no independent legal existence. She could not sue or be sued, sign contracts, retain her wages, own personal property, manage or control her real property, make a will, choose her own domicile, refuse to perform domestic services, decline her husband's sexual advances, or resist his physical or economic restraints. While the doctrine of coverture did not explicitly address names, coverture lowered women's status so pervasively that it undoubtedly helped lead to the social custom of women taking their husband's name when they married. This was just one more manifestation of the woman losing her own, separate, legal existence. Even so, it was not until Victorian times that the woman's loss of identity when she married grew to include "the loss of both her first and last names."[61] In more recent times, the custom has eroded, but many women still follow it though they are not required to.

Do women and men have the right to use any name they choose?

Yes. Despite the social custom of women taking their husband's names, our legal system has long recognized the right, under the common law, of any person to use any name she or he likes, as long as she or he is not doing so for a fraudulent purpose such as avoiding criminal prosecution or cheating one's creditors.

How does one change one's name?

To exercise this right in most states, one simply begins using a new name and notifies friends, associates, and creditors. It is a good idea to use the new name consistently and to change relevant legal documents, such as checkbooks, voter registration, driver's license and car registration, Social Security identification, credit cards, and tax returns.

There is another method one can use to change one's name. Most states have passed laws requiring state courts to provide a procedure for changing one's name. It is usually not necessary to use these procedures, however, as they are normally merely a convenient formality and not a requirement.[62] The advantage of the formal procedure is that it provides a court order and a public record and thus proves to everyone that the name change is legally binding.

If a woman wants to change her surname to that of her husband when she marries, are there any special steps she should take?

Generally, she can just start using her new name, pursuant to her common-law right to use any name she likes. In addition, many states have laws requiring people to reregister or notify authorities when their name changes "by marriage or otherwise." Such authorities should be notified by anyone who actually changes his or her name. The applicable government bureaucracies are generally those concerned with voting registration, driver's licenses, and car registration or certificates of title. Some laws have special requirements for people who are notaries public (for example, the law may require the notary to use her original name until her commission as a notary expires).

Should people who change their names in other ways upon marriage—for example, couples who choose a new third name or men who choose their wife's surname—follow the same steps?

Yes. They, too, have the common-law right to use any name they like, and they should check whether there are any state reregistration laws that apply to those who have changed their names. If they have problems with anyone about deviating from custom in this way, they can always use the formal name-change procedure to establish that the new name they have chosen is their legal name.

If a woman does not want to change her surname at marriage, does she have to take any special steps?

No. Since she did not change her name and since she has a common-law right to use any name she likes, she simply continues using the name she has always used.

In earlier years, women who did not change their surnames at marriage occasionally encountered resistance from government or commercial bureaucracies who presumed that the women had changed their names although they had not. The bureaucrats would then demand the women use their husband's name—for example, to vote or on their driver's license or credit cards. If the women refused, they could be denied the right to vote in their own name or to get the license or credit cards in that name. To avoid such problems, some women chose to use the formal name-change procedure to establish their right to continue using the name they had always used. When the women emerged from court with a judicial order to that effect, the bureaucratic opposition would cease. In the 1990s, few women are likely to face such resistance. If they do, they can rely on their common-law right to use the name of their choice.

Do women who changed their surname upon marriage and want to change it back to their premarriage name upon divorce have to take any special steps?

In theory, divorced women have the same common law right that others have to use any name they like and need merely begin using the name of their choice. In practice, the answer may be different in a few states. While many states have laws permitting women to get a name change as part of a divorce decree, some states may require women to change their name either through the divorce process or through the formal name-change procedure. A federal court took this approach in 1991 in a lawsuit brought by a divorced woman against the Utah Department of Motor Vehicles.[63] The department refused to issue a new driver's license to the woman in her premarriage name because she had not gone to court—either through the divorce process or through the formal name change procedure—to get the right to resume using this name and therefore had no official verification that it was her name. The court ruled against the woman's claim that she had a common-law right to use any name and insisted instead that she use the judicial process to exercise her choice.

Thus, in some states, divorcing women who wish to resume using their premarriage name may have to use either the divorce procedure or the formal name-change procedure to do so. To make the change quickly and avoid the necessity of using the formal name-change procedure, a woman seeking a divorce who wants to change her name should ask her lawyer to make sure it is part of the divorce decree. A woman who wishes to resume using her premarriage name can do so even if she has been awarded custody of the children and they bear his name.

Can a woman retain her birth surname for professional purposes, but adopt her husband's surname as her name for social purposes?

Yes, consistent with the common-law right to use any name one chooses, a woman should be able to use two different surnames for different purposes. It has long been common for women to practice law or medicine, for example, under their birth names while using a husband's surname for social purposes. Problems may arise, however, if a woman wants to maintain some but not all of her identification papers in her birth name. No court has specifically ruled on the issue, so it is possible that women doing so may face resistance; for example, a government agency might require that the woman register in her "real" name.

Can a man adopt his wife's surname at marriage?

Yes. Three state attorneys general—in Maine, Michigan, and Wisconsin—have issued opinions affirming this right.[64] Now that a few men are beginning to change their names at marriage, government agencies may have to be educated about a man's right to change his name to a woman's surname, just as it used to be necessary to educate them about the right of a woman not to change her name.

For example, in 1990 the New Jersey Division of Motor Vehicles, when confronted with a man who wanted to adopt his wife's name at marriage, at first prohibited him from doing so and then attempted to institute different, more onerous requirements for men who wished to adopt their wife's name, including a written explanation of why the new name was requested. After intervention by the local ACLU, however, the agency relented and issued a written directive that the same documents would be required (in this case, a marriage certificate) for both men and women.

What do the formal name-change procedures entail?

The procedures vary slightly from state to state but are generally not complicated. Most people can follow them on their own if they want to save money by avoiding a lawyer's fee.

Some states will not allow anyone to use the procedures unless she or he has been a county resident for six months or a year, but most do not impose this limitation. Usually the first step is to go to a courthouse and fill out a paper—often called a Petition for Change of Name—listing such standard items as current name, name desired, age, residence, and reason for change. The court clerk files this paper, usually for a filing fee, which can range from $10 to $75. The petitioner is then sometimes required to publish a notice of the proceedings in a local newspaper and present copies to the court to prove that this was done. Unfortunately, the cost of newspaper publication can be expensive—over $100, in some cases. The final step in some states is a short hearing before a judge, who will ask a few questions. If all goes smoothly, the petitioner then receives a legal document setting forth his or her new legal name. In some states, there is also a requirement to complete some additional official notification, such as publication in a newspaper.

Two cautionary notes should be added. First, the court will probably request reasons for the name change; the judge may probe to find out whether the petitioner is trying to defraud someone by the name change. To avoid this problem, it is wise for the petitioner to state explicitly that he or she has no intention to defraud anyone. There is no need to explain the personal reasons for name change to the judge; "personal preference" should be a sufficient explanation.

Second, if the judge turns down the petition, one of two things can be done: 1) an appeal of the decision; or 2) a refiling of the petition with another judge, if the local court allows it. Regardless of the approach, it is important to get a lawyer before proceeding further. An appeal to a higher court to reverse the judge's decision can be complicated and expensive and generally requires a lawyer's assistance. On the other hand, such appeals are usually successful.

For more details on formal name-change procedure, the reader can consult the particular state statute or call the clerk of the court, who is listed in the phone book, for the named court. If there is no such court in the phone book, the relevant court can be located by calling any state court.

Are there federal laws that protect a woman's right to choose her name?

Yes, in some important situations, but not for all purposes. The Equal Credit Opportunity Act gives a woman the right to open or to maintain a credit account using her birth surname, her husband's surname which she has adopted as her own, or a combined surname. Title VII of the 1964 Civil Rights Act can also be used to protect the right of women to use a name of their choice in the employment setting. In one case, a woman challenged her employer's policy of trying to force women who married to change their name to that of their husband. The employer—a Tennessee county health department—actually suspended a woman without pay because she refused to authorize a change on her personnel forms to reflect her husband's surname after she married. The federal court ruled that it was illegal sex discrimination to require married women, but not married men, to use their spouses' surnames on personnel forms.[65]

Does a married woman with a surname different from her husband's have a right to give her surname or a hyphenated surname to their child?

Usually—as long as both parents agree. This is an increasingly important issue since more women are not changing their surnames at marriage. The common practice in the United States has been to give the father's surname to the child. Several courts and state attorneys general, however, have recognized the common-law and constitutional rights of parents to choose a name for their children different from that of the father if the parents agree.[66] It is when parents disagree on the names children should use that most legal problems regarding children's names arise.

What legal impediments can there be to giving children different surnames?

When parents disagree about the names their children should use, judges tend to defer to the father's choice unless the children are very young, even if the mother has custody. There is no state law, however, that absolutely requires that a child be given the paternal surname.

In a few states, there *are* laws that limit the parents' choice of names. For example, in 1990 a federal court upheld a Nebraska law that requires parents to give a child the surname of one of the parents. In that case, an unmarried mother wanted to give her daughter not her own surname but a totally different one that the mother liked. The father had no objection. The court said that Nebraska law prohibited her choice.[67] Although the law seems to violate the constitutional right to choose the names of our children, the court upheld the law because it made record-keeping easier.

Moreover, there is generally a presumption that the husband's surname will be used in naming children. For example, a health department regulation in New Jersey requires that in order to give a marital child a surname other than that of the husband a mother must obtain the written consent of her husband, even though the mother's consent is not required for child to be given the husband's surname.[68] That regulation was being challenged in 1992 by the New Jersey ACLU.

Is there a way to challenge laws that limit women's rights to name their children?

They can be challenged as violating the common law principle of allowing any name. If the law contains different rules for mothers and fathers to name their children (as in the New Jersey regulation discussed above), it can be challenged under the federal or a state equal protection clause or a state equal rights amendment (see chapter 1).[69]

What if a mother and father disagree over the naming of a child?

This is the area where most litigation occurs.[70] Formerly, if the father contested the mother's right to name the child, he almost always won in legal proceedings. Some recent court decisions, however, have rejected a rule giving fathers first choice and have instead opted for a standard based on the "best interests of the child."[71] The trend is to apply the "best interests" standard to both initial disputes about naming,[72] as well as to later name changes for children such as those that occur during a divorce. Unless the children are very young, the courts still almost always award the naming right to the father. Several states have adopted, by statute or regulation, a rule that gives the naming right at birth to the custodial parent. In many name dispute cases in which mothers have prevailed, the woman has argued that, as custodial parent, she should be presumed to be acting in the children's "best interests" in deciding what names the children should use.

NOTES

1. The authors gratefully acknowledge the assistance of Sally Goldfarb, Senior Staff Attorney, NOW Legal Defense and Education Fund, in the preparation of this chapter.
2. L. Weitzman, *The Divorce Revolution: The Unexpected Social and Economic Consequences for Women and Children in America* (1985).
3. C. Lefcourt, *Women and the Law*, § 7A.05(2), at n.30 (1990).
4. *See generally* Weitzman, *supra* note 2.
5. *See, e.g., Garska v. McCoy*, 278 S.E.2d 357 (W. Va. 1981) (first state supreme court to adopt the primary caretaker presumption).
6. The current states' rules can be found in the charts (updated in the winter issue annually) in Freed & Walker, *Family Law in the Fifty States: An Overview*, 24 Fam. L.Q. 335–37 (1991).
7. Traditionally in those states property was classified according to who had purchased it or whose name it was in. Obviously, that led to major inequities since men were much more likely to acquire and hold title to property.
8. Freed & Walker, *supra* note 6.
9. *Id.*
10. In general, § 3B, the chapter on spousal support in C. Lefcourt, *Women and the Law* (1989), is an excellent source of information on this topic.
11. *See* Tex. Fam. Code Ann. § 3.63 (Vernon 1989). Texas permits alimony

by agreement of the parties. *Francis v. Francis*, 412 S.W.2d 29 (Tex. 1967).

12. C. Lefcourt, *Women and the Law*, § 3B.03(3) at n.79 (1989).

13. *Orr v. Orr*, 440 U.S. 268 (1979).

14. C. Lefcourt, *Women and the Law*, § 3B.01(1) (1989).

15. *Id.* at n.19.

16. Del. Code Ann. tit. 13, § 1512 (limit of 50% of length of marriage unless parties married 20 years or longer); Ind. Code Ann. § 31-1-11.5-11(e)(limit of 3 years unless spouse or child in custody of spouse is physically or mentally incapacitated); Kan. Stat. Ann. § 60-1610(b)(2)(limit of 121 months, subject to reinstatement).

17. Bureau of the Census, U.S. Dep't. of Commerce, *Child Support and Alimony: 1985 Current Population Reports* Series P-23, No. 152, at 6 (Aug. 1987).

18. Contempt is bringing a motion to enforce the original judgment. Execution is the seizure of a debtor's property to satisfy a judgment, generally done by a sheriff or other law enforcement officer pursuant to a writ resulting in a forced sale, the proceeds from which go to the satisfaction of the debt. Garnishment is a legal procedure where a court, sheriff, or clerk of the court demands that a third party who possesses money or property owing to a judgment debtor turn over a portion of the money or property to the judgment creditor in order to satisfy the judgment. Attachment is the act of seizing property to secure or satisfy a debt, usually authorized by court order. A lien is an encumbrance on property, where the property remains unaffected until its sale or transfer, at which time the lien asserts the claim of its holder against the proceeds from the sale.

19. Recent Census Bureau figures show that more than half of the 8.8 million mothers who were rearing children without the father's presence in the home did not have a child support order. Of those who had orders, less than half (48.2%) received the entire amount; the other half was divided almost evenly between those who received only partial payments (25.8%) and those who received no money (26%). Bureau of the Census, U.S. Dep't of Commerce, *Child Support and Alimony, supra* note 17. 1985," Series P-23, No. 152 (1987).

20. *See* 42 U.S.C. § 651 *et. seq.*

21. For further discussion, *see* Foster and Freed, *Spousal Rights in Retirement and Pension Benefits*, 16 J. Fam. L. 187 (1978).

22. 42 U.S.C. § 666.

23. *See generally* C. Lefcourt, *Women and the Law*, § 7 (1984).

24. *Gentry v. Gentry*, 798 S.W.2d 928 (Ky. 1990). Other courts that have recognized a change in the public policy regarding divorce and have thus enforced premarital agreements include *In re Marriage of Ingels,*

42 Colo. App. 245, 596 P.2d 1221 (1979); *In re Marriage of Dawley*, 17 Cal. 3d 342, 131 Cal. Rptr. 3 551 P.2d 323 (1976); *Posner v. Posner*, 233 So.2d at 381 (Fla. 1970).

25. *See Posner v. Posner*, 233 So.2d at 381 (Fla. 1970); *Burtoff v. Burtoff*, 418 A.2d 1085 (D.C. 1980).

26. In *Bridgeman v. Bridgeman*, 391 S.E.2d 367 (W. Va. 1990), the court refused to enforce a premarital agreement that allegedly consisted of the husband's courtship letters to the future Mrs. Bridgeman.

27. *See Williams v Williams*, 801 P.2d at 495, 498 (Ariz. App. 1990)(listing cases).

28. *Williams v. Williams*, 801 P.2d at 499.

29. *See generally* Younger, *Perspectives on Antenuptial Agreements*, 40 Rutgers L. Rev. 1059, 1073–86 (1988).

30. *Burtoff v. Burtoff*, 418 A.2d 1085 (D.C. 1980).

31. The Restatement (Second) of Contracts § 190 (2) (1981) employs such a "reasonableness" factor: "A promise that tends unreasonably to encourage divorce or separation is unenforceable on grounds of public policy."

32. The National Conference on Commissioners on Uniform State Laws, which recommends legislation to states, has drafted standards for upholding contracts. The text of the Uniform Premarital Agreement Act is contained in C. Lefcourt, *Women and the Law*, App. 7C (1984).

33. *Simeone v. Simeone*, 581 A.2d 162 (Pa. 1990).

34. N.Y. Dom. Rel. Law § 236 (B)(3) (1990). The Uniform Marital Property Act explicitly establishes the right to alter the Act's provisions by entering into marital agreements.

35. *Marvin v. Marvin*, 18 Cal. 3d 660, 134 Cal. Rptr. 815, 557 P.2d 106 (1976).

36. *E.g.*, *Whorton v. Dillingham*, 202 Cal. App. 3d 447, 248 Cal. Rptr. 405 (1988)(enforcing oral agreement between gay couple as severable from portion of the agreement regarding provision of sexual services).

37. *Braschi v. Stahl Associates Co.*, 74 N.Y.2d 201, 543 N.E.2d 49, 544 N.Y.S.2d 784 (1989); *accord East 10th St. Associates v. Goldstein*, 154 A.D.2d 142, 552 N.Y.S.2d 257 (1990)(extending *Braschi* definition of family to evictions from rent-stabilized apartments despite statutory language limiting "family members" to enumerate marital or blood relations).

38. *Braschi v. Stahl Associates Co.*, 544 N.Y.S.2d 784, 790, 74 N.Y.2d 201 (1989).

39. *Donovan*, Opinion and Decision After Remittitur at 2, No. 73 LA 385-107 (Cal. Workers Comp. App. Bd. Dec. 3, 1983).

40. Rivera, *Queer Law: Sexual Orientation Law in the Mid-Eighties, Part II*, 11 U. Dayton L. Rev. 275, 335 (1986). Only one jurisdiction, the

District of Columbia, specifically addresses sexual orientation in its custody law. It states that sexual orientation should not be a "conclusive consideration" in a custody determination. D.C. Code Ann. § 16-914(a)(1981).

41. In 1991 a court in Washington, D.C., upheld adoption by two lesbian mothers of each others' child. *In re Adoption of Minor (T.)(Petition of L.S.)*, 17 Fam. L. Rep. (BNA) 1523 (D.C. Super. Ct. 1991). *See generally* National Center for Lesbian Rights (NCLR), *Preserving and Protecting the Families of Lesbians and Gay Men* 6 (1990). The reader may contact NCLR, 1663 Mission Street, 5th Floor, San Francisco, CA 94103, to obtain citations to second-parent adoption cases. *See also* Patt, *Second Parent Adoption: When Crossing the Marital Barrier Is In A Child's Best Interests*, 3 Berkeley Women's L.J. 96 (1987–88).

42. *Alison D. v. Virginia M.*, 77 N.Y.2d 651 (1991).

43. Bartlett, *Rethinking Parenthood as an Exclusive Status: The Need for Legal Alternatives When the Promise of the Nuclear Family Has Failed*, 70 Va. L. Rev. 879, 946–47 (1984).

44. Polikoff, *This Child Does Have Two Mothers*, 78 Geo. L.J. 459, 491 (1990).

45. Or. Rev. Stat. § 109.119 (1989).

46. Polikoff, *supra*, note 44, at 491.

47. The authors gratefully acknowledge the assistance of Melanie S. Griffin, the executive director of the New Jersey Commission on Sex Discrimination in the Statutes, in the preparation of this section.

48. *The Killing Numbers*, Ms., Sept.–Oct. 1990, at 45.

49. C. Lefcourt, *Women and the Law*, § 9A.02[1][a], at n.5 (1987).

50. Helton, McFarlane, & Anderson, *Battered and Pregnant: A Prevalence Study*, 77 Am. J. Pub. Health 1337 (1987).

51. *See* W. Prosser, *Handbook of the Law of Torts* 136 (4th ed. 1971). As William Blackstone explained, "For, as he is to answer for her misbehavior, the law thought it reasonable to intrust him with this power of restraining her, by domestic chastisement." 1 W. Blackstone, Commentaries 445.

52. Eppler, *Battered Women and the Equal Protection Clause: Will the Constitution Help Them When the Police Won't?* 95 Yale L. J. 788, 792 (1986).

53. P. Finn & S. Colson, *Civil Protection Orders: Legislation, Current Court Practice, and Enforcement* 43 (1990).

54. Lefcourt, *Women and the Law*, § 9.02[3] (1988).

55. Lefcourt, *Women and the Law*, § 9.04 (1988).

56. Diana Russell, *Rape in Marriage* 23 (1990).

57. After the 1989 decision of the U.S. Supreme Court in *DeShaney v. Winnebago County Dept. of Social Services*, 109 S. Ct. 998 (1989),

women alleging a due process violation because the police failed to protect them from domestic violence must first show that the police had a "special relationship" or a specific duty to protect them. *See, e.g., Balistreri v. Pacifica Police Dept.*, 990 F.2d 696, 700 (9th Cir. 1990).

However, women have sometimes won on an alternative theory— that the police treat domestic abuse cases different than other cases, thus causing an equal protection violation. *E.g., Watson v. City of Kansas City, Kansas,* 857 F.2d 690 (10th Cir. 1988); *Bartalone v. County of Berrien,* 643 F. Supp. 574, 577 (W.D. Mich. 1986); *Thurman v. City of Torrington,* 595 F. Supp. 1521, 1527–29 (D. Conn. 1984). *See also Hynson v. City of Chester,* 864 F.2d 1026, 1027 n. 1 (3d Cir. 1988)(collecting cases). In order to win such a case, women must present statistics showing a lower level of police response to victims of domestic violence. *See generally* Eppler, *Battered Women and the Equal Protection Clause: Will the Constitution Help Them When the Police Won't?* 95 Yale L.J. 788 (1986).

58. "The victim receives no protection from the court with a mediated 'agreement not to batter.' And a process which involves both parties mediating the issue of violence implies, and allows the batterer to believe, that the victim is somehow at fault." National Council of Juvenile and Family Court Judges, *Family Violence: Improving Court Practice* 28 (1990).

59. Shu, *Lesbian Battery,* Ms., Sept.–Oct. 1990, at 48.

60. Thanks are extended to Priscilla Ruth MacDougall for her review and comments on this section.

61. Babcock, Freedman, Norton, & Ross, *Sex Discrimination and the Law: Causes and Remedies,* at 579 (1975). See pp. 579–83 for further historical information on married women's surnames and pp. 561–65 for a more complete discussion of coverture.

62. For example, in *Traugott v. Petit,* 404 A.2d 77 (R.I. 1979), the Supreme Court of Rhode Island ruled, in the case of a woman seeking a driver's license, that the formal name-change procedure was an "optional" procedure that supplemented the common-law right. Thus, a divorced woman did not have to use the formal name-change procedure but could instead change her name under the common law by consistently using her birth name.

63. *Jorgensen v. Larsen,* 1991 U.S. App. LEXIS 10627, *not officially reported,* 930 F.2d 922 (10th Cir. 1991). But see *Traugott v. Petit, supra* note 62, which ruled that the divorced woman did *not* have to use the formal name-change procedure.

64. Op. Att'y. Gen. Me. (Apr. 4, 1978); Op. Att'y. Gen. Mich. (Apr. 14, 1980); Op. Att'y. Gen. Wis. (Aug. 25, 1984).

65. *Allen v. Lovejoy*, 553 F.2d 522 (6th Cir. 1977).
66. *E.g.*, *Sydney v. Pingree*, 564 F. Supp. 412 (S.D. Fla. 1982)(invalidating on Fourteenth Amendment grounds a Florida statute requiring that a child conceived and born in wedlock be given the father's name on the birth certificate; the parents, Chris Ledbetter and Dean Skylar, wished to name their son Sidney Skybetter); *O'Brien v. Tilson*, 523 F. Supp. 494 (E.D.N.C. 1981)(holding similar North Carolina law violated both due process and equal protection); *Jech v. Burch*, 466 F. Supp. 714 (D. Hawaii 1979)(fused name); *Secretary of Com. v. City Clerk of Lowell*, 366 N.E.2d 717 (1977). Op. Atty. Gen. Mich. (Apr. 14, 1980); Op. Atty. Gen. Md. (Nov. 9, 1978); Op. Atty. Gen. Me. (Aug. 18, 1976); Op. Atty. Gen. Me. (May 5, 1976); Op. Atty. Gen. Alaska (May 5, 1976); Op. Atty. Gen. Conn. (Jan. 23, 1975); Op. Atty. Gen. Wis. (Oct. 7, 1974). *See generally* MacDougall, *The Right of Women to Name Their Children*, 3 Law & Inequality 91 (1985).
67. *Henne v. Wright*, 904 F.2d 1208 (8th Cir. 1990), *cert. denied*, 59 U.S.L.W. 3461 (Jan. 8, 1991).
68. N.J.A.C. 8:2-1.1.
69. Apart from a summary affirmance of a federal district court decision ruling that the Alabama Department of Public Safety could require a married woman to use her husband's surname in applying for a driver's license, the Supreme Court has not spoken on the question. *Forbush v. Wallace*, 341 F. Supp. 217, *aff'd mem.*, 405 U.S. 970 (1972). *Forbush* has been repudiated by numerous courts including the Alabama Supreme Court, which ruled that Alabama never had required a married woman to adopt her husband's name. *State v. Taylor*, 415 So. 2d 1043 (Ala. 1982). *Forbush*'s value as precedent is also undermined because it was decided before *Craig v. Boren*, 429 U.S. 190 (1976), the case that enunciated a more stringent standard of review for sex discrimination.
70. *See generally* MacDougall, *The Right of Women to Name Their Children*, 3 Law & Inequality 91 (1985).
71. The "best interests" standard is described in *Marriage of Schiffman*, 28 Cal. 3d 640, 169 Cal. Rptr. 918, 620 P.2d 579 (1980).
72. For example, the best interests standard was applied in a 1988 California case where a husband and wife separated before the birth of a child. The court ordered that the child's surname on the birth certificate should be hyphenated from both parents surnames, but for all other purposes the child would be known by the mother's surname. *In re Douglass*, 205 Cal. App. 3d 1046, 1055, 252 Cal. Rptr. 839, 844–45 (1988).

V

Reproductive Freedom

In a frontal assault on women's right to equality,[1] the Supreme Court's 1992 decision in *Planned Parenthood v. Casey*[2] stopped short, by the narrowest of margins, of overruling *Roe v. Wade*[3]—the 1973 landmark decision that struck down anti-abortion law and declared that women had a constitutional right to reproductive freedom. *Roe* thus remains the law of the land, although the Court is giving states enormous latitude to restrict access to abortion, further diluting the meaning of *Roe*. And with Justices Rehnquist, Scalia, Thomas, and White indicating they would overrule *Roe*, leaving these four Justices one vote shy of the five needed to abolish *Roe*, the right to reproductive freedom is in severe danger.

Since 1989, when the Court decided *Webster v. Reproductive Health Services*,[4] inviting state legislatures to limit women's ability to choose abortion, the Court has been presented with opportunities to overrule *Roe*. At each opportunity it has severely narrowed the parameters of reproductive freedom. First, in *Webster*, the Court upheld a state law prohibiting abortions in public facilities or by public employees and a requirement that twenty week fetuses be tested for viability. In 1990 the Court crippled young women's right to choose safe, legal abortions by upholding two versions of laws requiring parental involvement, in *Hodgson v. Minnesota*[5] and *Ohio v. Akron Center for Reproductive Health*.[6] In 1991 the Court endangered low-income women's reproductive freedom by sanctioning government restrictions that prevent federally funded birth control providers from discussing abortion with their patients. That case, *Rust v. Sullivan*,[7] renders the right guaranteed in *Roe* virtually meaningless for millions of low-income women nationwide who rely on federally funded facilities for family planning care and information. And in 1992 the Court upheld in *Casey* a Pennsylvania law that imposed even more onerous restrictions on the ability of women to obtain abortions—including a twenty-four-hour waiting period and a requirement that minors obtain the consent of one parent or a judge.

Indeed, the attack against reproductive freedom, while profoundly affecting all women, has affected and will continue to affect most severely low-income women and women of color, who comprise the majority of women seeking services from public facilities. *Rust* allows interference with the speech of federally funded physicians, and *Webster* and *Casey* permit states to pass new laws under which women may be prohibited from obtaining abortions and abortion-related services in public hospitals (though not in private facilities). And a series of Court decisions have allowed the federal government and many state governments to eliminate Medicaid funds for abortion. We know from pre-*Roe* days that low-income women and women of color suffer the most when safe, legal abortions are not available. Before *Roe*, 49% of the pregnancy-related deaths in New York were due to illegal abortions. Of these deaths, 50% of the women were African-American, and 44% were Puerto Rican.[8]

Although the overwhelming majority of Americans support the right to reproductive freedom, they only recently awakened to the grave threat to *Roe* in the Supreme Court. As a result, antichoice forces—which have been building strength since 1973—became disproportionately strong. They have been sheparding bills through state legislatures that would severely limit women's right to reproductive freedom. And the far right has been taking to the streets in greater numbers and using more harassing tactics than ever before.

Despite these threats, advocates for reproductive freedom have increased their efforts to protect past gains and improve access to reproductive health care. Instead of merely fighting antichoice proposals, advocates are pushing for repeal of current restrictions. In Congress and in selected state legislatures, prochoice leaders are introducing laws that will protect access to abortion and contraception should the Supreme Court overrule *Roe v. Wade*. Above all, activists are expanding their alliances to ensure that prochoice coalitions are representative of the voting public. Women of color, in particular, have been instrumental in rejuvenating the reproductive freedom movement.

This chapter discusses some of the main issues surrounding reproductive freedom and suggests steps that must be taken to preserve the right to reproductive freedom. Information pertaining to the status of laws in each state, can be obtained by calling the state American Civil Liberties Union office or by writing the National Abortion Rights Action League at 1101 14th St., N.W. Washington, D.C. 20005, for their 1991 state-by-state review of abortion rights.

THE RIGHT TO REPRODUCTIVE FREEDOM

How does *Casey* affect women's right to reproductive freedom under *Roe*?

Understanding the impact of *Casey* on women's rights under *Roe v. Wade* first requires understanding what *Roe v. Wade* decided. In *Roe v. Wade*[9] the Court identified constitutional limitations on the extent to which states may restrict a woman's decision to have an abortion. States may not prohibit or interfere with a woman's right to decide on an abortion, in consultation with her physician, during the first trimester of pregnancy. From then until viability (about the twenty-fourth to twenty-eighth week of pregnancy), the state can establish medical regulations governing abortion only if they are necessary to protect maternal health. After viability, the state can prohibit abortions except where they are necessary to protect the life or health of the woman.

The Court's rationale for this structure turned on the competing interests of the woman on the one hand and the state's desire to protect the woman and the fetus on the other. The Court ruled that the woman has a constitutional right to privacy but that the state also has an interest in protecting the health of the woman and may assert an interest in the potential life of the fetus in the last trimester before birth. Until the end of the first trimester, the mortality rate for childbirth is higher than it is for abortion; thus prior to that point, the state's interest in preserving a woman's health is not strong enough to justify regulations that interfere with the woman's choice, except that a state may require that the choice of abortion be made in consultation with a doctor. After the first trimester, however, the state's interest in protecting a woman's health may be asserted by regulations to that end. The state's interest further increases after viability, the point at which the fetus is potentially able to survive outside the woman's womb. After that point, i.e., after approximately twenty-four weeks of pregnancy, the state's interest in potential life can take precedence over the woman's right to privacy, and abortions can be prohibited except when necessary to preserve her life or health.

Casey did not overrule *Roe's* guarantee of a woman's right to choose abortion. Instead, in a sharply divided decision the Court applied a new test to determine whether a state law is unconstitutional—whether that law has the "purpose" or "effect" of placing a "substantial obstacle in the path of a woman seeking an abortion before the fetus attains viability." This test will encourage even more restrictions on the right to choose abortion free from government interference. The majority opinion, however, written by Justices O'Connor, Kennedy, and Souter, was called by Justice Blackmun, the author of *Roe v. Wade,* "an act of personal courage and constitutional principle." The issue of choice will now be before Congress, who has the power to pass the Freedom of Choice Act that legalizes abortion.

What has been the current strategy of antichoice activists?
The antichoice movement has developed and enthusiastically pursued a legal strategy for depriving women of their constitutional right to choose abortion. This strategy has been summarized by antichoice activists.

> There appear to be only three essential prerequisites [to overturning *Roe*]: statutes that confront the judiciary with abortion related issues must continue to be enacted; these statutes must be competently and vigorously defended; and the membership of the Supreme Court has to be altered so at least five justices are reasonably open to the possibility of reversing *Roe*.[10]

In addition, the antichoice lobby has pursued a strategy that recognizes that criminalizing abortion outright is not the only way to overrule *Roe*. As one author has observed:

> Instead of directly attacking the existence of a woman's right to reproductive freedom, their strategy has focused on imposing onerous regulations that interfere with women's access to abortion until all choice is effectively eliminated. If the Supreme Court were to uphold such restric-

tions, it could overrule *Roe,* at least in part, without any public admission that it was depriving women of their constitutional rights.[11]

The antichoice lobby has been effective in achieving its goals. It has brought the issue repeatedly before the Supreme Court by securing the enactment of unconstitutional legislation in the states. In addition, it may have achieved its third goal of creating a majority on the Court willing to overrule *Roe,* with four justices seeking to overturn *Roe,* three of whom were appointed by Presidents Reagan and Bush.

In addition to pursuing their goals in courts and legislatures, antichoice groups have taken to the streets. Far-right groups, such as Operation Rescue, have targeted clinic after clinic for prolonged demonstrations. The severity of their tactics has escalated, with ever-increasing incidents of harassment, trespass, and physical assault on women seeking abortions and on the clinic workers who provide them. These demonstrations have drawn an inordinate amount of press, thus amplifying the voice of the far-right faction of the antichoice movement. Creative attorneys have challenged Operation Rescue's actions under a civil rights act, Section 1985, that prohibits conspiracies to interfere with constitutional rights. But as of this writing, the Supreme Court is considering whether to accept the Bush administration's view that Section 1985 does not protect women seeking abortions from such conspiracies.[12]

How has the prochoice majority responded to the antichoice movement?

While the antichoice movement waged its battle, the prochoice majority in America remained relatively silent, relying on the courts to protect its fundamental rights. The press failed to educate the public on the antichoice movement's strategy, and perhaps as a result, voters elected Presidents Reagan and Bush on platforms that expressed outright hostility to women's reproductive rights.

Yet *Webster* increased public awareness of the mounting danger to abortion rights, and as a result the reproductive freedom movement remobilized. It seeks new adherents by attempting to address the wide spectrum of issues and day-to-day experiences that affect women of diverse backgrounds.

Prochoice demonstrations are on the increase across the country, and voters' attention has once again turned to reproductive freedom. Consequently, prochoice activists have become increasingly effective in defeating antichoice efforts.

For example, choice played a critical role in 1989 when voters elected prochoice candidates for governor in Virginia and New Jersey. Similarly, the November 1990 elections witnessed tremendous prochoice gains in many state legislatures that had been overwhelmingly antichoice as a result of the many years of prochoice voter complacency. In that same month, voters in Oregon defeated two antichoice ballot initiatives. By a margin of 67% to 33%, the voters rejected a ban on virtually all abortions (the ban exempted only those abortions necessary to save a woman's life or for some victims of rape or incest). They also defeated a measure that would have required a woman under the age of eighteen to notify a parent at least forty-eight hours before an abortion was to be performed. These legislative efforts will only intensify as more and more effort is placed on heading off and changing detrimental laws in the first instance, without resort to increasingly hostile courts.

How did state legislators react to *Webster?*
Over five-hundred abortion restrictions and bans were introduced in state legislatures in the wake of *Webster*. Prochoice forces have been able to defeat the vast majority of these antichoice efforts, although often by only the slimmest of margins. Yet new laws were enacted in seven states—Pennsylvania, South Carolina, West Virginia, Utah, Louisiana, North Dakota, and Mississippi—and one U.S. territory, Guam. The law in Pennsylvania was the first to be reviewed by the Court.

The new laws generally fall into three categories: abortion bans, "roadblock" laws, and minors' laws. The minors' laws, perhaps the most popular new legislation, are discussed below in a separate question. As to the other two types of laws, abortion bans have presented the most direct challenge to *Roe,* giving the new conservative majority on the Court the chance to implement the Republican party platform goal of reversing *Roe*. Under the "ban approach" (used by Utah, Louisiana, and Guam) all abortions are prohibited as a matter of criminal law, with limited exceptions—for an immediate danger to a woman's life and a few cases of rape and incest. There are sometimes exceptions for fetal abnormalities and threats to women's health as well. Frequently, the exceptions are so vaguely worded that physicians cannot tell when an abortion would be illegal. Thus, these laws interfere with the fundamental principle that those subject to a criminal law must be given fair notice that their behavior is illegal. Most fundamentally, however, they would deprive virtually all women of their right to abortion, if passed by the remaining states and upheld by the Reagan-Bush Court.

The "roadblock approach," in contrast to the "ban approach," does not seek to prohibit all abortions but sets burdensome obstacles in a woman's path to free and informed reproductive decision making. Mississippi and North Dakota adopted this approach with new laws that establish a mandatory delay and require women to receive state-devised abortion "information." Other roadblock techniques include mandatory spousal notification, state reporting requirements, and severe clinic licensing requirements.

Antichoice forces continue to introduce restrictive laws in many states, and there remains a strong possibility that, unless grassroots opposition grows, many of these efforts will be successful. The future success of the prochoice movement will be determined largely by the ability of prochoice supporters to win key electoral battles and by the ability of prochoice forces to build a political infrastructure that can effectively mobilize constituents in support of reproductive freedom. Although impressive prochoice gains have been achieved since the July 1989 *Webster* decision, antichoice political advantages built over the nearly two decades since *Roe* cannot be dismantled quickly.

What is the problem with mandatory delays and state-devised abortion information?

In the guise of protecting women's health, antichoice legislators have proposed laws that would require doctors to delay the performance of an abortion for twenty-four or forty-eight hours after the woman first gives her informed consent to the procedure. These laws also force doctors to give women specific information intended to discourage them from having the abortion—even if the information is irrelevant, unnecessary, or misleading. In reality, these laws serve no legitimate state interest and instead only threaten women's health.

These laws are not needed because women already take considerable time to make this decision of such obvious importance to them. Moreover, state laws, as well as the standards of the medical profession, ensure that health care practitioners will both provide women with accurate and unbiased information about their health care options and also obtain women's informed consent to the procedures.

But the proposed laws are not only unnecessary; they are also dangerous to women's health. Because there are no abortion providers in 83% of all United States counties, many women must travel long distances to obtain abortions. In addition, most clinics schedule abortion procedures only one or two days per week. As a result, mandatory 24- or 48-hour waiting periods can result in two-week delays, necessitating more costly and medically risky abortions.

Does a minor have a right to obtain an abortion without notice to, or the consent of, one or both parents?

Yes, but only in the states that have not enacted parental involvement laws. Every state in the United States protects the confidentiality of teenagers seeking medical advice and treatment for birth control, sexually transmitted diseases, pregnancy test, prenatal care, and childbirth. At the same time, however, an alarmingly high number of states have criminal laws mandating parental involvement in a young woman's abortion decision. The following thirty-five states now have laws on the books that prevent minors from obtaining abortions without parental consent or notice; of these, only the fifteen with asterisks were being enforced as of late 1991, however.[13]

35 States Requiring Parental Consent or Notice

Alabama*	Idaho
Alaska	Illinois
Arizona	Indiana*
Arkansas*	Kentucky
California	Louisiana*
Colorado	Massachusetts*
Delaware	Maryland
Florida	Michigan*
Georgia	Minnesota*

Mississippi   Rhode Island*
Missouri*   South Carolina*
Montana   South Dakota
Nebraska   Tennessee
Nevada   Utah*
New Mexico   Washington
North Dakota*   West Virginia
Ohio*   Wyoming*
Pennsylvania
(*Law currently being enforced)

Three states (Connecticut, Maine, and Wisconsin) require a minor to receive mandatory counseling that includes discussion of the possibility of consulting her parents.[14] But minors do not *have* to give parental notice or get parental consent in these three states or in the states with no laws on the subject. Nor do they have to in the twenty states listed above whose laws were *not* being enforced.

In the states with parental involvement laws, minors can avoid the requirements only if they can prove to a court that they are mature enough to make their own decision or that it would be in their best interest to get an abortion without involving their parents. Going to court in this way is called a *judicial bypass*. While nearly all of the states with parental involvement laws have some kind of judicial bypass, the willingness of judges to grant permission varies greatly from state to state. For example, judges in Ohio and Indiana routinely deny bypass requests, while judges in Massachusetts routinely grant them.

In two June 1990 decisions, the Supreme Court decided some, but not all, of the issues surrounding parental involvement laws. In *Hodgson v. Minnesota*,[15] the Court found unconstitutional a Minnesota law that required all young women to notify both of their biological parents before obtaining an abortion, without allowing the young women to seek any judicial bypass. The Court upheld a separate provision of the law, however, that also required young women to notify both parents but did provide for the judicial bypass. Thus, as long as young girls have a right to go to court to try to bypass their parents, state notification laws are permissible.[16]

On the same day, in *Ohio v. Akron Center for Reproductive*

Health,[17] the Court also upheld as constitutional an Ohio one-parent consent law that provided a judicial bypass alternative. The Court rejected "Rachel Roe's" claims that the bypass failed to adequately protect her anonymity and failed to provide for expeditious review by state courts. *Akron* thus virtually forecloses further federal legal challenges to one-parent consent laws that include a bypass.

Must a woman obtain her husband's consent or notify him before getting an abortion?

No. The Supreme Court has ruled that states may not force a woman to obtain her husband's consent for an abortion.[18] In rejecting the consent requirement, the Court reasoned that "inasmuch as it is the woman who physically bears the child and who is more directly and immediately affected by the pregnancy as between the two, the balance weighs in her favor."[19] The same can be said for "notice." And although the Court has never addressed the validity of husband or "father" notification requirements, many lower court decisions have found that the reasoning of "consent" cases applies equally to cases dealing with "notice."[20]

Nevertheless, Pennsylvania adopted a husband notification provision as the centerpiece of its 1989 restrictions on abortion.[21] The provision, which was found unconstitutional on appeal,[22] requires a woman to give the performing physician a sworn statement that she has notified her husband that she is about to have an abortion.

In the Pennsylvania challenge to the Supreme Court, ACLU attorneys advanced not only traditional "privacy" arguments but also invoked federal and state equal protection guarantees. One of their arguments was that state notice requirements are discriminatorily directed only at women. A husband who makes medical decisions that may affect his reproductive capacity is not required to notify his wife, for example. Thus, a wife need not be notified when her husband is sterilized, receives treatment for prostrate cancer, or takes a drug that affects his ability to procreate.

Another point is that one of the consequences of mandatory notice—forced childbearing—is a burden unique to women. States require that husbands be notified for the sole purpose of encouraging the man to interfere with the woman's abortion choice. Indeed, most of the statutes allow the notified husband to sue his wife to force her to carry the fetus to term. Only women suffer the health effects of carrying an unwanted pregnancy to term, and women—as the primary caretakers of children—are substantially more likely to suffer the loss of job and educational opportunities that result from bearing unwanted children.

Finally, mandatory notice is bad policy. The vast majority of women who choose abortion voluntarily involve the men in their lives with their decision making. For them, mandatory husband notification is unnecessary. For women in troubled or abusive marriages, on the other hand, husband notification will not foster marital communication, the purported goal of such requirements. Rather, the laws enable husbands to force their wives, through physical violence or economic or psychological coercion, to carry an unwanted pregnancy to term.

Nor does the physical harm exemption to notification laws solve this problem. Domestic violence occurs with alarming frequency in the United States and women are more likely to be battered and sexually abused while pregnant. Some of these women are psychologically unable to admit that they have been battered or to report the abuse to law enforcement officials as required by these laws, so the exemption does them no good. In addition, a limited exemption for physical harm ignores the fact that husbands also use economic or psychological coercion, threats of harm to children, or retaliation in future child custody or divorce proceedings to control their wives. Even though evidence of family violence has been well documented, states continue to consider these onerous husband notification requirements, lending increasing credibility to the condescending view that women are unable to make important life decisions independently.

Can low-income women obtain government funding for abortion?

Not federal funding; state funding is possible in some states but not in others. Congressional and state legislative action and a 1980 Supreme Court decision, *Harris v. McRae*,[23] have eliminated Medicaid funding for virtually all abortions in the vast majority of states. Since 1976, Congress has attached amendments, popularly known as the Hyde amendments, to the yearly appropriations bills for the U.S. Departments of Labor and Health and Human Services. These amendments restrict federal Medicaid funding of abortions to those cases in which an abortion is necessary to protect a low-income woman's life. President Bush has twice vetoed attempts to extend funding to low-income women who are the victims of rape or incest and to reinstate Medicaid funding in the District of Columbia, where the local legislature voted to provide such funding with D.C. taxpayer monies.

In *Harris v. McRae*, the Supreme Court ruled that the federal constitution does not require Medicaid to pay for medically necessary abortions, even though Medicaid pays for all other medically necessary procedures. The Court found that abortion restrictions in the funding context are different from other abortion regulations and that it is legitimate for a state to choose to promote fetal life by funding only childbirth and not abortion—even when a woman's health is sacrificed. By allowing a state to accomplish through a withdrawal of funds what it could not otherwise do directly, the decision radically undermined the constitutional protection that *Roe* gives low-income women.

The decision in *McRae* made clear, however, that Congress and the states are free to fund Medicaid abortions if they so choose, and the fight for Medicaid abortions has therefore been thrown back to the federal and state legislatures. Thus, a low-income woman's right to reproductive freedom has become more a product of where she lives than anything else. The federal government and most states have eliminated virtually all public funding for abortion. At least twenty-seven states and the District of Columbia will not provide Medicaid funding unless the woman's life is in danger (Alabama, Arizona, Colorado, Delaware, Florida, Georgia, Illinois, Indiana, Kansas, Kentucky, Louisiana, Maine, Michigan, Minnesota, Montana, Nevada, New Hampshire, New Mexico, North Dakota, Ohio, Oklahoma, Rhode Island, South Carolina, South Dakota, Tennessee, Texas, Utah). Eight states provide funding in limited circumstances (Idaho, Iowa, Maryland, Minnesota, Pennsylvania, Virginia, Wisconsin, Wyoming). Only twelve states fund most abortions (Alaska, California, Connecticut, Hawaii, Massachusetts, New Jersey, New York, North Carolina, Oregon, Vermont, Washington, West Virginia).[24]

How have low-income women been indirectly targeted by antichoice groups?

In addition to the explicit denial of Medicaid funds for abortions, numerous legal restrictions increase cost and decrease access for low-income women. Existing state laws that do not prohibit abortion outright may still use licensing or zoning requirements to make it prohibitively expensive to operate or establish clinics or obtain abortions. For example, in some states laws require that abortion clinics have unneeded blood supplies, knee or foot controlled sinks, wide hallways and elevators, and that they pay licensing fees. Challenges to these ordinances have met with both success and failure.[25]

In addition, some states have passed reporting and record keeping requirements that threaten the privacy of patients by failing to provide adequate protection for the confidentiality of the specified information. These requirements also unduly burden the clinics by mandating, for example, that a great deal of detailed and unnecessary information be reported to the state or that records be kept for many years. Some of these laws have been stricken as unconstitutional.[26]

Can a state prohibit abortions in public facilities?

Yes. In *Webster*, the Court upheld the statute's prohibition against abortions in public facilities, even in cases where the procedure is performed by a private physician and is fully paid for by the woman. The effect of this law will be particularly harsh in areas in which public facilities are the only places available to obtain abortions. In Missouri, for example, one public facility was responsible for 97 percent of all post-fifteen-week, hospital-based abortions in the state the year before the statute was enacted. Women who want such abortions will now have to travel long distances out of state, causing delays and increasing health risks.

In reaching this decision, the Court substantially extended its ruling in *Maher v. Roe*,[27] *Poelker v. Doe*, and *Harris v. McRae*,[28] although it vigorously denied that it was doing so.[29] Under *Maher, Poelker*, and *Harris*, states were free to promote childbirth over abortion by withholding public funds for abortions or by prohibiting public hospitals and staff at those hospitals from performing abortions.[30] But under *Webster*, states may be able to pass laws reaching even private doctors who perform abortions on private patients paying for services with private funds, if their admission privileges happen to be at a hospital or other medical facility that leases or rents equipment or land from state or local governments.[31]

Can states require that all abortions be performed in hospitals?

No. In 1973 the Court rejected hospitalization requirements for first-trimester abortions.[32] Ten years later, in *Akron v. Akron Center for Reproductive Health*,[33] the Court rejected a mandatory hospitalization requirement for all abortions performed after the first trimester. The Court reasoned that mandatory hospitalization did not increase a woman's safety and thus was not a reasonable health regulation.[34] It was also concerned about putting "a significant obstacle in the path of women seeking an abortion"[35] by making the abortion more expensive and forcing the woman to travel to find suitable abortion facilities.[36] Thus, although states may attempt to place burdensome restrictions on abortion clinics, they cannot flatly require that abortions be performed in hospitals.

Can federally funded doctors counsel about and refer for abortion?

Not in birth control programs that receive federal funds. The Supreme Court approved this result in the case of *Rust v. Sullivan*[37] in May 1991. In particular, the Court approved new regulations, promulgated in 1988 by the United States Department of Health and Human Services, that forbade providing information about abortion in Title X-funded facilities—that is, in federally funded birth control clinics for poor women.

Title X is a congressional program for funding family planning clinics for low-income women. These clinics provide low-income women with family planning medical care and information. By 1990 Title X, with an annual budget of $200 million, funded more than 4,000 clinics and was the single largest source of federal funds for family planning in the United States. Title X programs serve five million low-income women nationwide, many of whom are minors, and many of whom are women of color. The communities that Title X clinics serve suffer disproportionately high rates of teenage pregnancy, infant mortality, and sexually transmitted diseases. In many of these communities, the clinics receiving Title X funds are the only source of family planning services and information, or even of general health care.

When it established the program, Congress disallowed the use of Title X funds for abortion, but physicians in Title X-funded clinics were free to discuss abortion and to refer their patients to abortion providers. Title X-funded organizations could even offer abortion services, as long as they did so with non-Title X funds. Subsequently, Congress repeatedly rejected proposals to prohibit abortion counseling and referrals. In response, the executive branch unilaterally changed the regulations.

Under the 1988 regulations, clinic personnel must provide pregnant women with a list of facilities that promote the health of women and the "unborn child" when they refer the women to prenatal care providers. The list may include facilities that perform abortions but may not include clinics whose principal service is abortion; and the list may not exclude providers of prenatal care that do not perform or refer for abortion. In addition to this list and information to promote the health of the "unborn child" pending the referral, the only other information clinic personnel may provide is to tell women that "abortion is not an appropriate method of family planning." Clinic personnel, including physicians, may make no other response even in cases of the most obvious need—for example, if the patient were fourteen years old or had a condition such as AIDS, heart disease, or diabetes that would be aggravated by a continued pregnancy. Only in the most extreme situation—when a women's "pregnancy places her life in imminent peril"—may doctors refer the woman to an abortion provider.

The ACLU argued to the Supreme Court that the restrictions constitute impermissible viewpoint-based censorship: speech conveying the viewpoint favored by the current administration is allowed—and even compelled—while speech conveying the viewpoint disfavored by the current administration is banned. Furthermore, as the American Medical Association warned the Court, compelling doctors to provide incomplete information is drastically at odds with their legal and ethical duty to give patients full information. The regulations could even expose doctors to malpractice suits and loss of their licenses. But the Court rejected both arguments.

The regulations not only restrict the use of Title X funds but also require Title X-funded clinics to separate their Title X programs physically as well as financially from any program—funded with non-Title X sources—that provides abortion counseling, referral, or services. For many clinics, the expense of establishing a separate facility with separate staff would be prohibitive, but the Court accepted this requirement as well. Most organizations that receive Title X funds will thus be forced either to eliminate programs that offer abortion counseling or lose federal funding altogether. The loss to low-income women will be tremendous.

In upholding the Title X regulations, the Court left *Roe* technically intact. At the same time, it significantly under mined reproductive self-determination for perhaps the most vulnerable groups of women—the young and the poor. The majority in *Rust* explicitly recognized that the decision would adversely affect low-income women's ability to obtain health care but contended that this result was simply a product of their indigence[38]—not a matter for judicial concern. For those turned away from Title X clinics, the promise of choice embodied in *Roe* has become empty indeed.

What is the controversy over fetal tissue research?

The Bush administration has consistently supported a moratorium on the use of federal dollars for fetal tissue research on the grounds that support of such research would somehow promote abortion.[39] There is, however, no evidence to substantiate this assumption. Indeed, a recent report by the University of Minnesota Center for Biomedical Ethics found that "the available evidence does not prove or even suggest that large numbers of women are likely to choose to abort for the purpose of donating fetal tissue."[40]

The fetal research ban jeopardizes important medical advances as well as the lives of thousands of persons in the United States who are potential beneficiaries of such studies. Fetal tissues have been used for vital medical purposes for decades. Jonas Salk's development of the first polio vaccine, research that won the 1954 Nobel Prize in Medicine, began with cultures of fetal kidney cells. In the seventies, fetal tissue experiments allowed the developers of the rubella vaccine to show that the vaccine virus crossed the placenta and posed a risk to the fetus.

As a result, it became standard practice to avoid giving the rubella vaccine to pregnant women. Moreover, fetal experimentation was important in developing techniques to identify fetuses that had suffered from rubella infection.

Today, fetal research continues to contribute to knowledge that will help improve fetal, pediatric, and adult health. Among the areas of current study are the genetics of retinoblastoma, a life-threatening disease of children; the differentiation of cells in lymphoid cancers, such as leukemia; respiratory distress syndrome; a chicken pox vaccine; transplant rejection; sickle cell anemia; and some AIDS research. A distinct area of clinical research involves the transplantation of fetal tissues into seriously ill children and adults. In important experimental operations, doctors have transplanted fetal brain cells into the brains of people suffering from Parkinson's disease, an incurable condition that strikes as many as half a million Americans. Researchers have also reported promising results from transplants of fetal pancreatic cells into diabetics.

Researchers have warned that the federal government's funding policies for fetal tissue research has already greatly impaired scientific advances in this country.[41] Because the ban has so greatly disadvantaged American research and since women are so very unlikely to make abortion decisions based on the availability of fetal research, vigorous efforts are underway to restore federal funding.

CONTRACEPTION AND STERILIZATION

What choices are available for women today?

About 60 percent of all U.S. women between the ages of 15 and 44 practice contraception; of these, approximately 40 percent rely on female sterilization or vasectomy, while 60 percent use a reversible method. Reliance on female sterilization continued to increase in the eighties and became the leading method practiced among all married and formerly married women. Among never-married black women, sterilization increased most significantly between 1982 and 1988 and is now second only to oral contraceptives. Less-educated women also became sterilized in large numbers in recent years.[42] With so many women becoming sterilized, it is more important than ever to ensure that sterilization decisions are freely made by women themselves, a difficult task in light of this country's history of forced sterilization, especially of women of color.[43]

While oral contraceptives are still the most popular method for American women, their use declined markedly between 1973 and 1982 and then leveled off between 1982 and 1988. In addition, condoms became substantially more popular during the eighties, particularly among teenagers, and use of the cervical cap and spermicidal sponge increased although their use is still rare. At the same time, IUD use declined dramatically, from 2.2 million to .7 million. Among white never-married women, use of the diaphragm decreased sharply, as did periodic abstinence (the rhythm method and natural family planning) and foam.[44]

Have any new alternatives become available?
The only substantially new alternative that has become available recently in the United States is Norplant—a contraceptive device that takes the form of six matchbook-sized nonbiodegradable rubber capsules containing progestin levonorgestrel. Using a local anesthetic, a trained clinician inserts the capsules just under the skin on the inside of a woman's arm. Once implanted, Norplant provides extremely effective continuous protection for 5 years, at which time it must be replaced. The rate of accidental pregnancy in the first year of use is .2%; in the second year, .5%; and during years three to five, 1%.[45] When a woman wishes to discontinue the method, she must return to her health care provider, who will remove the implants under local anesthesia.

The most common undesirable effect of Norplant is disruption of the menstrual cycle. Most women using Norplant have an increase in the average number of bleeding days per cycle and a marked increase in the number of spotting days. Some women report headaches, depression, nervousness, fatigue, dizziness, and nausea.[46] The user may find that the implants are slightly visible, and the initial procedure is expensive.[47] Furthermore, because insertion and removal must be performed by clinical practitioners, women choosing Norplant must relinquish a certain amount of control over their own bodies.

Has an increased awareness of HIV infection affected contraceptive use?

Yes. Publicity surrounding AIDS has sparked condom sales and usage in recent years. Drugstore sales of condoms rose by 25% between 1986 and 1988. Sales of latex condoms with spermicide more than doubled over the same period.[48]

Recent studies of sexual activity among heterosexuals indicate that much of this increase in condom sales can be attributed to heterosexuals, who, although aware of HIV infection, have done little to curb their frequency of sexual contacts. One 1989 study of college women, for example, found little change in their sexual behavior over the last fourteen years: the proportion of college women who had engaged in intercourse at least once was 88% in 1975 and 87% in both 1986 and 1989. The study also found no significant difference over time in the average number of male partners chosen by sexually active women or in the percentage of women engaging in high-risk sexual practices. However, the percentage of sexually active women who reported that their partner always or almost always used a condom rose from 12% in 1974–75 to 21% in 1986 and to 41% in 1989. (The number of women whose partner "always" used a condom was significantly lower: 6% in 1974–75 and 21% in 1989.)[49]

Among all women, the reported percentage of condom users was even lower than the college rate: only 12% in 1982 and 15% in 1988.[50] Thus, despite increased awareness of AIDS, the vast majority of women still are unprotected. Accordingly, additional education directed specifically toward women is needed.

How has the use of oral contraceptives changed over time?

In 1990 a total of sixty million women worldwide relied on the pill, eleven million in the United States alone.[51] Despite fluctuations in the number of women taking the pill at any single point in time, the number of women who at some point in their lives have used the pill has remained remarkably stable over the years. A study conducted by the National Center for Health Statistics in 1987 found that while most women ultimately switch to another contraceptive method, approximately 80% of all U.S. women born since 1945 have used the pill at some time. Among women born after 1940, white women are more likely than women of color to have used the pill; but differences in "ever" usage according to race disappear among younger women. African-American women are most likely to have used oral contraceptives before age eighteen, and all women begin taking the pill at relatively young ages, almost always by age twenty-five, and use it for about five years, on average.[52]

How important is public funding of contraceptive services?
Approximately one in four U.S. women who use a reversible method of contraception rely on public funding, either through a family planning clinic or a private physician who is reimbursed by Medicaid. According to some recent studies, if publicly funded services were not available, these women would have between 1.2 million and 2.1 million unintended pregnancies a year—substantially more than the four hundred thousand they currently experience.[53] Therefore, public funding of contraceptive services is imperative.

Not all public funding schemes, however, are desirable or even constitutional. When public funding is used to push women into using one particular contraceptive method—such as Norplant or sterilization—it effectively denies women their reproductive freedom.[54] Such coercive family planning programs should be resisted.

How could Supreme Court decisions limiting "privacy" rights affect contraceptive choices?
A woman's right to make contraceptive choices freely is part of a larger constitutional right of "privacy" or "liberty." Decisions relating to contraception and procreation are among the many "decisions that an individual may make without unjustified governmental interference"[55] because they are "basic to individual dignity and autonomy."[56] Accordingly, any decision limiting privacy rights, in whatever context, could potentially affect women's right to make contraceptive decisions. Furthermore, contraception matters have always had a great impact on abortion issues, and vice versa, because the core concerns in both cases are so similar.

In the past, judicial reasoning from contraception cases was used to expand women's abortion rights. Today, however, when courts are sanctioning more and more restrictive abortion regulations, abortion cases may be used to approve new restrictions on access to contraceptives. Regressive abortion decisions may have their most immediate impact on teenage women's access to contraceptives. Encouraged by victories in abortion cases requiring parental involvement, anti-abortion groups are likely to press for mandatory parental involvement whenever a minor seeks contraception. In addition, if courts approve laws in the abortion context requiring husbands to be notified and women to receive antichoice counseling and undergo mandatory waiting periods courts may also sanction such restrictions in the larger family planning context.

Have recent reproductive freedom defeats affected public attitudes toward contraception?

Restrictive abortion decisions have contributed greatly to an atmosphere in which the importance of women's reproductive freedom has been trivialized and the state's ability to dictate the use of women's bodies has been enhanced. In testing the limits of this new climate, some prosecutors, judges, and legislators now seek to force women in the criminal justice system and other low-income women to practice contraception. In most cases, the contraception would be "voluntary" only in that no one would *physically* force a woman to undertake a particular method of contraception. However, when the choice is between poverty and contraception, or jail and contraception, any choice that exists is not truly free.

As of August 1991, at least one state had proposed enticing women on welfare to use Norplant by offering it free and by paying users a one-time $500 bonus, plus $50 for each year they continue with the method.[57] If this program were part of a larger program to improve all reproductive health care for women, it would be welcome. However, by targeting and bribing low-income women to use one specific contraceptive method, the state is limiting reproductive freedom, not enhancing it. In addition, the state is operating upon the classist and racist belief that low-income women are not equipped to make their own reproductive decisions. State funds would be better spent if they were to support a wide range of contraceptives, leaving individual women free to make their own decisions.

In addition, a judge in California has ordered a woman who pled guilty to one-time child abuse to use Norplant.[58] Court-ordered contraception should be ruled unconstitutional because it unnecessarily infringes upon women's rights to reproductive freedom and bodily integrity, as well as their right to refuse medical treatment. Alternative, less restrictive means of advancing rehabilitative goals are available in these cases. For example, instead of forced contraception, the state could offer mothering classes and close monitoring of family relationships to prevent future child abuse. Still, as long as our political and judicial climate remains hostile to women's reproductive freedom, pleas for court-ordered contraception are likely to continue to grow.

Far from being part of a new trend, the California probation case and the proposed state laws hark back to old-fashioned eugenics: plans designed to "improve" society by ensuring that "undesirables," usually low-income women, women of color, and differently abled women, do not reproduce. Unless this trend is stopped, it will be extended to restrict women's rights even further, to divert attention from core social problems, and to derail progress that could be made in solving these complex issues.

Has this regressive legal atmosphere affected pharmaceutical companies?

United States manufacturers exaggerate the pressure of the antichoice minority in order to legitimize their unwillingness to address women's reproductive concerns. In reality, their reluctance may stem from their own conservative outlook and their growing concern with guaranteed profits. And to be fair, manufacturers face the increasing costs of developing new contraceptives, threats of liability over currently used methods, and consumer distrust over certain methods, particularly in the wake of massive IUD failures. In addition, contraceptive technologies must pass more stringent Food and Drug Administration (FDA) requirements than most other drugs.[59] Testing is expensive and time consuming: "it would take 10.5 to 17.5 years to develop . . . a new female contraceptive agent and would cost $24 to $70 million—if everything goes well!"[60]

Because of these factors, the most notable trend in the contraceptive field in the United States is the steady decline of contraceptive research. Once a leader in the field, the United States now lags far behind. In fact, as of August 1991, only one manufacturer continued to undertake significant research on new contraceptive technologies. Accordingly, any breakthroughs are likely to come from outside the United States.

What are other trends in the provision of contraceptives?

In the wake of new technologies that would increase women's dependence upon the medical establishment, American women continue to seek greater control over their reproductive lives. As one group of doctors noted, women "want to be involved in choosing which methods to use; they want the methods to be completely voluntary; and, in some instances, they would like to be able to obtain their method anonymously and outside of the medical care system."[61] Thus, one major trend is toward "self-help." Self-help women's health groups, such as the Boston Women's Health Collective, have appeared across the country. Faced with new obstacles to safe and legal abortions, these organizations have gained a new sense of urgency. Modeling themselves after pre-*Roe* self-help groups, some of today's self-help groups are even teaching abortion methods, such as menstrual extraction.[62]

Another trend is a marked increase in the provision of contraceptive information. Greater emphasis has been placed on informed choice and, in turn, on informative patient package inserts. Due to the AIDS epidemic, contraceptive information is especially important. Ironically, today more than ever, a vocal conservative minority is attempting to block meaningful sex education.

Can women be sterilized without their informed consent?

Absolutely not.[63] Yet women have been and continue to be sterilized, either without their knowledge, without their consent, without knowing that the operation is permanent, or under such coercive circumstances that their formal acknowledgement of consent is meaningless. Sterilization abuse primarily affects low-income and minority women and the retarded.

The federal government funds 90 percent of the cost of sterilization under its Medicaid and family-planning programs. The Department of Health and Human Services (HHS), which is responsible for these programs, was ordered to issue regulations establishing requirements for informed consent for all federally funded sterilizations. The court order resulted from a suit brought on behalf of two twelve- and fourteen-year-old black girls in Alabama who were sterilized under a federal program without their parents' knowledge and consent. The court found that 100,000 to 150,000 persons had been sterilized annually under these federal programs, many of them minors and incompetents.[64]

The voluntary sterilization regulations[65] are similar to a law that regulates all sterilizations in the public and private sectors in New York City. The New York City law was fought for by women's and community groups attempting to curb sterilization abuse. The HHS regulations, which apply to both men and women, prohibit sterilization of anyone under twenty-one, require a thirty-day waiting period after written consent is given, and counseling in the person's own language about the irreversibility of the procedure and its risks, benefits, and alternatives. Consent cannot be obtained while a woman is in labor, is having an abortion, or is under the influence of drugs or alcohol. The regulations also prohibit the use of federal funds for sterilization of the mentally incompetent and institutionalized. The regulations provide that federal funds may not be used for hysterectomies done solely for the purpose of sterilization.

In addition, under the regulations a person cannot be asked to consent to sterilization as a condition for obtaining or continuing to receive welfare or other government benefits. Officials who coerce women into being sterilized by threatening to deprive them of such benefits may be fined or imprisoned.[66]

If fully implemented, the regulations might curb the most blatant forms of abuse. However, studies have shown that they are not uniformly followed and that some hospitals disregard them altogether.[67] Doctors in a Maryland hospital once admitted that they often flouted the regulations by not accepting federal funds and simply allowing the hospital to assume the costs.[68] The government's enforcement power is limited to withholding federal reimbursement.

Sterilization abuse can only be altered where there is community action to pressure local hospitals to follow the HHS regulations even in connection with sterilizations not paid for by federal funds. Any person who thinks he or she is a victim of abuse should contact the ACLU or a local attorney or complain to the state Medicaid office; a local women's group or the National Women's Health Network might also offer help.

Women who wish to obtain more information about sterilization abuse can write for *Women Under Attack*, CARASA, 386 Park Ave. S., New York, N.Y. 10016; or *Sterilization Resource Guide 9*, National Women's Health Network, 224 9th St., S.E. Washington, D.C. 20003.

What does the reproductive freedom movement have in common with the disability rights movement?

Both struggles are rooted in the belief that people have a right to control their own bodies and to make autonomous decisions without unwarranted governmental interference. To this end, advocates on behalf of reproductive freedom draw and learn from advocates for the rights of the disabled. In broadening the scope of the reproductive freedom movement, there has been a recent attempt to recognize the particular concerns of disabled women.

Along with low-income women and women of color, disabled women are most likely to be targets of sterilization abuse. Historically, forced sterilization has been the key tool of the eugenics movement. The aim of this movement was to apply the principles for improving "stock," such as animals, to human beings. The "unfit"—which included the "feeble minded, insane, epileptic, diseased, deaf and deformed"—were to be bred out of existence.[69] Similar thoughts lurk behind coerced sterilizations of disabled people today.

In addition, disabled women may also be forced to have abortions against their will and may be denied access to information that would help them make truly free procreative decisions. Although prenatal screening should be available to all women who desire it, care should be taken to ensure that it not be used to compel women to abort less than "perfect" fetuses. Only voluntary, *noncoercive*, genetics screening and counseling should be used. Moreover, reproductive freedom advocates should not prey upon fears about disability to push for abortion rights. As one advocate for both reproductive rights and disabled peoples' rights has stated:

> No woman should be forced to bear a child, abled or
> disabled; and no progressive social movement should ex-

ploit an oppressed group to further its ends. We do not
need . . . to list the conditions under which abortion is
acceptable. The right to abortion is not dependent upon
certain circumstances: it is our essential right to have control over our bodies.[70]

Another issue concerns the fact that disabled women are frequently denied access to contraceptives and gynecological services because of society's refusal to recognize their sexuality.
Similarly, disabled women with children face a myriad of parenting and custody issues, which should be included on the
reproductive freedom agenda. For a more complete discussion
of disabled women and reproductive freedom, see Adrienne
Ash, "Reproductive Technology and Disability," pages 59–101
in Taub and Cohen, eds., *Reproductive Laws for the 1990s: A
Briefing Handbook* (1988).

**What are the reproductive freedom concerns particular to
lesbians?**
Lesbians are, of course, concerned with the right to make
independent procreative decisions. The concern is particularly
acute today as they seek to have children more than ever before.
They are often frustrated in that desire, however. Many sperm
banks and fertility centers, for example, will not inseminate
lesbians. Similarly, due to the persistent, mistaken belief that
lesbians and gay men are necessarily "bad parents," they face
great difficulty in adopting children and serving as foster parents. Some states categorically exclude lesbians and gay men
from adoption and foster parent programs, while others allow
them to adopt only the children who, for whatever reasons, are
deemed "unadoptable."[71]
    An inclusive reproductive freedom movement must address
these issues. Just as the reproductive freedom movement has
much to learn from the disabled rights movement, so must the
reproductive freedom movement draw from the gay and lesbian
rights movement. All these struggles have much in common
as they seek to challenge deeply entrenched sex roles. The
fundamental values at stake in these cases are strikingly similar:
the rights to bodily integrity, intimate association, decisional
autonomy, and ultimately full equality.

Where can women obtain information about obtaining abortions?

The National Abortion Federation (NAF) has established a toll-free hotline to help women choose an abortion clinic. That number is 1 (800) 772-9100. The NAF also provides legal and medical information about abortion procedures. General information packets (*Having an Abortion: Your Guide to Good Care* and *Unsure about Your Pregnancy? A Guide to Making the Right Decision for You*) can be obtained by calling (202) 667-5881 or writing 1436 U Street, N.W., Suite 1003, Washington, D.C. 20009.

The National Abortion Rights Action League has an extensive list of publications that includes such materials as *Who Decides? A Reproductive Rights Issues Manual* ($5/copy), *Who Decides? A State by State Review of Abortion Rights* ($10/copy), *The Voices of Women* (free up to 10 copies), and a pamphlet *Choice Legal Abortion: Arguments Pro and Con* (free up to 99 copies and then 10¢/copy). A full list of publications can be obtained by calling (202) 408-4600 or writing NARAL, 1101 14th Street, N.W., Washington, D.C. 20005.

NOTES

1. Kathryn Kolbert, Julie Mertus, and Rachel Pine co-authored this chapter. Janet Benshoof, Lourdes Soto, Ann Teicher, Suzanne Lynn, and Madeline Kochen were original co-authors of this chapter. Dawn Johnsen of the National Abortion Rights Action League provided valuable comments and assistance.
2. Slip opinion No. 91-744 (June 29, 1992).
3. 410 U.S. 113 (1973).
4. 492 U.S. 490 (1989).
5. 497 U.S. _____, 110 S. Ct. 2926 (1990).
6. 497 U.S. _____, 110 S. Ct. 2972 (1990).
7. 111 S. Ct. 1759 (1991).
8. Emergency Memorandum: Effect of Pending Supreme Court Case on the Right of Women of Color to Choice. *Abortion on the Brink: The Supreme Court v. A Woman's Right to Choose*, published by the National Lawyer's Guild. *See generally* Nsiah-Jefferson, "Reproductive Law, Women of Color, and Low-Income Women," in *Reproductive Laws for the 1990s*, 17–58 (N. Taub & S. Cohen eds. 1988).

9. 410 U.S. 113 (1973).

10. Rosenblum & Marzen, "Strategies for Reversing *Roe v. Wade* through the Courts," in *Abortion and the Constitution: Reversing Roe v. Wade Through the Courts* 195, 209 (D. Horan, E. Grant, & P. Cunningham eds. 1987)(cited in Johnsen and Wilder, *Will Roe v. Wade Survive the Rehnquist Court?* 13 Nova L.R. 457, 459–60 (1989) at [hereinafter Johnsen & Wilder].

11. Johnsen & Wilder at 461.

12. *See National Organization for Women v. Operation Rescue*, 914 F.2d 582 (4th Cir. 1990), *cert. granted sub nom. Bray v. Alexandria Women's Health Clinic*, 111 S. Ct. 1070 (1991). *See also N.Y. State Nat'l Organization for Women v. Terry*, 886 F.2d 1339 (2d Cir. 1989), *cert. denied*, 110 S. Ct. 2206 (1990).

13. National Abortion Rights Action League, Who Decides?—A State by State Study of Abortion Rights, 1991 [hereinafter NARAL].

14. *Id.*

15. 110 S. Ct. 2926 (1990).

16. In addition, in *Hodgson* the Court upheld the statute's 48-hour mandatory waiting period.

17. 110 S. Ct. 2972 (1990).

18. *Planned Parenthood v. Danforth*, 428 U.S. 52, 67–72 (1976).

19. *Id.*

20. *See Conn v. Conn*, 525 N.E.2d 612 (Ind. Ct. App.), *aff'd & opinion adopted*, 526 N.E.2d 958 (Ind.), *cert. denied*, 488 U.S. 955 (1988) (husband's intervention rejected); *Coleman v. Coleman*, 57 Md. App. 755, 471 A.2d 1115 (1984) (same); *Doe v. Doe*, 365 Mass. 556, 314 N.E.2d 128 (1974) (same); *Doe v. Smith*, 527 N.E.2d 177 (Ind. 1988), *cert. denied*, 492 U.S. 919 (1989) (boyfriend's intervention rejected); *Jones v. Smith*, 278 So. 2d 339 (Fla. App. 1973), *cert. denied*, 415 U.S. 958 (1974)(same).

21. 18 Pa. Cons. Stat. Ann. § 3209 (Purdon 1983 and Supp. 1990).

22. *Planned Parenthood v. Casey*, 744 F. Supp. 1323 (E.D. Pa. 1990), *aff'd in part and rev'd in part*, 1991 U.S. App. *Lexis* 24792 (3d Cir. 1991).

23. 448 U.S. 297 (1980).

24. *See* NARAL at 184.

25. *See Ragsdale v. Turnock*, 841 F.2d 1358 (7th Cir. 1988); *Birth Control Centers, Inc. v. Reizen*, 743 F.2d 352 (6th Cir. 1984); *Deerfield Medical Center v. City of Deerfield Beach*, 661 F.2d 328 (5th Cir. Unit B 1981); *Mahoning Women's Center v. Hunter*, 610 F.2d 456 (6th Cir. 1979); *Planned Parenthood of Minnesota, Inc. v. Citizens for Community Action*, 558 F.2d 861 (8th Cir. 1977); *Friendship Medical Center, Ltd. v. Chicago Bd. of Health*, 505 F.2d 1141 (7th Cir. 1974); *Margaret*

S. v. Edwards, 488 F. Supp. 181 (E.D. La. 1980). *But see Baird v. Department of Public Health*, 599 F.2d 1098 (1st Cir. 1979); *Bossier City Medical Suite, Inc. v. City of Bossier City*, 483 F. Supp. 633 (W.D. La. 1980).

26. *See Thornburgh v. American College of Obstetricians and Gynecologists*, 476 U.S. 747 (1986); *Planned Parenthood v. Casey*, 744 F. Supp. 1323 (E.D. Pa. 1990); *Margaret S. v. Edwards*, 488 F. Supp. 181 (E.D. La. 1980); *Wynn v. Scott*, 449 F. Supp. 1302 (N.D. Ill. 1978), *aff'd sub nom. Wynn v. Carey*, 599 F.2d 193 (7th Cir. 1979). *But see Planned Parenthood v. Danforth*, 428 U.S. 52 (1976).

27. 432 U.S. 464 (1977).

28. 448 U.S. 297 (1980).

29. 492 U.S. at 507–11.

30. 491 U.S. at 508–09.

31. Justice O'Connor suggested, however, that a situation might arise in which the ban on the use of public facilities would operate in an unconstitutional manner. 492 U.S. at 523–24 (O'Connor, J., concurring in part and concurring in the judgment).

32. *Doe v. Bolton*, 410 U.S. 179 (1973).

33. 462 U.S. 416 (1983).

34. *Id.* at 434–39.

35. *Id.* at 434.

36. *Id.* at 434–35.

37. 111 S. Ct. 1759 (1991).

38. *Id.* at 1777–78.

39. Letter from Secretary of Health and Human Services Louis Sullivan to Dr. William Raub, Acting Director of the National Institutes for Health 1 (Nov. 2, 1989) (extending indefinitely the moratorium) [hereinafter Sullivan Letter].

40. University of Minnesota Center for Biomedical Ethics, *The Use of Human Fetal Tissues: Scientific, Ethical, and Policy Concerns* 262 (1990).

41. Donovan, *Funding Restrictions on Fetal Research: The Implications for Science and Health*, 22 Family Planning Perspectives 224 (1990).

42. Mosher, *Contraceptive Practice in the United States, 1982-1988*, 22 Family Planning Perspectives 198 (1990).

43. *See* Davis, *Racism, Birth Control and Reproductive Rights*, in *From Abortion to Reproductive Freedom: Transforming a Movement* 22–25 (M. G. Fried ed. 1990).

44. Mosher, *supra* note 42, at 201–4 (1990).

45. Bardin, *Norplant Contraceptive Implants*, 2 Obstetrics and Gynecology Report 96–102 (1990).

46. *Id.*

47. R. A. Hatcher, et. al., *Contraceptive Technology: 1990–1992* 307 (1990)(hereinafter *Contraceptive Technology*).

48. Moran, *Increase in Condom Sales Following AIDS Education and Publicity, United States*, 80 Am. J. of Pub. Health 607 (1990).

49. DeBuono, *Sexual Behavior of College Women in 1975, 1986 and 1989*, 322 New Eng. J. of Med. 821 (1990).

50. Mosher, *supra* note 44, at 201 (1990).

51. Althaus and Kaeser, *At Pill's 30th Birthday, Breast Cancer Question is Unresolved*, 22 Family Planning Perspectives 173 (1990).

52. Dawson, *Trends in Use of Oral Contraceptives—Data from the 1987 National Health Interview Study*, 22 Family Planning Perspectives 169 (1990).

53. Forrest and Singh, *Public-Sector Savings Resulting from Expenditures for Contraceptive Services*, 22 Family Planning Perspectives 6 (1990).

54. *See, e.g.*, Lewin, *A Plan to Pay Welfare Mothers for Birth Control*, N.Y. Times, Feb. 9, 1991 at A11, col. 4 (Kansas proposal to pay women $500 incentives to have Norplant implanted in their arms).

55. *Carey v. Population Services Int'l.*, 431 U.S. 678, 686 (1977).

56. *Thornburgh*, 476 U.S. at 772.

57. Lewin, *supra* note 54. In addition, a state legislator in Kansas, as well as legislators in Ohio and Louisiana have proposed mandatory Norplant for women convicted of certain drug offenses. Nowhere have such proposals been adopted.

58. Lewin, *Implanted Birth Control Device Renews Debate over Forced Contraception*, N.Y. Times, Jan. 10, 1991 at A20, col. 1.

59. *Contraceptive Technology* at 576.

60. *Id.* at 577, *citing* Lincoln & Kaeser, *Whatever Happened to the Contraceptive Revolution?* 20 Family Planning Perspectives 20–24 (1988).

61. *Contraceptive Technology* at 578.

62. *See* Punnett, "The Politics of Menstrual Extraction," *From Abortion to Reproductive Freedom: Transforming a Movement* 101 (M. G. Fried ed. 1990).

63. *See Skinner v. Oklahoma*, 316 U.S. 535 (1941).

64. *Relf v. Weinberger*, 565 F.2d 722 (D.C. Cir. 1977).

65. 45 C.F.R. § 205.35 (1979).

66. 42 U.S.C. § 300a-5, § 300a-8 (Supp. 1976).

67. R. McGarrah, *Sterilization Without Consent: Teaching Hospital Violations of HEW Regulations*, Health Research Group (Jan. 1975); T. Bogue and D. W. Sigelman, *Sterilization Report Number 3: Continuing Violations of Federal Sterilization Guidelines By Teaching Hospitals in 1979*, Public Citizen Health Research Group (Apr. 1979).

68. Kurtz, *Sterilization Widespread in Maryland: Hospitals Ignoring Federal Restrictions*, Washington Star, June 22, 1980.

69. Ann Finger, "Claiming *All* of Our Bodies: Reproductive Rights and Disabilities," 281, 283–84, in Arditti, Duelli Klein, & Minden, eds., *Test Tube Women* (1984); *see also* Carl Bajema, *Eugenics Then and Now* 15 (1976).

70. Finger, *supra* note 69, at 287.

71. *See, e.g. Opinion of the Justices,* 530 A.2d 21 (N.H. 1987)(opinion joined by then New Hampshire Justice and now U.S. Supreme Court Justice David Souter). *Compare In the Matter of J.S. & C.,* 324 A.2d 90 (N.J. Super. 1974), with *In re Jane B.,* 380 N.Y.S.2d 848 (1976) and *In re Adoption of Charles B.,* 522 N.E. 2d 884 (Ohio 1990).

VI
Liberty Rights During Pregnancy

Pregnancy and childbirth have traditionally furnished the justification for many elements of women's second-class citizenship. In the 1980s, new pregnancy-based threats arose. A number of doctors and hospitals sought to use the law to compel pregnant women to follow their advice—most commonly, by getting court orders forcing their patients to have caesarean sections rather than natural childbirth. Also, government prosecutors and courts sent women who used drugs while pregnant to jail as a kind of forced "medical treatment" for the fetus or as a punishment for using drugs while pregnant.[1] Government social workers with access to positive drug-test results sought to remove newborns from their mothers rather than provide treatment for both. And paradoxically, many drug treatment programs refused admission to pregnant women precisely because of their pregnancy.

These punitive approaches—justified in the name of fetal interests—were, ironically, often counterproductive. As one author has noted:

> allowing the government to demand that women comport themselves in the best interests of their fetus—as the government defines those best interests—would effectively create an adversarial relationship with the woman's own body that she could avoid only by aborting the pregnancy.[2]

Punishment involves other problems. It violates women's rights and ignores the complexity of women's lives. And it represents a search for a cheap and easy solution to difficult social problems that require the expenditure of money (drug treatment programs). Punishing women instead of providing them with the resources to become healthy may make the authorities feel better, but it does little to solve the core problems. For women's choices—as in the case of medical care for pregnancy and childbirth—are not always easy; and poverty and the lack of drug treatment and prenatal care may contribute more to an unhealthy pregnancy than a woman's own behavior.

FORCED CAESAREAN SECTIONS

Have courts forced women to have caesarean sections in lawsuits brought by doctors and hospitals?

In a few cases. One commentator has counted at least eleven instances where caesareans were ordered by a court after the women refused to consent to the operation.[3] But recent cases have led to better law. The most celebrated case occurred in 1987, when Angela Carder, a patient at George Washington University Medical Center who was twenty-six weeks pregnant and terminally ill with cancer, was forced to undergo a caesarean section against her will. She did not want the operation—perhaps because she was advised it might bring on her death immediately. She agreed that she would have a caesarean once the fetus reached twenty-eight weeks, but hospital officials feared she would not live that long. As a result, the hospital rushed to court for an order authorizing the surgery in an effort to save the fetus. The hospital did so without notifying her long-time physician, who later stated that he would have testified that the operation was "medically inadvisable *both for Angela Carder and for the fetus.*"[4] And indeed, shortly after the surgery, both died—the newborn within 2½ hours, Ms. Carder within 2 days.

On appeal, the court ruled that the trial court had used an inappropriate method to decide the case and should not have ordered the caesarean section.[5] Rather than weighing the interests of the fetus against the interests of the pregnant woman, the court should have used a "substituted" judgment approach, considering only Ms. Carder's own preference for her medical treatment.

Subsequently, the parents of Angela Carder enlisted the help of the ACLU Reproductive Freedom Project and sued the hospital for deprivation of human rights, discrimination, wrongful death, malpractice, and other claims arising out of its treatment of Ms. Carder. To settle the lawsuit, the hospital agreed in 1990 to establish a new policy governing its medical staff. That policy recognizes the right of pregnant patients to determine the course of medical treatment on behalf of themselves and their fetuses and to refuse medical recommendations. It provides:

Respect for autonomy does not end because an adult patient with capacity refuses a course of action strongly recommended by an attending physician. Nor do professional standards require that patients comply with every physician recommendation or that physicians agree to comply with every patient request. From this respect for both patient autonomy and for professional standards flows our strong preference for maintaining decision-making within the physician-patient relationship rather than having outsiders (e.g. courts) impose health care decisions on unwilling patients.[6]

The terms of the settlement agreement are consistent with the American Medical Association's policy on the issue. That policy recognizes that while women have a "moral responsibility to make reasonable efforts toward preserving fetal health, this . . . responsibility does not necessarily imply a legal duty to accept medical procedures in order to benefit the fetus."[7]

Indeed, physicians' predictions of medical outcomes are often wrong, as the death of Ms. Carder's twenty-six-week-old fetus demonstrated. The hospital may have hastened Ms. Carder's death by the operation; and had she been allowed to reject the operation, perhaps she could have survived until the twenty-eighth week of her pregnancy, when she was willing to have a cesarean and when her baby would have had a much better chance of survival.

Should pregnant women be forced by court order to have caesarean sections because their doctors recommend this as the best alternative for the fetus?

No. All persons, including women, possess a right to accept or refuse medical treatment, as the court in the Angela Carder case recognized. That court quoted an old Supreme Court opinion: "No right is held more sacred, [n]or is more carefully guarded . . . than the right of every individual to the possession and control of his own person, free from all restraint or interference of others."[8] Accordingly, physicians are required to obtain the informed consent of patients before initiating surgery or other medical intervention, and they cannot proceed if they do not. Further, the constitutional right to privacy, which is a central component of the right to liberty, is violated when one's body is subject to unwanted physical intrusion.[9]

Historically, this has been true even when one person sought to force another to submit to medical treatment in order to benefit the first person. As the *Carder* court pointed out, "[C]ourts do not compel one person to permit a significant intrusion upon his or her bodily integrity for the benefit of another person's health."[10] It gave the example of a judge who declined to order a man to donate bone marrow to his cousin, even though without the donation his cousin would die.

Of course, most people will probably be generous to their relatives in such situations, and most pregnant women will want to follow their doctor's advice. But the fact remains that the law has not compelled such generosity by brute force and should not do so here. Moreover, when pregnant women are forced to accept unwanted treatment, they are placed in an adversarial relationship with their physicians. If women cannot trust that their doctors will be responsive to their own wishes, they may avoid healthcare altogether. That would not be in the best interests of either the pregnant woman or the fetus. Finally, doctors are often wrong. While the *Carder* case provides the most vivid example, other examples come from the cases of pregnant women who evaded court orders to have caesarean sections and gave birth to healthy children without surgical intervention, despite the dire predictions of their doctors that their babies would die.

For all of these reasons, courts should rule that forced medical intervention violates the constitutional rights of pregnant women and is unsound as a matter of public policy.

DRUG USE DURING PREGNANCY

Can mothers be jailed because their children are born with traces of drugs in their system?

They have been, but such arrests are being challenged and upheld as unconstitutional. From 1988 through 1992, prosecutors arrested at least one hundred and fifty women after their newborns' urine indicated traces of cocaine.[11]

One problem with such arrests is that prosecutors have used

criminal laws in ways that were never intended when the laws were enacted. For example, Kentucky prosecutors charged Connie Welch with criminal child abuse and Florida prosecutors charged Jennifer Johnson with delivering drugs to her fetus via the umbilical cord because these women's newborns tested positive for drugs. Both of these women were convicted, and Connie Welch was sentenced to five years in jail. But the women had no notice that their drug use during pregnancy violated those laws. In the Welch case, the law was written to apply to the abuse of children, not fetuses. In the Johnson case, the law was written to apply to drug pushers who intentionally sell drugs on the street to children, not to the involuntary transfer of drugs via the umbilical cord. Accordingly, both convictions were overturned on appeal.

Another reason that prosecution of alcohol and drug dependent women is unconstitutional is that these women have been singled out while similar behavior engaged in by men remains immune from scrutiny. For example, men are not—and most likely never will be—arrested for child abuse after having used alcohol, morphine, or methadone, substances animal studies have revealed can affect sperm and thereby cause birth defects.[12]

The belief that prosecution is an appropriate approach to these cases is based on several erroneous assumptions. One assumption is that pregnant addicts are indifferent to the health of their fetuses or that they willfully seek to cause them harm. This may not be the case, however. Real resource constraints—such as poverty—may prevent addicted women from securing medical care during their pregnancies. Even when treatment is available, women may be stopped from getting help by the addiction, which typically involves loss of control over use of the drug even when there are serious consequences.

Another assumption is that treatment is readily available. Yet many treatment programs will not accept pregnant women because they fear liability for pregnancy-related problems or lack obstetrical services. In New York City, for example, 54% of the 78 drug treatment programs surveyed by a New York physician refused to treat pregnant women; 67% declined to treat all pregnant women on Medicaid; and 87% had no services available to pregnant women on Medicaid who were addicted to crack.[13] The American Civil Liberties Union Women's Rights

Project has sued two hospitals in New York City because of such discriminatory policies and is investigating the problem in other jurisdictions. And few of the programs that do accept pregnant women arrange for childcare, which makes it very difficult for women to avail themselves of the services that are available.

Yet a third erroneous assumption is that successful prosecutions will deter most pregnant women from alcohol or drug use. No studies have demonstrated this to be true, and it seems unlikely that deterrence would operate effectively on a person in the irrational grip of an addiction. In addition, the countervailing problem is that punitive measures may deter pregnant women from using the very health-related services that will most benefit themselves and their children, out of fear of being turned into the police by medical personnel.

For these reasons, almost all of the criminal indictments brought against such drug and alcohol dependent mothers have been dismissed. And numerous health and medical organizations have issued policies opposing the criminal prosecution of alcohol and drug dependant women including the National Association for Perinatal Addiction Research and Education; the Center for the Future of Children; the American Medical Association; the American Public Health Association; the American Academy of Pediatrics; American Society of Addiction Medicine; the March of Dimes; the National Association of Public Child Welfare Administrators; the American Nurses Association; the Coalition on Alcohol and Drug Dependent Women and Their Children; the Southern Regional Project on Infant Mortality; the American College of Nurse-Midwives; the National Abortion Rights Action League; the National Association of Maternal-Child Health Programs; the National Center for Clinical Infant Programs; the National Council on Alcohol and Drug Dependence; the National Perinatal Association; the National Society of Genetic Counselors; and the National Women's Health Network.

Can women lose custody of their children, solely because they are born testing positive for drugs?

In some states. Intermediate appellate courts in California, New York, Connecticut, and Michigan have allowed babies born with such test results to be removed immediately at birth,[14] although none of the states' highest courts has approved the practice. Evidence suggests this practice is not necessarily in children's best interests however, and the practice may violate women's due process rights to family integrity.

While a positive drug test combined with *other* indications of parental unfitness may suggest that a particular mother will not be able to provide adequate care for her child, many factors suggest that in the majority of cases medical treatment for the mother, rather than taking her child away, is better for the baby. First, a child's positive drug test is not necessarily evidence of child abuse or neglect, although it is often treated as conclusive proof of both. In fact, the tests are open to different interpretations. For example, a positive drug test indicates only that a drug was ingested within the last twenty-four to seventy-two hours; it does not distinguish between a one-time user and an addict. Moreover, drug tests are not always accurate; false positives are quite common, and their prevalence is magnified by the occurrence of human error in administering the tests. Even a genuine positive test result may not predict future harm to a child and therefore should not constitute sufficient evidence to conclude that a child is in such danger that it should be removed from its mother. Use of a positive toxicology as a sole trigger for removal is also contrary to laws mandating that preventive services be provided prior to removal in order to ensure that families remain intact as long as possible.

Even assuming that a positive toxicology is meaningful, automatic removal does not guarantee that a child's best interests will be served. For example, when a positive toxicology is used as sole proof of neglect, child welfare officials often fail to undertake even the most cursory review of the home. In one ACLU case in Nevada a social worker removed a newborn from its mother's care based solely on the social worker's belief that a positive test result was a sufficient indication of fetal alcohol syndrome. She never visited the home to assess the environment or attempted to obtain an opinion from a physician trained in diagnosing fetal alcohol syndrome. Three months later, and after considerable trauma for the mother, the court ordered the baby's return because social workers had failed to prove that the child suffered from fetal alcohol syndrome.

The acute shortage of foster care, particularly in major urban areas, also suggests that medical intervention to help the mother, rather than deprivation of custody, is frequently the best option. One hospital survey found that a number of drug-exposed newborns who were ready to leave the hospital had to remain there instead because of problems such as a lack of foster care or a delayed protective service evaluation.[15] And a Los Angeles pilot program reported that the 13 children in its program who had been exposed to drugs in utero were placed in a total of 35 foster homes before reaching the age of 3.[16] Children left to the care of a series of hospital attendants and foster homes may do better if the government monies spent on caring for these children in hospitals and foster care are used instead to treat their mothers and keep the family unit intact.

Positive toxicologies should be used for medical intervention, not as a basis for removal without additional proof of parental unfitness. Prior to declaring a parent unfit, social service agencies should consider a broad range of environmental factors relating to a parent's ability to care for a child, and they should assess the entire home environment. Anything less than a thorough evaluation of the family may cause its unnecessary dissolution.

Can hospitals release evidence of pregnant women's positive drug tests to law enforcement officials or social service workers without the women's consent?

Hospitals sometimes do so if they believe the tests provide evidence of child abuse. State child abuse laws generally allow health care workers to release medical records if they have a good faith belief that abuse has been committed. Yet patients' constitutional rights may be violated by the practice. When hospitals release women's medical records without their consent, the hospitals violate the patients' right to confidentiality. They also undermine the trust necessary for an effective doctor-patient relationship. In fact, women may avoid the health care system altogether, rather than risk punitive actions, a result that helps neither addicted women who are pregnant nor their fetuses.

There are a number of arguments that could be used to fight this practice in court, although it is far from clear that they will be successful. Constitutional liberty and privacy guarantees, as well as privacy statutes in some states, should prohibit hospitals from revealing patients' medical histories to county prosecutors or social service agencies.[17] The patients' privacy right, defined by the Supreme Court in another context as the "interest in avoiding disclosure of personal matters,"[18] may encompass a pregnant addict's right to nondisclosure of her medical history.[19] Indeed, medical records are ordinarily entitled to a high degree of protection, and courts have usually, but not always, upheld the sanctity of the doctor-patient relationship in the face of threats posed by reporting requirements.[20]

Another argument is that the information cannot be released to the state because it is effectively being used for the purpose of punishing pregnant women for their status as addicts. This argument is based on a 1962 Supreme Court case about a California law under which the status of being a narcotics addict was a crime; the court rejected the law as unconstitutional.[21]

Can drug treatment programs lawfully exclude pregnant women?

Perhaps not, under at least one state's human rights law. In the only challenge to this practice to date, the ACLU Women's Rights Project filed a class-action lawsuit against two private alcohol and drug treatment programs in New York City. The lawsuit relies on the New York State public accommodations law, which prohibits discrimination because of pregnancy in private facilities open to the general public.[22]

As noted above, many alcohol and drug treatment programs still discriminate against pregnant women. Few programs provide residential drug treatment programs for pregnant women and their children. Day treatment facilities, which are less effective than residential programs, offer the only alternative, and many will not treat pregnant women either, especially if the women are not drug free.

Discrimination appears to be most common when the treatment needed is detoxification, which may involve the use of mild sedatives, and the treatment program lacks prenatal care or obstetrical services. Programs often fear that such treatment may harm the fetus and therefore subject them to liability.

This result is problematic for a number of reasons. First, the professed concern for the fetus makes little sense given the harm that can occur if crack addiction or other alcohol or drug problems go untreated. Second, it is possible to provide detoxification services to pregnant women safely without risk to the woman or fetus. Third, traditional informed-consent doctrine should protect physicians and hospitals that properly advise patients of the risk associated with, and the alternatives to, a course of treatment. Fourth, liability concerns are somewhat suspect since no program has ever been sued by a woman or child for the effects of drug treatment in such circumstances. Finally, programs can set up referral networks or part-time obstetrical care or develop other resources to ensure that patients obtain the full range of services they need. In short, if society is truly serious about helping the children of alcohol and drug dependent women, dramatically increasing the number of treatment programs open to pregnant women will be the mark of that commitment.

NOTES

1. *See* Moss, K., *Recent Developments*, 13 Harv. Women's L.J. 278 (1990); Johnsen, D., *From Driving to Drugs*, 138 U. Pa. L. Rev. 179 (1989); Chasnoff, I., *Temporal Patterns of Cocaine Use in Pregnancy: Perinatal Outcome*, 261 JAMA 1741 (1989).
2. Johnsen, D., *supra* note 1 at 191.
3. Gallagher, J., *Prenatal Invasions and Interventions: What's Wrong with Fetal Rights*, 10 Harv. Women's L.J. 9, 11 and n.16 (1987). *E.g.*, *Jefferson v. Griffin Spaulding County Hospital Authority*, 274 S.E.2d 457 (Ga. 1981).
4. *In re A.C.*, 533 A.2d 611 (D.C. 1987), *vacated*, 539 A.2d 203 (D.C. 1988), *rev'd en banc*, 573 A.2d 1235, 1248 n.17 (D.C. App. 1990).
5. 573 A.2d 1235 (D.C. App. 1990).
6. In addition, the hospital agreed to appoint a "patient advocate" to the staff who is responsible for advising patients or their surrogates of pertinent hospital and medical staff policies; the institutional structure of the hospital; the terms of the settlement agreement; and the identity and responsibility of medical staff.
7. Cole, H., Section Editor, *Legal Interventions During Pregnancy: Court Ordered Medical Treatment and Legal Penalties for Potentially Harmful Behavior by Pregnant Women*, 264 JAMA 2663 n.8 (Nov. 28, 1990).
8. *Union Pacific Ry. Co. v. Botsford*, 141 U.S. 250, 251 (1891).
9. *Thornburgh v. Am. College of Obstetricians and Gynecologists*, 476 U.S. 747, 772 (1986).

10. 573 A.2d at 1243–44.

11. *See, e.g.*, *Reyes v. Superior Court*, 75 Cal. App. 3d 214 (4th Dist. 1977) (holding that felony child endangering statute did not include a woman's prenatal drug abuse); *People v. Stewart*, No. M508197, slip op. at 7–8 (San Diego Mun. Ct. Feb. 23, 1987) (finding criminal child support statute that explicitly covered "a child conceived but not yet born" not intended to impose additional legal duties on pregnant women); *State v. Andrews*, No. J0 68459, slip op. (Ohio C. P. June 19, 1989) (refusing to usurp legislature's role by extending child endangering law); *State v. Osmus*, 276 P.2d 469 (Wyo. 1954) (finding that child abuse statute was not intended to apply to an unborn child); *State v. Gray*, No. L-89-239, slip op. at 3 (Ohio Ct. App. Lucas Cty. Aug. 31, 1991) (upholding dismissal of child endangerment charges against a woman who gave birth to "an allegedly cocaine addicted baby" because "we are not persuaded that the General Assembly intended to make a criminal act of the passage of harmful substances from a mother to her child in the brief moments from birth to the severance of the umbilical cord"), *appeal docketed*, No. 90-1986 (Ohio Apr. 22, 1991); *People v. Hardy*, No. 128, 458, slip op. at 2 (Mich. App. Apr. 1, 1991); *Commonwealth v. Pellegrini*, No. 87970, slip op. at 8 (Mass. Sup. Ct. Oct. 15, 1990); *People v. Cox*, NO. 90-53545, slip op. at 9 (Mich. Cir. Ct. July 9, 1990); *State v. Carter*, No. 89-6274, slip op. at 2-3 (Fla. Escambia Cty. Ct. July 23, 1990) (dismissing drug delivery charges against a pregnant woman who delivered a baby who tested positive for cocaine metabolite), *appeal docketed*, No. 90-2261 (Fla. 1st DCA Sept. 18, 1990); *State v. Inzar*, slip op. at 1–2 (N.C. 1991)(dismissing charges of substance abuse against pregnant woman who allegedly used crack during her pregnancy) (appeal withdrawn); *People v. Welch*, No. 90-CA-1189-MR (Court of Appeals 1990); *contra Johnson v. State*, No. 89-1765 (Fla. 5th DCA Apr. 18, 1991)(*appeal docketed*, No. 77, 831 (Fla. 5th DCA).

12. Cohen, F., *Paternal Contributions to Birth Defects*, Nursing Clinics N. Am. (March 1986) at 49.

13. Chavkin, W., *Help, Don't Jail Addicted Mothers*, The N.Y. Times, July 18, 1989, at A21, col. 2.

14. *In re Valerie D.*, 25 Conn. App. 586 (1991); *In re Stephanal Tyesha*, 157 App. Div. 2d 322, 556 N.Y.S. 2d 280 (1990); *In re Troy D.*, 215 Cal. App. 3d 889, 898–99, 263 Cal. Rptr. 869 (1989); *Matter of Baby X*, 97 Mich. App. 253, 293 N.W. 2d 736 (1980); *In re Ruiz*, 27 Ohio Misc. 2d 31, 500 N.E. 2d 935 (1986).

15. Miller, G., *Addicted Infants and Their Mothers*, Zero to Three, vol. 9, no. 5, June 1989, at 21.

16. Interim Hearings on Parental Substance Abuse and Its Effects on the Fetus and Children Before the Senate Select Committee on Substance Abuse, California Legislature at 30 (1988)(statement of Carol Cole).

17. Courts may not agree, however. In *In re Troy D.*, 263 Cal. Rptr. 869, 872 (Cal. App. 4th Dist. 1989), for example, the court rejected plaintiff's argument that the hospital had violated the California Confidentiality of Medical Information Act by releasing her medical records. The court did not see any important public policy served by preventing disclosure of the newborn's records.

18. *Whalen v. Roe*, 429 U.S. 589, 599 (1977).

19. *See also United States v. Westinghouse Electric Corp.*, 638 F.2d 570 (3d Cir. 1980) (medical files); *Hawaii Psychiatric Society v. Ariyoshi*, 481 F. Supp. 1028, 1039 (D. Haw. 1979).

20. *See Thornburgh v. Am. College of Obstetrics and Gynecologists*, 476 U.S. 747, 765–68 (1986), later proceeding, *Am. College of Obstetrics and Gynecologists, Pennsylvania Section v. Thornburgh*, 656 F. Supp. 879, 889–90 (E.D. Pa. 1987) (striking down statutory provisions requiring reporting of information about women obtaining abortions, or resulting in such disclosure); *Jones v. Superior Court*, 174 Cal. Rptr. 148 (Cal. App. 4th Dist. 1981). *Compare Whalen v. Roe*, 429 U.S. 589 (1977).

21. *Robinson v. California*, 370 U.S. 660 (1962), *reh'g denied*, 371 U.S. 905 (1962).

22. *Elaine W. v. North General Hospital*, Index No. 6230/90 (N.Y. Sup. Ct., filed Nov. 23, 1989), brought under N.Y. Exec. Law § 296.

VII
The Criminal Justice System

SEXUAL ASSAULT

There has been a great deal of national attention recently focused on the issue of sexual assault, culminating with the trials of William Kennedy Smith and Mike Tyson in 1991 and 1992. These cases are significant because they signal an increased willingness by the state to prosecute cases where the alleged assailant knew the victim. However, obtaining convictions is still another matter, with "acquaintance" rape cases remaining the most difficult, especially where the alleged assailant is white, as in the Smith trial, or where the victim is minority, as in a recent case in which three white college students were acquitted of forced sodomy and sexual abuse of a Jamaican woman after getting her drunk at their fraternity house located at St. John's University in Queens, New York.[1]

On the other hand, rape law in the 1990s has substantially improved over the rape law that prevailed in the 1960s. The women's movement has achieved many reforms in the law, and there are now fewer hurdles to successful rape prosecutions than there once were. This section discusses how the law has improved so that victims of rape will be encouraged to pursue their criminal remedies. It also discusses remaining problem areas and offers suggestions for further reform so that even more victims can be helped in the future.

What is rape?

There is no simple definition. Historically, most state laws defined rape as English common law did, as occurring when a man engaged in sexual intercourse with a woman not his wife, by force or threat of force, against her will and without her consent.[2] This definition—and court rules requiring special corroboration in rape cases and physical resistance by the woman—reflected several highly sexist stereotypes: that mar-

ried women are rightfully the property of their husbands; that
women falsely accuse men of rape to extract revenge; and that
a woman must physically resist an attack to demonstrate that
she does not consent.[3] Each of these notions has made it difficult
to convict men of rape.[4]

Advocates have successfully reformed many state laws. Many
state legislatures and courts, for example, have expanded the
definition of rape to include rape occurring within a marriage.
Some have abandoned the "utmost resistance" requirement
under which women had to put their lives virtually at risk by
fierce resistance before the state would say rape had occurred.
"Sexual conduct" has also been redefined to reach not only
vaginal penetration but also oral and anal penetration[5] and any
sexual contact.[6] A number of states have eliminated the special
corroboration rules—unique to the crime of rape—that refuse
to allow rape convictions based solely on the victim's testimony.[7] Even more states, and the federal government, have
placed stringent limits on the rapist's ability to use the woman's
past sexual history to avoid a rape conviction.[8] These changes
reflect a more enlightened view of what constitutes sexual
violence. They have not been uniformly adopted by state legislatures and courts, however, and they fail to address perhaps
the biggest problem: successfully prosecuting rapists where the
victim was afraid to resist and did not do so because of such
factors as the man's larger size, his greater age or authority, his
threatening appearance and manner, the isolation of the spot,
or threats that he might harm her in various nonphysical ways.
In such situations, even if her explicit "no" makes it clear that
she did not consent, the law has sometimes found the rapist
not guilty and converted her lack of resistance into a false
consent.

What legal doctrines have been used to require that women resist in order to prove a rape case?

An early legal doctrine required "utmost resistance." The
woman virtually had to put her own life at risk in order to
establish that she was raped. The classic definition was given
by a court in 1906.

> [N]ot only must there be entire absence of mental con-
> sent or assent, but there must be the most vehement

exercise of every physical means or faculty within the woman's power to resist the penetration of her person and this must be shown to persist until the offense is consummated.[9]

The danger was obvious. If she fought this hard, the rapist might kill her. Indeed, police often advised women in these situations not to fight back, for precisely that reason. So some states replaced this standard in the 1950s and 1960s with one requiring "reasonable," rather than "utmost," resistance. While this was a mild step forward, it still kept the focus of attention in the criminal trial on the *woman's* actions, rather than the *rapist's*, and it still required that she resist to demonstrate that she did not consent. Her word was not enough.

As Harvard Law Professor Susan Estrich observes in her book *Real Rape*, this standard protected men who ignored women who said "no" but did not fight back physically. It assumed that women do not always mean it when they say "no," do not know what they want, lack honesty and integrity, enjoy physical struggle as a sexual stimulant, and will abuse the power they have in relationships at the expense of innocent men.[10] As a result, many men who have ignored a woman's "no" have been protected, and many women who have resisted their assailants have been injured.

To counter the harms caused by the "resistance" requirement, another reform effort emerged in the 1970s and 1980s. Professor Estrich explains that reformers tried to shift the explicit focus of the law from the woman's resistance to the rapist's use of force. Accordingly, the influential Model Penal Code defined rape "as sexual intercourse where the man 'compels her to submit by force or by threat of imminent death, serious bodily injury, extreme pain or kidnapping, to be inflicted on anyone,'" and many states followed suit.[11] Resistance—physical demonstration that the woman did not consent—was no longer supposed to be an issue.

But Professor Estrich contends that the courts defined "force" in such a way that they shifted the focus right back to the woman's resistance—at least in what she calls "simple rape" (when the defendant knew his victim and neither beat nor threatened her with a weapon) cases.[12] Requiring male force as proof worked in rape cases where the assailant was a stranger who used guns or knives. Many courts refused to convict, however, in rape cases where the man was an acquaintance and did not use such weapons. While the women in these cases said no, they were often too scared to resist—that is, to fight back— for reasons such as a prior beating by the man, or his size or intimidating demeanor. In such cases, the courts used the woman's lack of physical resistance to find that the assailant had not used the *force* that the law required to convict him of rape. So while resistance was no longer relevant to the issue of whether she consented, it became relevant to the issue of whether he used force. And without the requisite force, she lost—even if she did not consent and said so very clearly.

Professor Estrich describes as one example of this approach a 1984 North Carolina case where the appeals court threw out a rapist's conviction.[13] During a six-month relationship the man had struck her, and she ended the relationship after one of these episodes. He later approached her and made threats such as "grabb[ing] her arm and stat[ing] that she was coming with him," threatening to "'fix' her face to show he 'was not playing,'" and telling her he had a "'right' to have intercourse with her" in response to her statement that the relationship was over.[14] Subsequently, at the house of one of the defendant's friends, he asked her if she was "ready," and the victim told him she did not want to have sexual relations. The defendant pulled her up from the chair, undressed her, pushed her legs apart, and penetrated her. She cried. These facts created a paradox for the court. Professor Estrich explains:

> The court explicitly says that the sexual intercourse was without the woman's consent. It also says that there was no force. In other words, the woman was not forced to engage in sex (as proven by her failure to resist), but the sex she engaged in was against her will. . . . Apparently, [the judges] could not understand the woman's reaction. For me, it is not at all difficult to understand that a woman who had been beaten repeatedly, who had been a passive victim of both violence and sex during the "consensual" relationship, who had sought to escape from the man, who is confronted and threatened by him, who summons the courage to tell him their relationship is over only to be answered by his assertion of a "right" to sex, would not

fight his advances. She did not fight; she cried. It is the reaction of "sissies" in playground fights. It is the reaction of people who have already been beaten, or never had the power to fight in the first place. It is, from my reading, the most common reaction of women to rape.[15]

What can be done to reform the law to make conviction possible in simple rape cases, where the assailant is an acquaintance who uses no weapons, and the woman makes clear that she does not want to have sex but is too scared to resist?
A reform in the 1990s would be to seek enactment of new rape statutes explicitly stating that courts shall not require the woman to resist as a precondition for a conviction. Instead, convictions could be obtained upon a showing that the woman clearly said no and that she was afraid to resist. Moreover, it should be enough that she was actually scared; her fear should not be held up against the standard of some hypothetical "reasonable" person. This standard would shift the burden to men to determine if the woman actually consented to sexual relations. If she said that she did not, he would proceed at his own risk. As Professor Estrich has said, "'Consent' should be defined so that no means no."[16]

Must a victim immediately report an attack?
No. For many years the law required victims to report an attack to the police immediately. The requirement was called the *hue and cry doctrine* and reflected the view that "a willing participant in sexual relations [may become] a vindictive complainant [at a later date]."[17] This requirement has never been imposed for other crimes. While the requirement no longer survives, the Model Penal Code still requires that a complaint be "prompt" and defines "prompt" as occurring within three months of the assault.[18] Most states, however, do not require victims to file a report within a specified period of time. But they will allow the defense to introduce evidence of the time it took for the victim to make the complaint.[19] On the other hand, courts may also accept evidence of Rape Trauma Syndrome (RTS) to explain a victim's delay in reporting a rape,[20] although juries may still choose—as in the St. John's case—not to believe it.

What is Rape Trauma Syndrome?

Some women who have been raped suffer emotional harm to the extent that it causes behavioral and psychological responses that lead them to act in ways that cast doubt on the veracity of their charge. Typical behavior may include delayed reporting of an offense, reluctance to discuss the rape, recantations of allegations of abuse, or continued contact with the assailant.[21]

Victims of sexual assault have sought to have experts testify in court to explain these behaviors as typical of a condition known as *Rape Trauma Syndrome*. This testimony may be useful to rebut jurors' misconceptions about a rape victim's behavior. For example, a victim who denied being raped to her friends or who asked the assailant not to tell anyone could have an expert testify that this is typical of Rape Trauma Syndrome. The expert could also describe the clinical symptoms that victims of Rape Trauma Syndrome display and state whether the victim has it.[22] Experts are usually not allowed to offer an opinion as to whether the victim was in fact raped, however.[23]

Can a defendant inquire into a woman's past sexual history as part of his defense?

Sometimes, but important legal reforms have sharply limited this practice. Courts used to view women's past sexual history as relevant either to the issue of whether a woman consented in the charged rape case or whether she was inherently culpable, or both. The myth was that if a woman was "unchaste," i.e., consented to intercourse with one man, she would consent to intercourse with any man. This often resulted in the admission of a victim's past sexual history, which protected women who had little, if any, prior sexual experience but punished those who did. The admission, at trial, of evidence of past sexual history humiliated many victims, violated their right to privacy, in effect put *them* on trial, and led juries not to convict in situations where the woman *had* been raped but had previously had consensual sex with other men.

Many states and the federal government have now enacted rape shield laws, which prohibit using evidence about a victim's past sexual history in the rapist's trial unless a defendant can show that the evidence is relevant and meets other strict standards. While most evidence of a victim's prior sexual conduct will be kept out of the trial, the judge can admit such evidence if the defendant is using it to show that other men were the source of the semen or injuries involved in the trial.[24] Similarly, the alleged rapist can try to prove that the victim once engaged in consensual intercourse *with him* and thereby attempt to prove that she consented this time.[25] This exception makes it especially difficult to prove rape when the victim had a prior relationship with the accused.

In some cases, defendants have charged courts with violating their right to a fair trial for excluding evidence of a victim's prior sexual history. While there may sometimes be a potential conflict between the rights of the defendant, on one hand, and those of the victim, on the other hand, this exclusion does not deprive an accused to a fair trial any more than do rules of evidence barring hearsay, opinion evidence, and privileged communications. Moreover, court rules sometimes give the defendant a special break. For example, the prosecution usually cannot introduce evidence that the rapist committed other "prior bad acts" such as raping other women.[26] The ACLU has therefore adopted a policy that requires trial judges to keep out irrelevant testimony, control cross-examination and argument, and eliminate prejudicial instructions unique to rape in order to protect victims from unnecessary violation of their right to sexual privacy without detracting from the fairness of the trial. Closed hearings can also be used to ascertain the relevance of any proposed line of testimony or cross-examination that may involve a witness's prior sexual history. Courts can also be required to state whether the history is relevant or irrelevant, and why, so that appellate courts can monitor these rulings.

ACLU policy also provides that the relevance of the prior sexual history of either the complainant or the defendant in rape[27] cases should be determined free from sexist assumption. The criteria used in admitting evidence of prior sexual history in rape cases must apply equally to the prosecution and the defense.

May a husband be convicted of raping his wife?

Historically, the law denied married women protection against rape by their husbands because married women were presumed to consent to all marital sex and could not therefore— in theory—be raped.[28] The marital rape exception was also premised on the belief that it would promote disharmony in the marital relationship if women were allowed to prosecute their husbands for rape.[29] These theories ignored reality. As one author has observed, "The marital rape exemption creates, fosters, and encourages not marital intimacy, harmony, or reconciliation, but a separate state of sovereignty ungoverned by law and insulated from state interference."[30]

Reform in this area is still necessary. While men may now be found guilty of raping their wives in some states, the marital rape exemption still existed in some form in thirty-nine states as of 1988.[31] In some states, rape within a marriage is defined as a lower level of criminality, or only certain kinds of marital rape are criminalized—for example, where the parties have formally separated.[32]

Must a woman have corroborating evidence for a successful prosecution of her attacker?

No. Historically, a woman's word alone was not enough. Courts required that her testimony be "corroborated," a requirement that evolved from the stereotype that women will lie about such matters.[33] Corroboration often required evidence of physical injury, the availability of witnesses, and other such evidence. Yet the corroboration requirement created a strange catch-22. As one commentator has noted, "Rape without resistance makes corroboration of every element essential; but the absence of resistance makes corroboration of nonconsent almost impossible to establish."[34]

Today, because of legal reform, only Nebraska has a specific corroboration requirement.[35] Yet where there is no corroborating witness, courts may provide juries with what are called *cautionary instructions.* They consist of warnings that rape is a charge easily made by the victim, that rape is a difficult charge to disprove, and that the testimony of the victim requires more careful scrutiny by the jury than does the testimony of the other witnesses in the trial.[36] Cautionary instructions are prejudicial and obsolete and should be eliminated where they are still used. Due process safeguards, such as the right to present witnesses, the right to counsel, and the presumption of innocence, ensure that the defendant will receive a fair trial.[37] Even without cautionary instructions or the actual requirement of them, this and other stereotypes still affect the way juries decide cases.[38] Thus, further reforms in the law are needed in those states that still use this approach.

What can be done to make the laws more effective?

While some states have abolished special corroboration rules and tried to narrow the physical resistance requirement, and other states have passed rape shield laws and narrowed the marital rape exception, much remains to be done. All special rules applied solely in rape trials must be done away with. There should be no corroboration requirement, no inferences drawn from the fact that a woman didn't go to the police right away, no physical resistance requirement (either to show lack of consent or the use of force), and no marital rape exception. Reform also requires enactment of rape shield laws in all states. There should be no inference because she has had prior sexual experiences, even with the defendant himself. Men who fail to respond to clear signals that a woman does not want to engage in sexual intercourse should be held responsible, as Professor Estrich has recommended.[39] The requirement that a woman be penetrated should also be abolished because women can still be humiliated and their privacy invaded by other forms of touching.

Reform must also reach beyond the law itself. Where necessary, police must be trained to avoid making salacious inquiries of women who have been raped. Courts must be sensitized to the humiliating consequences that may result from cross-examination of the victim concerning her past sexual history. Judges, police, and society-at-large need to be made aware of the unfairness of a system that still often fails to treat sexual assault as a crime against women, especially in cases of simple rape.

How do women go about changing rules in states where few or no reforms have occurred?

The first effort should take place in actual trials, where lawyers can ask the court to change judge-made rules. Feminist groups should contact prosecutors to try to convince them to raise these issues. Women victims should try to retain their own lawyers, in addition to the lawyer provided by the state, to represent them while they are testifying, and these lawyers should also challenge special rules applied solely to rape. If change cannot be achieved through the courts, a drive should be launched in the state legislatures to abolish special rules for rape.

Women should also seek new laws setting lower penalties for rape, penalties parallel to those imposed for aggravated assault, for instance. Although it sounds anomalous to urge lower sentences, this could actually help to assure more convictions. Experts are convinced that one reason the special evidence rules have been created, and so few convictions obtained, is the understandable reluctance to give a man a long sentence for the act of rape. If the penalties are lowered to a more realistic level, the emotional climate in favor of the accused will be reduced.

Can any practical measures be adopted to help the rape victim?

There are several practical steps women can take to avoid humiliating treatment in places where this is still a problem. Until these measures are undertaken, women will remain victims of the police, lawyers, and judges, in addition to sexual aggressors.

First, when a victim reports the crime, she should take a strong friend along—possibly one who is a lawyer or law student—someone who is cool, calm, sure of herself, and will stand up for her friend's rights at a time when she may be least able to do so. The role of the friend will be to help the victim assert her rights and to protect her against salacious questioning (such as forcing the victim to repeat all the details of the rape over and over to inordinately curious male police officers).

Second, a victim should refuse to answer questions about her past sex life. This is no one's business, and it is irrelevant to whether or not she has been raped. Even if the police insist that previous sexual experience is relevant because of the special evidence rules, the victim should reply that she will be challenging those rules and will not answer. If this does not suffice, she can go to the inquiring officers' superiors, if necessary.

Third, a victim should take a friend with her when the police send her to a doctor or hospital. The friend will help the victim object to improper treatment. One of the most frequent complaints rape victims make concerns the rude, abrupt, and hostile medical examinations they are given by police doctors. Such doctors often refuse to treat the victim but merely examine her to make sure that she has been raped. A victim should then also go to her own doctor who, presumably, will provide her with complete physical care.

An important service that women's groups could perform in this area is to meet with the police medical authorities to explain the problems with present procedures and attitudes, in order to get considerate treatment for rape victims. Another service could be to set up a panel of doctors (especially women doctors) who would be willing to give post-rape treatment in cases where police medical treatment is inadequate and women do not have family doctors they can go to immediately. The women's groups could publicize a phone number for rape victims; women who call would be given the name of a doctor who would see them. Groups can establish rape crisis centers. They could also train women who are on hand to accompany victims when they make their reports to the police; their services could be offered at the same time the woman calls in for a doctor's name. Women's groups would thus develop relationships with sympathetic doctors and gain firsthand knowledge of the types of abuse most prevalent at police stations. Experience in developing a service of the kind suggested could provide ammunition for later organizational efforts to make the police change their practices.

Fourth, a victim should discuss with the prosecutor the evidence he or she will be using at the time of the trial and the kinds of questions she, the victim, will be asked, both by the prosecutor and by the lawyer for the accused rapist. The prosecutor will need to know the answers to some of these questions in order to learn what information the defendant may try to use, but the victim can advise the prosecutor if she finds some of the questions humiliating and unnecessary and can request that such questions not be asked or that objections be raised to such questions by the defendant's lawyer. The victim should go over the prosecutor's head, if necessary.

Fifth, if she can afford it, a victim should try to get her own lawyer for the trial. This should be someone who will object if improper questions, based on the special evidence rules, are asked of the victim by the defendant's lawyer. Of course, the victim will have to answer if the court orders her to do so—

that is, if her lawyer has been unsuccessful in getting the court to rule that the particular questions are unnecessary.

Theoretically the prosecutor should raise objections, but she or he sometimes will not, and the result can be humiliating for the victim if she doesn't have a lawyer whose special role is to protect her interests. The victim's lawyer, in fact, should explain to the judge that he or she is there to protect the victim's reputation. The prosecutor or the victim's lawyer should also discuss with her in advance the kinds of evidence that will be used at the trial so that she understands what will happen once she is in the courtroom.

Sixth, women's groups should meet with police and prosecuting attorneys to explain what women find objectionable about present procedures, and they should seek systemic change in procedures.

Seventh, women should use employment discrimination laws to get more women into police forces, the district attorney's office, and on the bench. A major part of the problem is that rape victims frequently face an essentially all-male system from the moment they report the crime to the day of the trial. There are men in our society who believe that women have secret fantasies of being raped; there are men in our society who have secret fantasies of raping women. Victims of rape will face people with such biases less frequently only if women organize to affect change and equal employment representation in the field of criminal justice. But change in this area will not be accomplished easily. Women will be dealing with very conservative forces. Police, lawyers, and judges may be accustomed to handling rape cases in one way. They will not welcome reports from women that they themselves are mistreating rape victims and that reforms are necessary to correct such mistreatment. Nevertheless, this is the avenue that must be taken.

What can women's paralegal groups do in this area?

They can operate rape crisis centers to help women who have been raped. Such centers can start rape hotlines and can provide counseling (or referrals) for rape victims; advocates to help victims in their contacts with police, hospitals, and courts; companionship; general information; speakers' bureaus; classes in self-defense; and public relations information for the media.

Help for victims of rape and information on starting a rape

crisis center can be obtained by calling or writing the following organizations.

D.C. Rape Crisis Center
P.O. Box 21005
Washington, D.C. 20009
(202) 232-0203

National Coalition Against Sexual Assault
P.O. Box 21378
Washington, D.C. 20009
(202) 483-7165
(between 1 and 4 pm EST)

TREATMENT OF WOMEN IN PRISON

Historically, little attention was paid to the problems faced by women in prison.[40] Women comprised a small portion of the entire prison population, and since they were incarcerated primarily for nonviolent crimes, they constituted less of a threat. But women in prison are growing in numbers, and the problems they face are many. This has placed increasing pressure on a system that never had the capacity to adequately address the problems facing women in prison in the first place. Women have never received adequate medical care, they have been the victims of sexual harassment or rape, they have received less favorable education and work opportunities and other treatment than that afforded male prisoners, and they have suffered unique burdens associated with being the primary caregiver in their families. The advent of the AIDS crisis and the increasing incidence of alcohol and drug dependency among women prisoners have made it especially difficult to meet the needs of this population adequately. And overcrowding in prisons has exacerbated all of these problems.[41]

In the last decade, as the result of the proliferation of advocates for women prisoners, courts have intervened to protect their constitutional and statutory rights in a number of areas, although the major reforms occur in federal and state legislatures.

Who are the women in prison and why are their numbers increasing?

Demographic profiles reflect the following facts about women in prison. Forty-nine percent are African-American, and almost 13% are Hispanic.[42] Eighty percent of the women in prison are mothers, and 70% are single mothers.[43] Twenty-five percent of these women are pregnant or postpartum at some time during their incarceration.[44] Women in prison tend to be young: 73% are under the age of thirty.[45] Furthermore, 30% of women in state prisons have less than an eighth-grade education.[46] And the average female offender first started using alcohol or drugs between the ages of thirteen and fourteen.[47]

Most women in prison have committed nonviolent crimes. Their crimes are frequently economic in nature, such as prostitution and forgery.[48] One recent survey found that drug offenses and property crimes account for half of the crimes committed by women.[49] Similarly, the Federal Bureau of Prisons estimates that almost 60% of women in custody in the federal system are serving sentences for drug offenses.[50] In many cases, women are in prison because of new mandatory sentencing laws.

Do women retain any rights when they are incarcerated?

Yes. The courts have held that prisoners do not forfeit all rights by reason of their conviction and incarceration. The Eighth Amendment, which protects against cruel and unusual punishment, has been used to challenge harmful conditions of confinement,[51] and has afforded women the right to adequate medical care.[52] Title IX and the Equal Protection Clause have also been used to obtain educational, vocational, and work opportunities equal to those received by male prisoners.[53]

The Fourth Amendment, which protects people from unreasonable searches and seizures, has not been interpreted by courts to provide much protection to prisoners, however. For example, body and cell searches are permissible.[54] The Due Process Clause has been applied most effectively to challenge punishment for disciplinary violations,[55] but it has not afforded much protection to prisoners who undergo changes in their prison classification or cell assignments or who are transferred to a different facility, unless a prison regulation or state law has established a liberty interest. Prison officials can also limit religious expression so long as the policies are "reasonably related to legitimate penological interests."[56] For more information on this topic, see the ACLU handbook, *The Rights of Prisoners* (Southern Illinois University Press 1988).

What special problems do women face in prison?

While many of these concerns relate to both men and women, women face special problems.

Relations with children. Because so many incarcerated women are single mothers, the issue of family contact and reunification is of critical importance to them. Yet as of 1988, only ten state statutes attempted to address the difficulties facing incarcerated mothers and newborns.[57] In the absence of legislation and national standards, many women are deprived of contact with their children and many children are deprived of contact with their mothers. The child welfare system, which often takes children into foster care after women are convicted of crimes, frequently fails to keep mothers appraised of their children's whereabouts or involved in the process of reunification of the family unit. Since many states have only one prison for women, contact is also hindered by geographical separation.[58] Twelve percent of women in federal prisons are pregnant at any given time,[59] and those who give birth in prison are frequently separated from their child within forty-eight hours. The children are placed either with family members or in foster care. Only a few states allow women to retain physical custody of their children while incarcerated.[60]

Only two courts have ruled on whether women may retain custody after incarceration.[61] Both have held that incarcerated women do not have a right to the physical custody of their children.[62] In some states, however, women may keep their children in prison nurseries, or they may reside in community residences with their children.[63] In California, for example, the Mother-Infant Care Program allows low-security women prisoners, with children under six years of age, to serve their sentences in one of seven halfway houses statewide. Mothers receive parenting classes, counseling, vocational training, and college classes.[64]

Vocational training and work opportunities. Women in prison need vocational and educational training, yet these opportunities are limited. Most vocational programs provide training for traditionally female jobs with limited earning potential. Yet some of these programs have been successfully challenged under the Equal Protection Clause. In 1979, for example, women inmates in Michigan won an important lawsuit challenging discrimination at the Huron Valley Women's Facility.[65] The prison offered vocational training in only five broad areas—office occupations, food services, graphic arts, building maintenance, and general shop. Men had access to twenty different vocational programs, including automobile servicing, heating and air conditioning, machine shop, and drafting. Even where both men and women received training in the same broad area, the men's training was superior; where women were taught home cooking skills, men learned commercial cooking skills. As a result, the judge ordered Michigan to take comprehensive action, including upgrading the women's post-secondary education program, undertaking an extensive vocational counseling and testing program to inform women of the job possibilities and wage scales in traditionally male fields, giving women apprenticeship training and prison industry programs, as well as work passes and correctional camp work, and installing a legal education program for women.

Health care. Lack of health care is a major problem for most, if not all, women in prison. Many women are pregnant, have alcohol or drug dependence problems, need routine gynecological care, and suffer from depression, poor nutrition, or sexually transmitted diseases. AIDS has hit this population particularly hard. Although it is difficult to assess accurately the actual numbers of those who are HIV positive and those with AIDS because numbers reported to the federal government are based on self-reports by prison and correctional authorities, the National Institute of Justice estimated that there were 6,985 confirmed AIDS cases in federal, state, and county correctional systems in 1991.[66] This figure does not include all those who are HIV positive, which would substantially increase the number. Yet prison facilities do not provide the services necessary to meet the needs presented by these health care problems. The lack of national standards defining the level of care that should be provided exacerbates the problem.[67]

Pregnant women, in particular, face serious hardships. Correctional systems frequently have inadequate prenatal protocols, staff, equipment, and resident obstetricians or obstetrical care.[68] They deprive pregnant prisoners of adequate nutrition and exercise and subject them to inappropriate and dangerous methods of physical restraint.[69] The failure to provide appropriate services has resulted in infant deaths, late-term miscarriages, stillbirths, unnecessary hysterectomies, and emotional trauma resulting from the inability to secure medical care.[70]

Can male prison guards be employed in prisons in which women are incarcerated?

Yes. The ACLU opposes blanket bans on employing correctional personnel of one sex in a prison for members of the opposite sex. Such a policy constitutes sex discrimination and violates the civil rights and civil liberties of the employee. At the same time, the ACLU supports the personal privacy rights of prisoners who should not be forced to display their bodies to, or be subjected to pat downs, strip searches or body cavity searches by, correctional personnel of the opposite sex.

Prison officials can, and must, develop policies and practices that accommodate the rights of both employees and prisoners. Examples include using privacy curtains for prisoners to change behind; not assigning correctional personnel of the opposite sex to patrol the shower and bathroom areas; and requiring that all pat downs, strip searches, and body cavity searches be conducted by personnel of the same sex. There must be no adverse employment consequences for correctional personnel who are not permitted to perform these tasks in order to preserve the privacy rights of prisoners of the opposite sex. The restriction on employee duties with privacy implications should also be defined as narrowly as possible, consistent with those privacy rights.

How can conditions for women in prison be improved?

There are many avenues advocates may use to improve conditions for women in prison. Litigation is one of the most obvious methods and has enabled many women to enforce their rights. For example, in 1977 the first lawsuit brought on behalf of women in prison was brought in New York,[71] alleging that the prison's medical and record-keeping procedures caused substantial delays in medical care, that the methods of screening medical complaints were grossly inadequate, and that plaintiffs were denied adequate access to medical staff. The court ruled that these failures violated the constitution and ordered remedial measures.

More recently, pregnant women have initiated lawsuits seeking to improve prenatal and postpartum care. Legal Services for Prisoners with Children brought three suits in five years against California's largest women's prison and two California county jails.[72] One lawsuit, *Harris v. McCarthy*,[73] resulted in the creation of a pregnancy-related health care team, implementation of protocols for normal and high risk pregnancies, and identification of an obstetrics managing physician who would establish a general plan of care for every pregnant women in prison.[74]

In another lawsuit, *Rios v. Rowland*,[75] plaintiffs charged the California Department of Corrections (CDC) with failing to implement the Mother-Infant Care Program. Under the terms of the settlement agreement, the CDC is now required, among other things, to notify women of the program within one week after they are taken into custody; pregnant women are allowed to submit applications prior to delivery; and the CDC is required to maintain regional waiting lists of eligible prisoners. In the third lawsuit, *West v. Manson*,[76] prison officials agreed to provide pregnant prisoners with extra milk and bran, other special dietary supplements, prenatal vitamins, and access to prenatal classes. They also agreed not to impose physical restraints, such as the use of leg irons, without medical approval.

But litigation is not enough. National protocols need to be developed and implemented in both the federal and state prison systems. Advocacy groups can pressure their state legislatures to improve medical care and provide more and better drug treatment programs and programs for incarcerated mothers and their children. For a thorough bibliography on the subject, write the ACLU National Prison Project.

Who can women contact to get involved?

ACLU National Prison Project
1875 Connecticut Avenue, NW
Suite 400
Washington, DC 20036
(202) 234-4830

National Women's Law Center
Prison Project
1616 P Street, N.W.
Washington, DC 20036
(202) 328-5160

Legal Services for Prisoners with Children
1535 Mission St, 2nd Floor
San Francisco, CA 94103
(415) 255-7036

Aid to Imprisoned Mothers, Inc.
957 N. Highland Ave., N.E.
Atlanta, GA 30306
(404) 881-8291

Chicago Legal Aid to Incarcerated Mothers
205 W. Randolph Street, Suite 501
Chicago, Illinois 60606
(312) 332-5537

DISCRIMINATORY LAW ENFORCEMENT: PROSTITUTION

Do women and men have the same right to engage in commercial sexual activity?

Not in one sense. Female prostitutes can be sent to prison because they have had sex with male customers; their male sexual partners are generally not subject to any penalty for the very sex acts for which the women are incarcerated. The disparity results both from unequal laws and from unequal or selective enforcement of the laws. Some states have laws that make criminal only the act of having sex in return for the *receipt* of money. They do not make criminal the act of having sex in return for *giving* money.[77]

Other states do have laws making the act of giving money for sex a crime, albeit a lesser crime than receiving money for sex. But most officials who administer the criminal justice system are male, and male police, lawyers, and judges usually do not arrest, prosecute, or convict men for the crimes of "patronizing a prostitute" or "aiding and abetting." When enforcement is

attempted against male customers, there is often a strong public
outcry against the unfairness of harming their reputations.

Can unequal prostitution laws be challenged as violating constitutional principles?

Yes. The main theories are that women are denied their right
to equal protection, due process, and privacy under those laws.
For example, women prostitutes have argued that laws that
prohibit women from engaging in prostitution but do not prohibit men from patronizing a prostitute are unconstitutional
under both the federal and state constitutions. Such an argument has usually lost, generally on the theory that it is permissible to target sellers of an illicit service more heavily that buy-
ers.[78] Women prostitutes have also brought a different kind of
constitutional challenge to prostitution laws—one focused on
comparing the treatment of the female prostitute to that of the
male prostitute, rather than that of the male customer. This
approach has been more successful, but the result has been to
allow the prosecution of male prostitutes rather than to end the
prosecution of female prostitutes. For example, an Alaska court
used the Alaska ERA to strike the word "female" out of the
state prostitution law; that left the prostitution law still in existence and applying equally to both male and female prostitutes.
Similarly, a Massachusetts court interpreted a state law to reach
both male and female prostitutes in order to avoid the equal
protection problem that would exist if it continued to apply
only to women.[79]

Can the selective enforcement against women of prostitution laws that apply to both men and women be challenged?

Yes. There have been some cases in which female prostitutes
have successfully challenged a police department "selective
enforcement" policy pervasive in enforcing prostitution laws—
that is, the practice of arresting female prostitutes and not
arresting male customers where the law is broad enough to
allow arrest of both seller and buyer.[80] In one successful case,
there was police testimony stating it was department policy not
to arrest male customers of prostitutes, and the court ruled that
this violated the state ERA.[81] Others courts, however, have
condoned discriminatory enforcement. For example, in a California case, the court refused to find sex discrimination in

the pattern of enforcing the prostitution law primarily against female prostitutes and not against male customers. The theory was that it was permissible to concentrate on the "'profiteer,' rather than the customer, of commercial vice."[82]

What alternatives are there to criminal penalties for prostitution?

One possibility is decriminalization. Another is the licensing of prostitutes and other forms of regulation. Regulated prostitution has been permitted for years in Europe, with no noticeable harmful effect. One author who studied prostitution, with a specific focus on Boston, recommended that private, adult prostitution be decriminalized and that both solicitation and houses of prostitution be regulated through zoning and licensing laws.[83] There is no evidence that criminalization has decreased prostitution. As one author noted, "The laws and general strategy of repression seem to have had remarkably little effect on the prostitution economy."[84]

Yet another alternative is actively seeking enforcement of the various laws that can be used against the male customer, or enactment of new state laws to cover their participation in sex-for-money activities. A really firm campaign to do this—instead of challenging enforcement of the laws directed against women—might create a threat that would encourage some men to join the effort to get rid of the laws altogether.

Do prostitutes have a remedy for abuse by their patrons?

Although no state recognizes the beating of a prostitute by a patron to be domestic abuse, there is certainly evidence that many men hire prostitutes not only for sex, but to have a victim who is unable to complain to the police. Some shelters and other programs for battered women are starting to recognize this pattern and offer shelter and services to prostitutes.

Should prostitutes be subjected to mandatory testing for venereal diseases, such as syphilis, gonorrhea, or HIV, when their male customers are not subject to such testing?

No. This is both silly science and bad law. Venereal disease can spread from the man to the woman just as it can spread from the woman to the man. Testing only one partner in a sexual transaction obviously does little to halt the spread of the disease.

Although twenty-four states in 1991 had some sort of mandatory HIV testing of prostitutes and other sex offenders,[85] mandatory testing of prostitutes is vulnerable to legal challenge on equal protection, sex discrimination, and Fourth Amendment grounds.[86] Moreover, as a practical matter, targeting prostitutes for forced testing simply will not work as a prevention strategy. If there is any group that will be driven underground by such a policy, it is prostitutes.

An alternative to mandatory testing of prostitutes and their male customers would be a program of required venereal disease counseling (which would offer testing on a voluntary basis) for both prostitutes and their customers, similar to the programs required of persons convicted of driving while intoxicated. As with any counseling and testing program, confidentiality and antidiscrimination protections should be enforced.

NOTES

1. Shipp, E. R., *Sexual Assault Case: St. John's Verdict Touches Off Debate*, N.Y. Times, July 25, 1991, at B1.
2. Estrich, S., *Real Rape* 8 (1987). This chapter has relied heavily upon her book *Real Rape* (Harvard University Press, 1987) (hereinafter Estrich).
3. Estrich, *supra* note 2.
4. It is very important to recognize, however, that African-American men have often been falsely accused of raping white women. *See* Davis, A., *Women, Race and Class* 172–201 (1983) (hereinafter Davis). The fraudulent rape charge, as Ms. Davis explained, "stands out as one of the most formidable artifices invented by racism." *Id.* at 173.
5. Some states have made rape a gender-neutral crime; both perpetrators and victims may be men and women. *See, e.g.*, Ill. Rev. Stat. ch. 38, para. 12–13(a)(l) (1987).
6. Estrich at 83.
7. *See* Conn. Gen. Stat. Ann. § 53a-68 (1975), as repealed by acts 1969, No. 828, § 69, No. 74-131; Fla. Stat. Ann. § 794.022 (1965), as added by L. 1974, ch. 74-121; Iowa Code Ann. § 782.4 (West 1950), as repealed and re-enacted by acts 1974, ch. 1271, § l; Mich. Comp. Laws § 750.520(h)(1968), as amended by L. 195, ch. 109, § 6; N.M. Stat. Ann. § 40A-9-25 (1953), as amended by L. 1975, ch. 109, § 6;

N.Y. Penal Law § 130.16 (McKinney 1975), as added by L. 1974, ch. 14, § 1 (under this enactment corroboration no longer is required unless incapacity to consent is at issue); Pa. Stat. Ann. tit. 18, § 3106 (1973), as amended by acts 1976, No. 53, § 2; Wash. Rev. Code, ch. 9, § 79 (1963), as amended by L. 1975 (1st ex. sess.), ch. 14, § 2. This list is current as of 1984.

8. Cal. Evid. Code § 782 (West 1966), as added by stats. 1974, ch. 569, § l; Colo. Rev. Stat. Ann. § 18-3-407 (1973), as repealed and re-enacted by L. 1975, at 630, § l; Fla. Stat. Ann. § 794.022 (1965), as amended by L. 1974. ch. 74-121; Haw. Rev. Stat. § 37-707 (1968), as amended by L. 1974, ch. 83; Ind. Code Ann. §§ 35-l-32.5.1 *et seq.* (Burns 1975), as added by acts 1975, ch. 322; Iowa Code Ann. § 782 (West 1950) as added by acts 1974, ch. 1271; Mich. Comp. Laws Ann. § 750.520j (1968) as amended by acts 1974, No. 266; Mont. Codes Ann. § 94-5-503 (Supp. 1975), as amended by L. 1975, ch. 2, 129; Neb. Rev. Stat. § 28-408.05 (1975), as amended by L. 1975, L.B. 23, § 9; Nev. Rev. Stat. §§ 48.2, 50.4 (1968), as amended by acts 1975, at 600; N.M. Stat. Ann. § 40A-9-26 (1953), as amended by L. 1975, ch. 109, § 7; N.Y. Crim. Proc. Code § 60-42 (McKinney 1965), as added by L. 1975, ch. 230, § l; N.D. Cent. Code §§ 12.1-20-14, -15 (1976), as added by L. 1975, ch. 118; Ore. Rev. Stat., § 163.475 (1975), as amended by L. 1975, ch. 743, § 2; Pa. Stat. Ann., tit. 18, § 3104 (Purdon 1973), as amended by acts 1976, No. 53, § l; S.D. Codified Laws Ann. § 22-45-l (1969), as added by L. 1975, ch. 169, § 3; Tenn. Code Ann. § 40-2445 (1975), as added by L. 1975, ch. 44, § l; Tex. Penal Code § 21.13 (1974), as added by Acts 1975, ch. 203, § 3; Wash. Rev. Code § 9.79 (1961), as amended by L. 1975 (1st ex. sess.), ch. 14. See also Fed. R. Evid. 412. This list is updated as of 1984.
9. *Brown v. State*, 106 N.W. 536, 539 (Wis. 1906).
10. Estrich at 38–40.
11. Estrich at 59.
12. Estrich at 60–71.
13. Estrich at 60–62.
14. Estrich at 61.
15. *Id*.
16. Estrich at 102.
17. *See* Dubois, D., *Prompt Complaint*, 53 Brooklyn L. Rev. 1087, 1101 (1988).
18. Fischer, K., *Defining the Boundaries of Admissible Expert Psychological Testimony on Rape Trauma Syndrome*, U. of Ill. L. Rev. 691, 695 at n.34 (hereinafter Fischer).
19. *Id*.
20. *Id*. at 714.

21. Fischer at 712.

22. *Id.* at 715.

23. *Id.* at 725.

24. Fed. R. Evid. at 412(b)(2)(A); *See generally* Winters, K., *Federal Rape-Shield Statute,* 43 U. of Miami L. Rev. 947 (1989) (hereinafter Winters).

25. Fed. R. Evid. 412(b)(2)(B). *See generally* Winters at 959–60.

26. Fed. R. Evid. 404(b).

27. While sexist assumptions and practices cause harm most often to victims of rape or attempted rape, their rights can be protected if statutes and courts treat rape as a form of sexual assault. The ACLU recommends that standards and procedures be developed to apply to all forms of sexual assault and that the phrase "sexual assault" be used instead of "rape" in policy statements and laws in order to remove special legal disabilities from rape complainants.

28. West, R., *Equality Theory, Marital Rape and the Promise of the Fourteenth Amendment,* 42 Fla. L. Rev. 45, 64 (1990) (hereinafter West).

29. *Id.*

30. West at 71.

31. Comment, *For Better or Worse: Marital Rape,* 15 N. Ky. L. Rev. 611, 621–22 & n. 72 (1988).

32. West at 46.

33. Estrich at 43 (citing Note, *Corroborating Charges of Rape,* 67 Colum. L. Rev. (1967) at 1137–38).

34. Estrich at 47.

35. Fischer at n.36.

36. Morris, A., *Cautionary Instructions,* 1988 Duke L. J. 154 at 157 and n.20 (1988).

37. *People v. Rincon-Pineda,* 14 Cal. 3d 864, 878, 538 P.2d 247 (Cal. 1975).

38. *See, e.g.,* LaFree, G., *Rape and Criminal Justice: The Social Construction of Sexual Assault* (1989) at 201–3.

39. Estrich at 95–104.

40. The authors gratefully acknowledge the help of Alexa Freeman, of the ACLU Prison Project, Brenda Smith, director of the Women in Prison Project of the National Women's Law Center, and Ellen Barry, director of Legal Services for Prisoners with Children, for their invaluable assistance with this section.

41. In 1989 the female prison population grew by 24% and by another 7% in the first half of 1990. "Women in Prison: Growing Numbers, Growing Problems," National Women's Law Center, 1875 Connecticut Ave, NW, Suite 400, Washington, D.C. 20036 (hereinafter Growing

Numbers) at l. In 1989, for example, the number of women at the California Correctional Institution for Women was more that 220% over design capacity. E. Barry, L., *Recent Developments*, 12 Harv. Women's L.J. 189 (1989) at 195 (hereinafter Barry). In contrast, the male prison population grew only 12%. *Id. See also* Estimates and Statistical Analysis, Offender Information Services Branch, California Department of Corrections, Weekly Report, 1989.

42. Women Prisoners: A Profile. National Women's Law Center at 1 (hereinafter Profile).

43. Growing Numbers at l.

44. Profile at 1.

45. *Id.*

46. *The Female Offender*, Am. Correctional Ass'n. 3 (1990).

47. *Id.* at 6.

48. Barry at 190.

49. Growing Numbers at 1.

50. *Id.*

51. *Rhodes v. Chapman*, 452 U.S. 337 (1981).

52. *Estelle v. Gamble*, 429 U.S. 97 (1976), *reh'g den.*, 429 U.S. 1066 (1977).

53. *Glover v. Johnson*, 721 F. Supp. 808 (E.D. Mich. 1989); *Canterino v. Wilson*, 546 F. Supp. 174 (W.D. Ky. 1982); *Canterino v. Barber*, 564 F. Supp. 711 (W.D. Ky. 1983); *Bukhari v. Hutto*, 487 F. Supp. 1162 (E.D. Va. 1980).

54. *Bell v. Wolfish*, 441 U.S. 520 (1979).

55. *Wolff v. McDonnell*, 418 U.S. 539 (1974).

56. *O'Lone v. Estate of Shabazz*, 482 U.S. 342 (1987).

57. Deck, M. *Incarcerated Mothers and Their Infants: Separation or Legislation?* 29 B.C.L. Rev. 689 at 690 n.12 (1988) (hereinafter Deck).

58. *See Pitts v. Meese*, 684 F.2d 303 (D.D.C. 1987); *Pitts v. Thornburgh*, 866 F.2d 1450 (D.C. Cir. 1989).

59. *Behind Bars, Keeping Mother and Child Together*, N.Y. Times, Sept. 23, 1990, at _____.

60. Only New York currently allows children to remain in a nursery until the child reaches one year of age. N.Y. Correct. Law. 611 (McKinney 1968). The following states allow alternative placement of mothers with children in halfway house settings. *E.g.*, Cal. Penal Code § 34103425 (West 1982); Conn. Gen. Stat. Ann. § 18-69 a; Ill. Ann. Stat. ch. 38, para. 1003-6-2(g) (Smith-Hurd 1982); N.C. Gen. Stat. § 148-44 (1983); W. Va. Code § 28-5-8 (1986). *See* Deck at 700.

61. *Southerland v. Thigpen*, 784 F.2d 713 (5th Cir. 1986); *Pendergrass v. Toombs*, 546 P.2d 1103 (Or. App. 1976).

62. *Id.*

63. Deck at 699.
64. *Rios v. Rowland,* Civ. No. 330211 (Super. Ct. City and County of Sacramento, filed June 5, 1985).
65. *Glover v. Johnson,* 478 F. Supp. 1075 (E.D. Mich. 1979). For the subsequent history of this case, see *Glover v. Johnson,* 721 F. Supp. 808 (E.D. Mich. 1989).
66. "1991 Update: AIDS in Correctional Facilities," National Institute of Justice: Issues and Practices (U.S. Dep't. of Justice, July 1991) at 12–13.
67. Gaballe and Stone, *The New Focus on Medical Care Issues in Women's Prison Cases,* 15 National Prison Project 1 (1988).
68. *Jones v. Dyer,* No. H-114154-0 (Cal. Super. Ct., Alameda County); *Yeager v. Smith,* No. CV-F-87-493-REC (E.D. Cal., filed Sept. 2, 1987).
69. Barry at 190.
70. Barry at 196–201.
71. *Todaro v. Ward,* 431 F. Supp. 1129 (S.D.N.Y. 1977), *aff'd,* 565 F.2d 48 (2d Cir. 1977).
72. *Harris v. McCarthy,* No. 85-6002 JGD (C.D. Cal. filed Sept. 11, 1985); *Jones v. Dyer,* No. H-114154-0 (Cal. Super. Ct., Alameda County, filed Feb. 25, 1986); *Yeager v. Smith,* No. CV-F-87-493-REC (E.D. Cal. filed Sept. 2, 1987). *E.g.,* Barry, *supra.*
73. No. 85-6002 JGD (C.D. Cal. filed Sept. 11, 1985).
74. Barry at 196–97.
75. No. 330211 and 333240 (Super. Ct. of Cal. 1990).
76. No. H83-366 (D. Conn. filed May 9, 1983).
77. *Commonwealth v. King,* 372 N.E.2d 196 (Mass. 1977), discusses one such law. The Massachusetts legislature later rewrote the statute to cover the customer, too, as discussed in *Commonwealth v. An Unnamed Defendant,* 22 Mass. App. 230, 492 N.E.2d 1184 (1986). The Hawaii statute discussed in *State v. Tookes,* 67 Haw. 608, 699 P.2d 983 (1985), also appears to apply only to prostitutes and not to customers.
78. *State v. Tookes,* 699 P.2d 983, 988 (Haw. 1985); *Commonwealth v. King,* 372 N.E.2d 196, 204 (Mass. 1977); *See State v. Sandoval,* 649 P.2d 485, 487 (N.M. 1982) (upholding law that has higher penalties for prostitution than for patronizing prostitutes).
79. *Plas v. State,* 598 P.2d 966 (Alaska 1979); *King, supra,* note 78 at n.1.
80. *Commonwealth v. An Unnamed Defendant,* 492 N.E.2d 1184, 1186 (Mass. 1986); *Riemer v. Jensen,* 17 Crim. L. Rep. 2042 (Cal. 1975). *See King, supra* note 78, n.1, 372 N.E.2d at 207 (proof of failure to prosecute male prostitutes would be grounds for dismissing action seeking to prosecute female prostitutes).

81. *Commonwealth v. An Unnamed Defendant,* 492 N.E.2d 1184, 1186 (Mass. 1986).

82. *People v. Superior Court,* 562 P.2d 1315, 1320 (Cal. 1977); *See also In re Dora P.,* 68 A.D.2d 719, 418 N.Y.S.2d 597 (1979).

83. Milman, *New Rules for the Oldest Profession: Should We Change Our Prostitution Laws?,* 3 Harv. Women's L.J. 1, 63–64 (1980).

84. Hobson, *Uneasy Virtue: The Politics of Prostitution and the American Reform Tradition* 156 (1988).

85. Wall Street Journal, Jan. 3, 1991, at B2.

86. *But see People v. Adams,* 149 Ill.2d 331, 597 N.E.2d 574 (1992) (upholding constitutionality of testing).

VIII
Education

In 1837 Oberlin College made history by admitting women to a college for the first time in the United States. Yet, admission did not ensure equality. At first, women were considered too weak minded to take the same course work as men—it was thought their minds couldn't assimilate "men's" fare. The college preserved a clear aura of male dominance in other areas as well. Women were required to wash the male students' clothes, care for their rooms, and serve them at table. Nor were women permitted to speak publicly. Lucy Stone, the famous feminist and an early Oberlin graduate, refused to write a commencement essay because a male student would have read it to the audience.[1]

Given this beginning, it is not too surprising that academia is still afflicted with deep-seated but largely unrecognized sexism. Although male dominance continues today, women are challenging it with new—though limited—legal weapons.

Are there clearly defined national rights against discrimination in education?

Yes, but with certain limitations. In the 1970s Congress finally discovered the subject of sex discrimination in the nation's schools and colleges and passed a variety of laws designed to end sex discrimination in education. These laws, however, have some limitations that do not exist in the employment discrimination laws. The most far-reaching of the education laws—Title IX of the Education Amendments of 1972 Act (usually referred to as Title IX)[2]—forbids sex discrimination in public and private schools receiving federal money, and thus provides important protection to women in academia. But, as initially passed, it specifically allowed several forms of discrimination, and Congress has added to this list over the years. Also, the agency enforcing the law, originally the Department of Health, Education and Welfare, now the Department of Education, has permitted some forms of discrimination in its regulations. Until 1979 it was not even clear whether women could sue discriminatory schools (they can).

Then in 1984 the Supreme Court dealt Title IX (and similar civil rights laws) a major blow. The Court limited the scope of the law by ruling that the particular program or activity in which the discrimination took place was not covered by the law unless it directly received federal funding. This cramped reading of the law was remedied in 1988, when the Congress passed the Civil Rights Restoration Act over President Reagan's veto. This act restored the earlier interpretation of Title IX. Once an institution receives federal funding for any one of its programs or activities, it is prohibited from discriminating in *all* its programs and activities. However, in the interim, there was an absence of the major litigation that would have established a national definition of women's rights in the academic world, as lawsuits under the comparable employment discrimination laws have done.

Other laws passed by Congress are much narrower in scope than Title IX or suffer from other limitations. One law, an amendment to the Public Health Service Act,[3] addresses only the problem of sex discrimination against students in the health professions. Another law, Title II of the 1976 Amendments to the Vocational Education Act of 1963,[4] dealt with the important problem of sex discrimination in vocational schools. Congress also amended Title IV of the 1964 Civil Rights Act[5] to allow the attorney general to sue public schools and colleges for sex discriminatory policies. In a rare action, the attorney general used the law in 1990 to challenge a state college, the Virginia Military Institute, for its practice of barring all women from attending.

In yet another law, the Equal Educational Opportunities Act of 1974,[6] Congress acted ambiguously. In a grand preface, it declared that "all children enrolled in public schools are entitled to equal educational opportunity without regard to race, color, sex, or national origin." But the small print inexplicably allowed various forms of sex discrimination (e.g., while the law prohibits discrimination against teachers and staff on the basis of race, it fails to mention deliberate segregation by sex or employment discrimination based on sex).[7] Despite the wide variety of new laws passed in the 1970s, then, the gaps in coverage and the relative lack of litigation under them has led to an inadequate definition of what constitutes illegal sex discrimination in academia, or worse, to explicit permission to practice some forms of sex discrimination.

The picture has been slightly different in the area of constitutional doctrine. As chapter 1 indicates, the Equal Protection Clause of the Fourteenth Amendment can be used to attack discrimination carried out by state or local governments. Consequently, women can sue public elementary, junior high, and senior high schools, and state colleges and universities for practicing sex discrimination in violation of the Fourteenth Amendment and have done so. The courts' reaction to these lawsuits has been mixed.

Although many laws exist to attack sex discrimination in academia, there is still much work to be done. Some important examples are the *de facto* sex segregation in many vocational, professional, and graduate education programs, which in turn leads to and reinforces existing sex segregation in the employment world; the small number of women in top administrative and faculty positions; and the exclusion of women from many sports or the severe underfunding and lack of support for other sports of interest to women. These problems are exacerbated by the tendency of standardized tests—used to determine admissions, placement, and the allocation of scholarships—to discriminate against women.

The section below discusses the rights of women to equal educational opportunity under the Equal Protection Clause and the various federal statutes, with a focus on Title IX. In reading this section, the reader should bear in mind that although the issue discussed may refer to a particular statute or to the Equal Protection Clause, it may be possible in future lawsuits to assert the same right under other statutes or possibly under state laws as well. Thus the function of the first section is to alert readers to different kinds of discrimination that are practiced in academia. The second section describes procedures for seeking redress under different laws, as well as the remedies that are available (e.g., school admission, job promotion, attorneys' fees).

RIGHTS TO EQUAL EDUCATIONAL OPPORTUNITY UNDER THE EQUAL PROTECTION CLAUSE AND FEDERAL STATUTES

Both public and private schools play a vital role in educating women in this country. Despite many differences between them in ideology, educational philosophy, and affiliation, public and private schools share one trait: both frequently discriminate against women. However, all laws do not apply equally to all schools, and distinctions must be kept in mind when considering whether a particular practice at a particular school is illegal under a particular law. The Equal Protection Clause applies to public, but not private, schools because of the requirement of "state action." Similarly Title IV of the 1964 Civil Rights Act and the Equal Educational Opportunities Act of 1974 apply only to public schools. On the other hand, Title IX applies to most educational institutions that receive federal money and therefore reaches the discriminatory practices of many private schools and colleges as well as public ones. Laws dealing with discrimination in schools for health professionals and in vocational education likewise apply only to institutions that receive federal money. Thus, those private institutions that do not receive federal money can discriminate with impunity.

Do women have the right to attend all-male public schools?
Under the federal Equal Protection Clause, the answer has been sometimes yes, sometimes no. In an important 1982 case brought by the ACLU the Supreme Court ruled that the Mississippi University for Women could not exclude men from its School of Nursing.[8] Justice O'Conner, the first woman to sit on the Supreme Court, wrote the Court's opinion and decisively rejected the state's "educational affirmative action" rationale for its ban on men. She noted that most nurses are women, so that the all-female policy reinforced traditional stereotypes of nursing as a woman's field. She also pointed out that there is evidence that the exclusion of men from nursing helps to depress nurses' wages—in other words, that the all-female policy may actually work to women's disadvantage.

There have been other favorable cases as well. Women scored an important victory when they succeeded in desegregating the previously all-male University of Virginia at Charlottesville, the most prestigious school of the state university system.[9] High school students knocked down the all-male barrier at the highly rated Stuyvesant High School in New York City. Concerned parents forced the equally prestigious Boston Latin and Girls Latin public schools to use the same admissions standards for boys and girls, thus allowing some girls into the over 300-year-old, formerly all-male Boston Latin.[10] And a San Francisco girl won the right to attend Lowell, a top academic high school that imposed a higher admissions standard for girls than for boys in order to equalize the number of male and female students. The school's justification for this discrimination—that a balance of the sexes was essential for a good high school education—was found insufficient.[11]

In another situation the plaintiff was not successful when she relied on the federal Equal Protection Clause, but several years later another group of young women achieved an important victory by using their state equal rights amendment. In 1976 a Philadelphia girl was denied admission to the all-male Central High, one of the city's two academic high schools and the one with the best reputation and the most prestigious graduates. The other academic school, the all-female Girls High, was good but, as its name suggests, not quite on a par with "Central." The appellate court ruled in favor of "separate but equal." It ignored the superior science facilities and reputation of Central and said instead that Central and Girls High were comparable in quality, academic standing, and prestige. However, virtually no factual record was developed in that case; it was litigated on the legal principle rather than on the facts. The Supreme Court agreed with this result but gave no reasons.[12] In 1983, with a more complete record of the differences between the two schools, the state courts ruled in favor of the plaintiffs under the state's ERA and required Central High School to admit girls.[13]

More recently, a district court in Michigan ruled that the opening of an all-male academy by the Detroit Board of Education could be blocked since it was likely that the operation of such a facility would violate both the federal and Michigan Constitutions, as well as Title IX and several state laws.[14] The policy of sex segregation was justified by the board on the grounds that the academy was experimental, and the data collected from the three-year project would benefit female students as well. Furthermore, the board argued that coeducational programs had failed to adequately meet the needs of young urban males. Yet the board's claim that "the coeducational factor" was causing existing educational programs to fail was discounted by the court, as school officials had presented "no evidence that the educational system is failing urban males because females attend schools with males." In fact, the court observed, "the educational system is also failing females." The court did not reach the question of the constitutionality of separate-but-equal schools since no all-female academy was yet available to students. However, in barring women from admission to the new academy and in failing to provide an all-female facility, the court ruled that board was denying the rights of women to equal educational opportunities.

Where does this leave us? It is hard to say. First, the *Mississippi University* decision was limited. It outlawed only the ban on men at the nursing school and did not explicitly reach the ban on men in the rest of the university. Second, since Mississippi did not have an all-male school, and Detroit did not have an all-female academy, the question of whether separate-but-equal schools violate the Constitution remains unanswered. Further litigation will be needed on these issues before we know where the Supreme Court stands.

Perhaps motivated by the desire to keep the races from mixing sexually, some school districts, faced with court orders to desegregate by race, put all the girls (black and white) in separate schools from all the boys (black and white). Under the Equal Educational Opportunities Act of 1974, federal courts have struck down such plans by southern school districts to use sex segregation in order to avoid complete racial integration.[15] So far this law has been successfully applied only in the context of racial integration, but women may try to use it to gain admission to other sex-segregated schools. Another possible statute to use in attacking sex segregation in schools is Title IV of the Civil Rights Act of 1964.

Title IX also prohibits one-sex schools, but only undergraduate, graduate, professional, and vocational schools that receive federal funding are affected. Other single-sex schools are theoretically permitted to exclude the other sex. However, Title IX yields to the Equal Protection Clause when the two are in conflict.

Is single-sex education ever preferable for women?

Feminists are divided on this issue. In 1990 the board of trustees of Mills College, a women's college in California, attempted to follow a growing trend in single-sex institutions of higher education and go "coed." As is often the case, this step was not contemplated for ideological or pedagogical reasons but rather as a means of survival; applications to single-sex schools are way down. There was a hue and cry from the student body, many of whom claimed that women do better in an all-female environment, and the plan was abandoned. The students' theory was based in part on studies done in the 1970s that showed that women who had graduated from single-sex colleges in the previous decades had achieved a disproportionate number of leadership roles in later life.[16] However, at the time those women attended women's colleges many of the prestigious colleges—including Harvard, Yale, and Princeton—as well as many smaller, quality colleges and the military service academies, did not admit women at all. Thus, the most talented women of previous generations who desired to attend highly selective institutions often had little choice but to attend all women's colleges, such as the so-called Seven Sisters (many of which are now coed). These studies of success in later life have not been replicated since the barriers to women in the once all male schools have largely come down.

Furthermore, while the idea of a supportive all-female atmosphere continues to appeal to some women, it does not jibe with the long-range goal of complete sexual equality. It implies that women cannot compete with men in an academic setting, and we know that is simply not the case. Nowadays, the vast majority of talented young women are voting with their feet by simply not applying to single-sex colleges in sufficient numbers to keep them viable.

What schools are prohibited from discriminating by Title IX?

Title IX covers any school—from the preschool through graduate level—that receives federal funds. It applies to religious schools, but specific practices may be exempt, e.g., if a particular religion's tenets require the sex discrimination the school practices. (If the religion's tenets do not require sex discrimination, then the school's practices are reached.)

What discriminatory practices does Title IX prohibit?
Title IX provides:

No person in the United States shall, on the basis of sex, be excluded from participation in, be denied the benefits of, or be subject to discrimination under any education program or activity receiving Federal financial assistance.

In 1975, after a three-year delay, the Department of Health, Education and Welfare (HEW, the agency that administered Title IX until 1980[17]) finally published regulations defining which discriminatory practices are forbidden.[18] Some of the regulations are comprehensive. Others are clearly compromises and thus arguably unconstitutional since they specifically permit some forms of discrimination. The most important regulations will be discussed below.

Admissions

Does Title IX prohibit sex discrimination in school admissions processes?
In some but not all types of schools. Title IX does not prohibit discriminatory practices in preschool, elementary, and secondary schools, whether public or private; private undergraduate colleges; public undergraduate colleges that have always been single-sex institutions;[19] and military schools, which are defined as schools training individuals for the United States military services or for the merchant marines.[20] At least as far as Title IX is concerned, such schools may either exclude women completely, set up quota systems to limit their enrollment, or demand that women meet higher admissions standards then men. Public and private vocational schools at all levels, already integrated public undergraduate colleges, and public and private graduate and professional schools are prohibited from using discriminatory admissions policies.

Despite these gaps in Title IX coverage, however, there are other ways to attack single-sex policies. Thus, if a woman is denied admission to an all-male school protected by Title IX she should still sue the school under the Equal Protection Clause and other statutes, if possible, and in the process attack the Title IX provision as unconstitutional. In fact, this is what Joe Hogan did in his successful effort to attend the Mississippi University for Women. The Supreme Court accepted his view that the Equal Protection Clause guaranteed his right to attend the school, despite the Title IX language.

Of course, once schools admit women, they must treat them in a nondiscriminatory manner in all other respects.

School Organizations

Does Title IX permit any school organizations to discriminate?

Yes. Although most school organizations and activities are forbidden to discriminate on the basis of sex, a 1974 amendment to Title IX permitted college sororities and fraternities to limit membership to one sex and allowed such groups as the YMCA, YWCA, Girl Scouts, Boy Scouts, and Camp Fire Girls to exclude members of the opposite sex.[21] Congress amended the law once again in 1976 to exempt certain American Legion activities, such as Boys State, Boys Nation, Girls State, and Girls Nation. The 1976 amendment also permits schools to sponsor mother-daughter and father-son activities with the condition that if such activities are provided for boys, girls must be given the opportunity for "reasonably comparable" activities.[22] Although Title IX allows this and other forms of sex discrimination, it does not protect these actions from constitutional attack under the Equal Protection Clause or from attack under Title IX's implementing regulations.[23]

Campus Living

Does Title IX permit schools to discriminate in providing housing for students?

Yes and no. Title IX specifically allows the practice of segregating living facilities by sex. This is not a clear-cut issue; many students prefer sex-segregated dormitories, and a prohibition would eliminate the possibility of choice in this area. Others want coed dorms, and they will not be helped by Title IX, although the law does not limit the school's option to provide integrated living facilities either for all students or for students who wish accommodations of this kind.

Do college women have the right to equal treatment in campus housing rules?

Yes. The Title IX regulations do require schools that provide housing for men to provide housing for women that is comparable in quality and cost.[24] For instance, a university cannot house its male students in two-room private suites while crowding its female students into dormitory doubles. The number of housing units made available to women must be in proportion to the number of women who apply for housing. In addition, schools must take steps to ensure that off-campus housing is available to men and women on the same terms. Also the regulations for Title IX explicitly prohibit colleges from applying different housing rules and regulations to men and women, charging them different fees, or offering them different benefits or services, such as free cleaning for men only.[25] On-campus residency requirements, curfews, and other parietal rules for women only are now also illegal.

Financial Aid and Tuition

May educational institutions award scholarships that are explicitly restricted to one sex or discriminate in the award of financial aid in other ways?

The Title IX regulations forbid sex discrimination in financial assistance.[26] Schools may not give male and female students different types or amounts of financial aid, nor may they use different eligibility requirements for males and females. For instance, a school may not give scholarships to all men with a 3.0 average but only to women who have a 3.5 average, nor may it award larger scholarships to men than to women with the same financial need.

Once again the regulations do not forbid certain forms of discrimination. A school may administer sex-restricted scholarships and fellowships established by will or trust or by foreign governments (e.g., the Rhodes Scholarships, which were once restricted to men) with the provision that the overall effect must not be to discriminate against women. Women who are otherwise eligible for financial aid must not be denied aid because of a shortage of unrestricted funds. Thus, the school cannot make scholarships available to men with less need or lower academic qualifications simply because there are more endowed scholarships available for men.

If a women who is married to a nonresident attends a state university in her home state, can she be forced to pay nonresident tuition rates because of her husband's out-of-state residence?

Not if she can show she is in fact a resident of the state. State universities often charge nonresidents higher tuition rates than residents pay. In determining residency, some universities apply the common-law rule that a married woman's residence follows that of her husband instead of the modern view that each may establish his or her own residence. As a result, married women students sometimes discover they are classified as nonresidents for tuition purposes although they may have lived in the state since birth. (Of course, nonresident women benefit from such rules when they become eligible for lower in-state tuition by marrying a state resident. Either way, such rules discriminate on the basis of sex and marital status.) This practice can be attacked on several grounds.

Married women at state universities in Pennsylvania who had been charged out-of-state tuition because their husbands were nonresidents sued the universities and demanded a return of the excess tuition. Rejecting the universities' argument that administrative convenience and the preservation of fiscal integrity required the residency rule, the judge decided that the rule violated the Equal Protection Clause. He ordered the universities to stop presuming that out-of-state husbands determined the residence of their wives and to refund excess charges to any woman who could prove she was entitled to the lower in-state rate.[27]

Another avenue of relief may be available under state law. At least one state, California, has passed a law providing that for tuition purposes a married women may establish her own residence without regard to that of her husband.[28] In addition, Title IX regulations specifically forbid sex discrimination in applying residency rules to determine eligibility for in-state tuition or fees.[29] Thus a state could not apply the common-law rule that a wife's domicile is that of her husband.

Coursework and Textbooks

Do girls have the right to take the same courses as boys and to refuse to take girls-only courses?

Yes. With a few exceptions, the Title IX regulations forbid excluding a girl (or boy) from a class or activity because of sex or offering separate courses to girls and boys. This applies to courses in health, physical education, industrial arts, business, vocational and technical subjects, home economics, and music as well as traditionally integrated courses. Schools may group students in physical education according to physical ability and may separate girls and boys for participating in wrestling, boxing, rugby, ice hockey, football, basketball, and other contact sports. Sex education classes may also be held in separate sessions for girls and boys in elementary and secondary schools but not in post-secondary education.[30] Choruses that are selected on the basis of vocal range are permitted to be one—or predominantly one—sex.[31]

A few girls have succeeded in challenging discriminatory course assignments—such as metalworking for boys and home economics for girls—under the Equal Protection Clause.[32] Under this theory, girls cannot be forced to take a course that is required for girls but not for boys. The threat of a lawsuit may motivate a recalcitrant board of education to eliminate illegal course segregation.[33]

May school counselors steer girls into courses "suitable" for females or advise them to prepare only for jobs that women have traditionally held?

No. This common practice violates Title IX regulations. Counselors may not indirectly preserve male-only courses, like woodworking, by channeling girls into more "feminine" fields, or discourage girls from taking what may be considered masculine subjects like physics or calculus.[34] However, such discrimination is often insidious and difficult to eradicate because counselors are unaware of their own biases or honestly believe they are merely being realistic about the job opportunities for women. Schools that find that a disproportionate number of boys or girls are enrolled in a particular course or program of study are required to investigate the situation in the school's counseling and testing program, but it is doubtful that such self-monitoring is very effective.

Many of the standardized vocational interest tests employed by counselors to assist people in making the "right" career choice have a built-in sex bias. Tests often use different questionnaires for males and females or evaluate boys' and girls' answers according to different standards so that a boy and a girl giving the same answers would get different career advice. They may rate a boy's aptitude for jobs traditionally held by men and a girl's for jobs traditionally held by women, rather than rating both boys and girls for all jobs. Such discriminatory tests and counseling materials are now forbidden by Title IX regulations. Parents' and women's groups should investigate the tests used in their community schools to make sure these discriminatory tests are not still being used.

May schools use textbooks that show women only in traditionally female jobs or that contain other sexual stereotypes?
Yes. Although gender-based textbooks tend to socialize girls into subservient "female" roles and to reinforce the stereotypes of women as passive, dependent, emotional creatures, the regulations issued under Title IX specifically exempt textbooks and other curricular materials from coverage under the law.[35] The reason is a possible conflict with the First Amendment to the Constitution, which protects freedom of speech and press from government interference.[36]

However, there may be other avenues to address this issue. For example, California has legislation requiring schools to use instructional materials that portray the contributions of women in all fields and forbidding the use of materials that treat women as inferior.[37] Many women's groups work to develop unbiased textbooks, educational materials, and courses and to eliminate sex-role stereotyping in schools.[38] In response to their efforts, other states may have adopted laws or official directives to replace, forbid, or supplement discriminatory textbooks and other materials.

Pregnant and Parenting Students

May a school exclude pregnant students or unwed mothers?
No. Title IX regulations forbid schools to exclude pregnant students or students who have had a child or an abortion.[39]

Pregnant students may ask to attend special schools or educational programs, but their requests must be truly voluntary. Schools cannot pressure pregnant students into withdrawing from regular courses or refuse to allow them to return after their babies are born. A pregnant student must also be allowed to take a leave of absence for as long as her physician thinks necessary and later resume school attendance, even though the school does not usually permit leaves of absence. If the school maintains a separate, voluntary program for pregnant girls, it must be comparable in quality to that offered to other students.

In addition to laws prohibiting discrimination on the basis of sex (usually interpreted nowadays to include pregnancy), a number of states—including California, the District of Columbia, Florida, Minnesota, New York, Oregon, Rhode Island, and Wisconsin—also have laws or programs designed to encourage pregnant and parenting students to remain in school and to provide various services to the students. [40]

Several equal protection decisions rendered before the passage of Title IX concluded that students' constitutional rights were violated when they were excluded from school solely on account of pregnancy, marital, or familial status. In lawsuits seeking reinstatement to educational programs after expulsion or suspension on account of pregnancy or parenthood, plaintiffs usually won. [41] Subsequently, Title IX provided a statutory basis to buttress the earlier case law. Since then, other courts have also rejected, on constitutional grounds, efforts to punish students or teachers for their decisions concerning parenting [42] and marriage. [43]

May students who are pregnant, married, or parents be excluded from extracurricular activities?

This practice is forbidden by Title IX regulations. [44] In addition, a number of courts have ruled that married or parenting students cannot be barred from extracurricular activities in an effort to discourage early marriage or to curb discussions of sex. A Texas judge decided that a sixteen-year-old girl who had been married and divorced and had then given her child up for adoption, could not be excluded from such extracurricular activities as chess, choir, drama, and the National Honor Society. He emphasized that she was an exceptionally good student and that success in these activities would enhance her chances of getting into college or winning a scholarship.[45] In another case, a school was ordered to allow a married high school senior to participate in extracurricular activities and other school functions. The judge decided that the school regulation, whose sole purpose was to punish perfectly legal marriages, infringed upon the girl's fundamental right to marry.[46] Several married male high school students have also won the right to play on varsity or interscholastic athletic teams.[47] However, at least one more recent decision suggests that the National Honor Society, which admits students on the basis of character, leadership, service and scholarship, can exclude pregnant girls on grounds of "immorality."[48]

Must health insurance benefits offered by educational institutions provide coverage for pregnancy and pregnancy-related conditions?

Yes, except that they are not required to cover abortions. Title IX regulations require that pregnancy and childbirth be treated the same as other medical conditions under health insurance plans offered by covered educational institutions.[49] The Civil Rights Restoration Act, which was otherwise necessary to the continued vitality of Title IX, contained a provision that allows institutions not to cover abortions in such plans. However, they may not discriminate against a student if she has had an abortion.

Sexual Harassment

Are women protected against sexual harassment in schools under Title IX?

Yes. Federal courts have uniformly ruled that Title IX prohibits sexual harassment.[50] The Supreme Court recently ruled that Title IX also allows victims of such discrimination to recover monetary damages to compensate them for their losses. The case, *Franklin v. Gwinnett County School District*,[51] involved a Georgia high school student. Her Supreme Court brief explained that "beginning in the fall of 1986, when she was in the tenth grade, she was subjected to a continuing course of

intentional sexual harassment, culminating in forced intercourse, by Andrew Hill, a sports coach and teacher employed
by the District."[52] School officials initially ignored her complaints, and it was not until March 1988 that they launched an
official investigation. Once they did, the investigator quickly
concluded that the sexual harassment allegations were true,
and Hill was forced to resign. The Education Department,
which is charged with enforcing Title IX, concluded that his
resignation and the school's implementation of grievance procedures was enough to bring the school into compliance with
Title IX. But Christine Franklin did not agree. She brought a
lawsuit to recover money damages as well.

The Court's decision to award damages has implications for
teachers as well as students. Teachers who have experienced
sexual harassment and other forms of intentional sex discrimination now have a reason to sue under Title IX in addition to
under Title VII of the Civil Rights Act, because Title VII has
a cap on damages, while Title IX does not.

Athletic Programs

**Do women have an equal right to participate in school
athletic programs?**
In the 1970s the struggle of women to win equal athletic
opportunities produced numerous lawsuits and a great deal of
controversy. Most of the young women who have used the
Equal Protection Clause or state discrimination laws to challenge their exclusion from their all-male teams have succeeded—at least in noncontact sports. Young women in Minnesota, Nebraska, Colorado, Tennessee, and Kansas established
their right to join all-male golf, tennis, cross-country track,
cross-country skiing, soccer, and baseball teams.[53] In at least
two cases, a physically qualified girl even won the right to
play.[54]

On the other hand, young women in Illinois[55] fared less well,
and in Tennessee an attempt to strike down restrictive playing
rules failed. A female guard who wanted her team to play
"boys'" rules persuaded a lower-level judge that the special
girls' basketball rules (e.g., split court, guards prohibited from

shooting) denied her equal protection and handicapped her in competing for a college athletic scholarship. Although Tennessee was one of only five states that imposed separate boy-girl rules, the appellate court upheld the rules in a decision based on the necessity of maintaining separate male and female basketball teams.

> When the classification, as here, related to athletic activity, it must be apparent that its basis is the distinct difference in physical characteristics and capabilities between the sexes and that the differences are reflected in the sport of basketball by how the game itself is played. It takes little imagination to realize that were play and competition not separated by sex, the great bulk of the females would quickly be eliminated from participation and denied any meaningful opportunity for athletic involvement. Since there are such differences in physical characteristics and capabilities, we see no reason why the rules governing play cannot be tailored to accommodate them without running afoul of the Equal Protection Clause.[56]

The successful athletic discrimination suits against all-male teams have generally been brought under the Equal Protection Clause by individuals suing only on their own behalf (not on behalf of an entire "class" of girls) and have involved noncontact sports. The absence of a girls' team seems to be a critical factor in the decisions allowing girls to play with boys. Several courts, however, have explicitly expressed reservations about integrated teams in contact sports. Despite those reservations, in two lawsuits under state equal rights amendments, courts have struck down restrictions on girls' participation even in contact sports. In Pennsylvania, a judge found unconstitutional a bylaw of an interscholastic athletic association that prohibited high school girls from practicing or competing with boys in football, basketball, wrestling, soccer, baseball, and several other sports. He ruled that girls must be permitted to play on boys' teams, even where there were separate girls' teams.[57] In Washington two high school girls who had qualified for the boys' football team won the right to play with their teammates when state judges ruled that the athletic association's regulation that barred their participation violated the state equal rights amendment.[58]

On the other hand, the regulations issued under Title IX provide very little protection against this form of discrimination in athletics.[59] Although in theory schools may not bar any student from playing in interscholastic or intramural athletics because of sex, in practice the regulations permit schools to sponsor separate teams for girls and boys when team selection is based on "competitive skill" or the activity is a contact sport[60] and thus to bar girls from all of these male sports teams. Most teams are covered by one or the other of these exceptions. If the school has only one team, however, girls must be allowed to try out for it—unless it involves a contact sport. Young women who have the skills to make the all-male teams permitted by these regulations might want to challenge them as unconstitutional sex discrimination.

Importantly, however, the regulations also mandate "equal athletic opportunities" for both sexes, though they do not require equal amounts of money to be spent on girls and boys. These regulations can be used to improve inadequate segregated female sports programs in many instances. In *Haffer v. Temple*,[61] for example, one court accepted the theory that school spending could be challenged under Title IX by refusing to dismiss a case challenging differential spending in athletic programs for girls and boys. The case was ultimately settled.

What strategy is best for women and girls who seek equal athletic opportunities?

Women must make some difficult strategy decisions in seeking to establish equal rights to participate in athletic programs. Should they ask for equal funding for separate male and female sports, integrated sports programs, or a combination of the two? The latter is probably the most desirable. Integrated sports provide the opportunity for the most athletically talented girls to compete with athletically talented boys. By also asking the schools to fund sports diverse enough to attract most girls and by insisting (in the political arena) that the average per student expenditure be equal for boys and girls, women would also provide opportunities for those girls who are not interested in, or lack the muscular development for, some of the traditionally male sports. More adequate funding of different sports than are currently emphasized would also help those boys with a similar lack of interest in or muscular development for sports like football. Eventually the schools might find themselves providing meaningful athletic programs for all students, sorting individuals into sports roughly by interest and skill rather than by sex.

Testing

Does Title IX prohibit the use of tests that have the effect of discriminating on the basis of sex?

Yes. In 1989 a federal district court in New York enjoined the New York State Department of Education from exclusive reliance on the Scholastic Aptitude Test (SAT) for the award of state merit scholarships. The court reasoned that the test had a discriminatory impact on young women in violation of Title IX regulations.[62] For example, girls were 53% of the competitors for the scholarships in 1987, but they received only 28% of the Empire State Scholarships ($2000 a year and renewable for 5 years for each recipient). With the help of the ACLU, Khadijah Sharif brought the case, along with nine other New York State high school seniors, all young women with exemplary high school records and high—but not high enough— SAT scores to qualify for these coveted scholarships. They showed that women, on the average, score 60 points below men on the SAT (50 points on the math portion and 10 points on the verbal portion) despite the facts that women do slightly better than men in both high school and college grades and that the SAT is supposed to predict a person's first year college grades. The judge also found that while the SAT is designed to predict college grades, the scholarship program was supposed to reward high school performance, and the SAT was not a measure of high school performance.

There are a number of such standardized tests that have the effect of discriminating on the basis of sex and are misused in the educational context, thus limiting the opportunities of young women (and occasionally also young men). This will be a fruitful area of inquiry in the future.

Vocational Education

What laws protect women from discrimination in vocational education?

Discrimination in vocational education has helped to concentrate women in domestic, clerical, and other low-paying, low-status, dead-end positions, while men monopolize the more lucrative skilled-craft jobs in trade and industry. A major factor in perpetuating this pattern is the virtual exclusion of women from many occupational training programs.

To alter this situation, Congress amended the Vocational Education Act in 1976 to require states to take affirmative steps to end sex discrimination in vocational education.[63] To qualify for federal money, states must collect data on the enrollment of women in training programs, reduce sex-role stereotyping and sex bias in job-training programs, and assist schools in making vocational education opportunities available to women. The law also provides grants to states for job training for homemakers who are seeking paid employment and for women in traditionally female jobs who want employment in "male" fields.

States that do not comply with the law risk the termination of federal funds. The law does not specifically authorize women to bring private lawsuits to enforce its provisions, but it is possible that such a lawsuit might be allowed.

In addition, Title IX forbids sex discrimination in all school policies—whether admissions, course assignments, or financial aid—in those vocational schools that receive federal money, and most do. Thus it should be possible to challenge all-male or all-female vocational schools under Title IX, as well as otherwise integrated schools with single-sex vocational programs. In some cases, the Equal Educational Opportunities Act of 1974, Title IV of the 1964 Civil Rights Act, and the Equal Protection Clause also could be used to challenge the assignment of students to vocational schools or programs on the basis of sex.[64]

Do students in the health professions have any additional rights against discrimination by their schools?

Yes, under an amendment to the Public Health Service Act. Two sections, 799A and 855 (formerly 845), specifically prohibit schools and training programs in the health professions from discriminating against students on the basis of their sex.[65] The prohibition applies only to schools and programs receiving financial assistance under Titles VII and VIII of the Public Health Service Act, but the vast majority of these schools do receive such assistance. The prohibition also applies to hospitals insofar as they operate medical schools, training programs, or even internships. Those affected may now protest and seek legal redress if a hospital refuses to hire women interns, if a medical school limits its enrollment of women or refuses to admit people over thirty (which affects women more than men), or if a nursing school refuses to admit men.

In 1975 HEW issued regulations[66] to interpret these sections of the Public Health Services Act. The regulations, which are independent of those under Title IX, afford stronger protection against discrimination in admissions, but omit athletic programs and provide less protection against discriminatory employment practices. Otherwise they parallel the Title IX regulations in the areas of student housing, student financial aid, equal benefits and services to men and women, and the treatment of pregnant and married students.

Faculty

Are teachers, other school employees, and students protected against employment discrimination by the sex discrimination provisions of the Public Health Service Act (PHSA) and Title IX of the Education Amendments of 1972 Act?

Yes. In 1982 the Supreme Court ended a long legal controversy on this issue. It ruled that Title IX protects employees in federally funded education programs from discrimination on the basis of sex in their employment.[67] Thus, Title IX helps teachers, administrators, and other school employees, as well as students. There has never been any real doubt over whether the PHSA covers employment discrimination; it does. But it protects only those teachers and employees who work directly with students.

Are there laws that protect teachers against sex discriminatory employment practices?

Yes. Both Title VII of the 1964 Civil Rights Act and the Equal Pay Act have been amended to protect teachers against sex discrimination. They are discussed in chapter 2, "Employment Discrimination."

Should teachers use all laws available to combat discriminatory practices?

Yes, since this maximizes the pressure on school officials. Teachers now have a wide range of remedies: court action under Titles IV and VII of the 1964 Civil Right Act, the Equal Pay Act, Title IX, and the Equal Protection Clause (if they are public school employees) and differing forms of agency action under Executive Order 11246 (contract cutoff), Title IX (grant, loan, and contract cutoff), and the Public Health Service Act.

State Laws

Do any state laws prohibit sex discrimination in education?

Yes. Many states now have laws forbidding at least some forms of discrimination, some of them modeled on Title IX. Other state statutes prohibit types of discrimination not covered by federal law. In addition, women in the states that have adopted state equal rights amendments[68] may challenge discriminatory practices in public facilities or those facilities with state involvement as violations of the state constitution.

A few other states have laws prohibiting educational discrimination on the basis of race, religion, or national origin but not sex. It is difficult to know how effective these laws are. Some, administered by state civil rights agencies, provide for complaint procedure and full enforcement powers. Others merely forbid some forms of discrimination and provide no apparent enforcement mechanism. Even where there is a comprehensive program on paper, personnel in state agencies and courts can undermine the effectiveness of the programs, as can a lack of funding.

Women who have encountered discrimination should check whether their states have laws prohibiting sex discrimination and whether these laws are adequately enforced. Because the Department of Education has been so slow in handling complaints since HEW enforcement responsibility passed to it in 1980, women should file their complaints with the appropriate state agency as well as with the U.S. Department of Education's regional office. In some cases the state agency may be able to get quicker results. Filing complaints in both places will also maximize pressure on schools to correct their discriminatory practices.

In states without laws on this subject, women should work for the inclusion of provisions in existing civil rights laws forbidding sex discrimination in education or for passage of comprehensive laws prohibiting all forms of educational discrimination. If the problem is the lack of enforcement of an existing law, women should lobby for adequate funding for the agency charged with enforcing the law, for the hiring and training of capable, dedicated staff, and for appointment of a director with a strong history of working against sex discrimination as well as other forms of illegal discrimination.

PROCEDURES TO FOLLOW IN SEEKING REMEDIES

A right that exists only in theory does no one any good. For example, a school principal may be acting illegally by preventing a young woman from enrolling in a course just because she is a woman, but until the principal has been forced to stop, the woman merely has a theoretical right not to be discriminated against. She has not gotten the results she needs. Occasionally a woman can change the situation by telling the principal (or other authority) that she has a right to do certain things and by referring the official to the appropriate law or appropriate enforcement agency; if the official then changes his or her actions, the woman has gotten her result. All too often, however, a lawsuit or some other legal action is required to enforce her rights.

The rights guaranteed by the Equal Protection Clause and the various federal statutes are generally enforced in different ways. If a woman sues under the Equal Protection Clause or Title IX, she can ask for an end to the discrimination. But if the Department of Education rather than the individual woman takes action under Title IX, the remedy might include a cutoff of federal funds to the offending school, although in almost all cases the Department of Education will seek to end the discrimination through conciliation. Also, administrative action in the form of a threatened cutoff of funds often comes too late (if at all) to help the individual victim of discrimination.

The Equal Protection Clause

How can a women challenge a discriminatory practice under the Equal Protection Clause?

A women can enforce rights under the Equal Protection Clause by bringing a lawsuit against the discriminating school or official. Of course, she will need a lawyer, preferably one experienced in the area of women's rights.

Usually a woman in this type of situation sues for an injunction—a court order telling someone to do something or ordering them to stop doing something. For instance, a judge can order a school to admit women or to stop enforcing a rule that applies only to female students. Occasionally a woman also sues for money damages or some other award. An equal protection claim against officials may be combined in a single lawsuit with a challenge to the discriminatory practice under one of the federal laws discussed here.

It used to be possible to combine both federal and state law and constitutional claims in a single lawsuit in federal court. But since a Supreme Court decision in 1984,[69] it is no longer permissible to sue state officials in federal court using state laws; this can now only be done in state courts. Thus it may be necessary either to bring such combined cases in state court or to bring separate lawsuits when this seems advisable. Women who are considering such cases should consult an experienced attorney on the best course of action.

Cases that have already established certain discriminatory practices as illegal under the Equal Protection Clause are discussed in section A of this chapter. It is important to remember, however, that the Equal Protection Clause prohibits discrimination only by public schools and colleges.

The Equal Educational Opportunities Act

How can women enforce rights under the Equal Educational Opportunities Act?

This statute is enforced in two ways: A women may bring a lawsuit in a federal district court to enforce her rights, or the United States attorney general may begin one on her behalf. The attorney general is also authorized to intervene in lawsuits begun by private individuals.[70]

Title IV of the 1964 Civil Rights Act

How can women enforce rights under Title IV?[71]

This law only permits the attorney general to sue a discriminatory school or college. Thus, a women's role is limited to requesting that the attorney general bring such a lawsuit when she has been discriminated against or is aware of a discriminatory practice.

What kinds of discriminatory practices can be attacked in such a lawsuit?

To date, the attorney general has used Title IV principally to desegregate public schools. But in 1990 the Justice Department also sued the Virginia Military Institute over its refusal to admit women.[72]

In the course of the desegregation lawsuits, Justice Department lawyers have also attacked other forms of discrimination—both against students and teachers—but these moves have always been incidental to the main issue of desegregation. This seems to indicate that Title IV can be used against all of the forms of sex discrimination mentioned in this chapter but that the Justice Department may not be inclined to do so unless women raise these issues in the context of segregated schools. Women should, nonetheless, request the Justice Department to fight other forms of educational discrimination in integrated schools, if for no other reason then to help educate Justice Department lawyers on other sex discrimination issues. Title IV applies both to lower schools and to colleges, so complaints about college-level discrimination should also be sent to the department.

How can women request that the attorney general bring such lawsuits?

They can send a letter to:

Attorney General of the United States Department
    of Justice
10th and Constitution Avenue, N.W.
Washington, D.C. 20530
Attention: General Litigation Section Civil Rights
    Division.

At the elementary and secondary level, the letter should be sent by the parents of affected children. At the college level, women students can raise the complaint.

In the letter, the complainant should describe the school system and the discriminatory practices and give as many facts as possible. It also helps to identify other women who share the same problem. The Justice Department will be more interested if it is a widespread problem because the attorney general must certify that the lawsuit will further desegregation efforts. Although it is impossible to know whether the Justice Department will follow through, it is probably worthwhile to make the effort—certainly so for women who cannot find or afford their own lawyers. Even for those who have access to counsel, requests for attorney general intervention may serve as a means of publicizing the discrimination and awakening government officials to its existence and effects.

Title IX

How are discriminatory schools punished under Title IX?

Any federal agency that awards money—whether as grants, loans, or contracts—to a school can cancel that assistance if it finds that the school discriminates. The agency may also refuse to award such assistance in the future or refer the case to the Justice Department for a lawsuit against the school. Although many federal agencies administer grant programs to educational institutions, the Department of Education is the main grantor and as such is the chief enforcement agency.

The threat of a cutoff of federal money is a powerful weapon since many schools depend on this money for a major portion of their budget. Of course, the Department of Education must be willing to make this threat and to carry through in the event of noncompliance if the law is to be effective. So far the agency has never done so.

Are there any other ways to enforce rights under Title IX?

Yes. In 1979 the Supreme Court explicitly ruled that women may bring their own suits in federal court under Title IX against discriminatory schools.[73] In addition, the Justice Department (through the attorney general) can bring such lawsuits.

How can women enforce their rights under Title IX?

If they want a Department of Education investigation—
which threatens the school with a possible cutoff of federal
funds—they should send a letter detailing their charges of
discrimination and the name and address of the school involved
to the nearest regional office of the Department of Education
or to:

Assistant Secretary for Civil Rights
Office of Civil Rights
Department of Education
330 C Street, S.W.
Washington, D.C. 20202-1100

The steps for filing complaints are detailed in the chapter on
employment discrimination (see chapter 2). Most importantly,
though this must be done within 180 days of the discriminatory
action complained of and should include as many facts as possible about the school's practices. For example, it could give
statistical evidence of discrimination (e.g., percentages of men
and women enrolled in different programs). Charges need not
be limited to those the complainant is sure she can prove—she
should add those she thinks may be true (it is the responsibility
of the Department of Education to investigate and prove or
disprove the charges). Likewise, the complaint should address
practices the complainant only suspects are discriminatory,
whether or not legal authority already supports her. Only by
raising new issues will new law be made. If possible, the name
of the federal program that gives money to the school should
be included. However, the Department of Education will find
out which agency gives grants to the school if the complainant
isn't sure. The department will also send the letter to the proper
federal agency if it is not in charge of the grant program (or
programs) at the school.

Once the Department of Education receives the charge, it
must investigate and possibly hold a hearing to find out whether
the school discriminates. Women complainants may participate
in these hearings only as witnesses or as "friends of the court."
They may not present their side of the matter by having an
attorney call witnesses or present evidence. Only Department
of Education lawyers do these things unless a special arrangement is made. However, if a woman is unhappy with the

results, she can ask a United States court of appeals to review the Department of Education action. Sometimes women's organizations may also be allowed to participate as "friends of the court," which means they can offer their opinion as to what the result should be, but they cannot present evidence or control the course of the hearing unless they are invited to do so.

If a woman wants to bring her own lawsuit in federal court attacking discriminatory education practices forbidden by Title IX, she can do so. She need only find a lawyer to bring suit for her; there is no requirement that the woman file anything with the Department of Education before suing. Attorneys' fees are available to prevailing plaintiffs in such cases, and they may also be able to win damages, as explained in the section on sexual harassment, above.

How can a woman assist (or pressure) the Department of Education while it is handling her complaint?
Nothing is guaranteed to work, but the following steps may help mobilize the bureaucracy. First, the initial letter to the department should provide as much information as possible, especially such useful items as the names, addresses, and phone numbers of people who should be interviewed. If several people have suffered from the same discrimination (e.g., five other girls were excluded from the same shop class), all of them should join in the complaint. This guarantees that if the situation of one of the complainant changes before the department takes action, there will be someone else who can assist it in correcting the discriminatory practice.

Any letters received from department officials should be answered quickly. If they do not get a reply within a reasonable time, they will conclude that the complainant is no longer interested in pursuing the complaint and will close the investigation.

The complainant should call the department regional office to find out the name and phone number of the investigator assigned to the complaint and should maintain friendly contact with this person. The department still has a great deal of discretion over which cases it handles and how thoroughly it investigates them. A complainant who is cooperative and remains interested in resolving her case may receive more attention. If nothing seems to be happening on a complaint, she can call the department to find out what action is being taken or planned. She can also contact the congressperson for her district and tell him or her about the discrimination and the lack of action on it. A letter from a congressperson to the department's regional office may work wonders.

Should women who want to challenge discriminatory practices in public schools use both the Equal Protection Clause and Title IX of the Education Amendments of 1972 Act?

It depends. Each provides a different remedy, and both together would maximize the pressure on school officials. Women should remember, though, that Title IX allows many public schools to follow various discriminatory admission policies. In these instances, the Equal Protection Clause provides the only remedy. (Women students at private schools, of course, can use only Title IX and not the Equal Protection Clause because of the lack of "state action.")

The Public Health Service Act

How are the antidiscrimination provisions of the Public Health Service Act enforced?

The Department of Health and Human Services must cancel any federal financial assistance—whether in the form of a grant, a loan guarantee, or a subsidy on interest payments—received under Titles VII or VIII of the Public Health Service Act by a school or program that discriminates. Theoretically, cancellation can occur in three ways. If the school fails to give HHS a written assurance that it will not discriminate, HHS must cut off or refuse to award the funds. HHS also conducts routine reviews to check for discrimination. And finally, someone can file a complaint with HHS, charging a program with discrimination. HHS would then conduct a hearing and cancel any financial assistance if it finds discrimination. Although the women discriminated against will not be allowed to participate in these hearings except as witnesses or "friends of the court," they will be able to ask a federal court to review HHS action.

A complaint can be filed by sending a letter describing the charges to the nearest Health and Human Services regional office or to:

Director, Office of Civil Rights
Department of Health and Human Services
Suite 5400, Cohen Building
330 Independence Avenue, S.W.
Washington, D.C. 20201.

Although there has been no court ruling on the point, it may also be possible to sue the discriminatory schools in federal court, under the same theory used to allow private lawsuits under Title IX.

Are there any differences between the sex discrimination provisions of the Public Health Service Act and those of Title IX?
Yes. The Public Health Service Act does not contain the numerous exceptions that Title IX does. Thus, women in the health professions who are not helped by Title IX—such as applicants to private undergraduate schools—may still be able to get relief under the Public Health Service Act.

Should women who can challenge sex discrimination under both laws do so?
Yes. This may help maximize the pressure on the school, even though the remedy under both laws is of the same nature—a cutoff of federal funds.

New Legislation

What provisions of Title IX need to be strengthened?
First, a strengthened Title IX would not exempt any school or admission policy from coverage. Even religious schools would be forbidden to discriminate since the law would cover only schools receiving federal funds. If a religious school wants to discriminate, it should not be allowed to do so with federal money, particularly since part of that money comes from female taxpayers. The special exemptions for admissions policies should also be eliminated. Finally, all the other specific discriminatory policies allowed under Title IX or the regulations should be eliminated.
An excellent source of technical information about and assis-

tance in action to eradicate sex discrimination on college campuses is:

The Project on the Status and Education of Women
Association of American Colleges
1818 R St., N.W.
Washington, D.C. 20009
(202) 387-3760.

(The project's newsletter is *On Campus with Women*.)
Other groups that work on education discrimination issues include:

PEER (Project on Equal Education Rights)
99 Hudson Street
New York, New York 10007
(212) 925-6635.

Another group, the National Women's Law Center, provides legal advice and representation to women experiencing sex discrimination in educational programs and for groups working to strengthen federal policies for sex equity in education. They also have excellent legal training materials on sex discrimination in education. Their address is:

National Women's Law Center
1616 P Street, N.W.
Washington, D.C. 20036
(202) 328-5160

NOTES

1. E. Flexner, *Country of Struggle* 29–30 and n. 13 (1970).
2. 20 U.S.C. § 1681 *et seq.*
3. 42 U.S.C. §§ 295h-9, 298b-2.
4. 20 U.S.C. § 2301 *et seq.*
5. 42 U.S.C. § 2000c-6.
6. 20 U.S.C. § 1701 *et seq.*
7. Of course, there is a wide variety of other laws prohibiting sex discrimination in employment, including academic employment. See chapter 2.
8. *Mississippi University for Women v. Hogan*, 458 U.S. 718, 102 S. Ct. 3331 (1982).

9. *Kirstein v. Rector and Visitors of University of Virginia*, 309 F. Supp. 184 (E.D. Va. 1970).

10. *Bray v. Lee*, 337 F. Supp. 934 (D. Mass. 1972). A few boys are also now attending the former Girls Latin School.

11. *Berkelman v. San Francisco Unified School District*, 501 F.2d 1264 (9th Cir. 1974).

12. The Supreme Court affirmed the decision without an opinion. *Vorchheimer v. School District of Philadelphia*, 532 F. 2d 880 (3d Cir. 1976), aff'd by an equally divided court, 430 U.S. 703 (1977).

13. *Newberg v. Board of Public Education*, 478 A.2d 1352 (Pa. Super 1984).

14. *Garret v. Board of Education of the School District of the City of Detroit*, 775 F. Supp. 1004 (E.D. Mich., 1991).

15. *U.S. v. Hinds County School Board*, 560 F.2d 619 (5th Cir. 1977); *Haymon v. Jefferson Parish School Board*, C.A. No. 77-396 (E.D. La. Oct. 21, 1977).

16. *See Mississippi University for Women v. Hogan*, 458 U.S. 718, 738–9 (1982) (Powell, dissenting).

17. In 1980 the new federal Department of Education took over the responsibility for enforcement of Title IX from HEW.

18. 45 C.F.R. pt. 86.

19. When this book was first published, the number of single-sex public undergraduate colleges was fairly small and included the United States military service academies, which now admit women. These schools were exempt from Title IX coverage in two ways: 1) some were military schools; 2) they had always been single-sex, public undergraduate colleges.

20. Women were admitted to the military academies by amendment to the Defense Appropriation Authorization Act of 1976. 10 U.S.C. § 4342 note (Supp. V. 1975). Women must meet the same academic and other standards required of men for appointment, admission, training, graduation, and commissioning (with slight modifications for physiological differences). However, the number of women admitted has been severely restricted "consistent with the needs of the services." (See chapter 11 for a discussion of sex discrimination in the military.)

21. 20 U.S.C. § 1681(a)(6) (Supp. V, 1975).

22. 20 U.S.C.A. § 1681(a)(7) and (8) (Supp. 1977).

23. *See Iron Arrow Honor Soc. v. Schweiker*, 652 F.2d 445 (5th Cir. 1981)(regulation authorizing secretary to cutoff federal funds to university where university gives "substantial assistance" to honor society that excludes women).

24. 34 C.F.R. § 106.32.

25. 34 C.F.R. § 106.32.

26. 34 C.F.R. § 106.37.

27. *Samuel v. University of Pittsburgh*, 375 F. Supp. 1119 (W.D. Pa. 1974). On appeal the court ruled that the women were entitled to restitution and that requiring each student to sue individually to recover her money imposed an undue burden. 538 F.2d 991 (3d Cir. 1976). The Supreme Court has never ruled on this issue but has ruled favorably in an analogous case. *Vlandis v. Kline*, 412 U.S. 441 (1973).

28. Cal. Educ. Code § 22847 (West 1974). Other states may have similar laws.

29. 34 C.F.R. § 106.31(b)(6).

30. 34 C.F.R. § 106.34(e).

31. 34 C.F.R. § 106.34.

32. *Sanchez v. Brown*, C.A. No. 69-C-1615 (E.D.N.Y. 1971).

33. State statutes in New York and Massachusetts prohibit the exclusion of either sex from courses. In addition, the Pennsylvania Commissioner of Education has issued a broad directive against discrimination in education that includes a prohibition against excluding either sex from courses. Other states may have similar rulings.

34. 34 C.F.R. § 106.36.

35. 34 C.F.R. § 106.42.

36. The Women's Educational Equity Act of 1974 authorizes grants to public agencies and private nonprofit organizations to develop, evaluate, and distribute nondiscriminatory curricula, textbooks, and counseling tests in order to promote equality in education. 20 U.S.C. § 3042(a)(1)(A) and (D)(1990).

37. Cal. Educ. Code §§ 9246 (West 1973).

38. *See Sex Discrimination: The Textbook Case*, 62 Cal. L. Rev. 1312 (1974) for a discussion of the effects of textbook stereotypes and the efforts to eliminate biased books in California, Pennsylvania, and Kalamazoo, Michigan.

39. 34 C.F.R. § 106.40.

40. *See Equal Educational Opportunities for Pregnant and Parenting Students: Meshing the Rights with the Realities*, a report by the Women's Rights Project of the American Civil Liberties Union *et al.* for an outline of and citation to these state laws, as well as a complete discussion of Title IX and constitutional provisions pertaining to the rights of pregnant and parenting students.

41. *See, e.g., Perry B. Grenada Municipal Separate School District*, 300 F. Supp. 748 (N.D. Miss. 1969); *Ordway v. Hargraves*, 323 F. Supp. 1155 (D. Mass. 1971); *Shull v. Columbus Municipal Separate School District*, 338 F. Supp. 1376 (N.D. Miss. 1972). *But cf. Houston v.*

Prosser, 361 F. Supp. 295 (N.D. Ga. 1973). (The district court held that no fundamental right was violated by school's expulsion of a pregnant student and subsequent imposition of condition that she could only resume studies in a night school, notwithstanding the allegation that rights to education and to procreation were impaired by this action. Nevertheless, the court granted relief to plaintiff since an additional requirement of the night program was payment of tuition and a textbook fee, which the indigent plaintiff could not afford. Thus, the court found the school system's action violated the Fourteenth Amendment's Equal Protection Clause.)

42. *See, e.g., Eckmann v. Board of Education of Hawthorn School District*, 636 F. Supp. 1214 (N.D. Ill. 1986) (affirming jury's finding that school board violated teacher's constitutional rights by discharging her on account of her decision to have and raise a child as a single parent).

43. *See, e.g., Street v. Cobb County Sch. District.*, 520 F. Supp. 1170 (N.D. Ga. 1981) (finding that school district violated student's constitutional rights by attempting to exclude her from day program after she began to reside with her boyfriend where district would have allowed a similarly situated married student to attend day school.)

44. 34 C.F.R. § 106.40.

45. *Romans v. Crenshaw*, 354 F. Supp. 868 (S.D. Tex. 1971).

46. *Holt v. Shelton*, 341 F. Supp. 821 (M.D. Tenn. 1972).

47. *Davis v. Meek*, 344 F. Supp. 298 (N.D. Ohio 1972); *Moran v. School District 7, Yellowstone County*, 350 F. Supp. 1180 (D. Mont. 1972); *Hollon v. Mathis Independent School District.* 358 F. Supp. 1269 (S.D. Tex. 1973), *vacated*, 491 F.2D 92 (5th Cir. 1974).

48. *Pfeifer v. Marion Center Area School District*, 700 F. Supp. 269 (W.D. Pa. 1988). *But see Wort v. Vierling*, 778 F.2d 1233 (7th Cir. 1985).

49. 34 C.F.R. § 106.40(4).

50. *See, e.g., Lipsett v. University of Puerto Rico*, 864 F.2d 881 (1st Cir. 1988); *Moire v. Temple University School of Medicine*, 613 F. Supp. 1360 (E.D. Pa. 1985), *aff'd mem.*, 800 F.2d 1126 (3d Cir. 1986).

51. *Franklin v. Gwinnett County School District*, _____ U.S. _____, 112 S. Ct. 1028 (1992).

52. Brief for Petitioner, at 2, *Franklin v. Gwinnett County School District*, *supra.*

53. *Brenden v. Independent School District*, 477 F.2d 1292 (8th Cir. 1973); *Bednar v. Nebraska School Athletic Association*, 531 F.2d 922 (8th Cir. 1976); *Reed v. Nebraska School Activities Association*, 341 F. Supp. 258 (D. Neb. 1972); *Hoover v. Meiklejohn*, 430 F. Supp.

164 (D. Colo. 1977); *Carnes v. Tennessee Secondary School Athletic Association*, 415 F. Supp. 569 (E.D. Tenn. 1976); *Gilpin v. Kansas State High School Activities Association, Inc.*, 377 F. Supp. 1233 (D. Kan. 1973).

54. *Clinton v. Nagy*, 411 F. Supp. 1396 (N.D. Ohio 1974); *Balsey v. North Hunterdon Regional School Dist. Bd. of Educ.*, 568 A.2d 895 (N.J. 1990).

55. *Bucha v. Illinois High School Association*, 351 F. Supp. 69 (N.D. Ill. 1972).

56. *Cape v. Tennessee Secondary School Athletic Association*, 563 F.2d 793 (6th Cir. 1977), *rev'd*, 424 F. Supp. 732 (E.D. Tenn. 1976).

57. *Commonwealth by Packel v. Pennsylvania Interscholastic Athletic Association*, 334 A.2d 839 (Commw. Ct. 1975).

58. *Darrin v. Gould*, 540 P.2d 882 (Wash. 1975); *See also Attorney Gen'l v. Mass. Interscholastic Athletic Association, Inc.*, 393 N.E.2d 284 (Mass. 1979)(rule prohibiting boys from playing on a girl's team was invalid under equal rights amendment and statute barring sex discrimination).

59. 34 C.F.R. § 106.41. These regulations are expanded on in a subsequent policy interpretation, set forth in 44 F.R. 71413-23 (Dec. 11, 1979).

60. The regulations define "contact sports as boxing, wrestling, football, rugby, ice hockey, basketball, and other sports involving bodily contact."

61. 678 F. Supp. 517 (E.D. Pa. 1987).

62. *Sharif v. New York State Department of Education*, 709 F. Supp. 345 (S.D.N.Y. 1989).

63. Title II of the 1976 Amendments to the Vocational Education Act of 1963, 20 U.S.C.A. § 2301 *et seq.* (Supp. 1977), For details, see *Achieving Sex Equality in Vocational Education: A Citizen's Guide to the 1976 Vocational Education Amendment*, available from Lawyers' Committee for Civil Rights Under Law, Federal Education Project, 733 15th St. N.W., Washington, D.C. 20005.

64. Readers interested in sex discrimination in vocational education should read the Title IX guidelines on this subject, found at 34 C.F.R. pt. 106, appendix A, with text at 34 C.F.R. pt. 100, appendix B.

65. 42 U.S.C. §§ 292d, 298b-2.

66. 45 C.F.R. pt. 83.

67. *North Haven Board of Education v. Bell*, 456 U.S. 512 (1982).

68. Alaska, Colorado, Connecticut, Hawaii, Illinois, Maryland, Massachusetts, Montana, New Hampshire, New Mexico, Pennsylvania, Texas, Utah, Virginia, Washington, and Wyoming.

69. *Pennhurst State School & Hospital v. Halderman,* 465 U.S. 89 (1984).
70. 20 U.S.C. §§ 1706, 1709 (Supp. 1977).
71. 42 U.S.C. §§ 2000c-6 (Supp. V 1975).
72. C. A. No. 90-0126-R (W.D. Va. 1990).
73. *Cannon v. University of Chicago,* 441 U.S. 677 (1979).

IX

Insurance

How does insurance discriminate against women and men?
Insurance is one of the few areas of American life where
blatant discrimination on the basis of sex is still permitted.[1]
Insurance companies often classify policyholders by groupings,
and while most of those groupings are unobjectionable (such as
charging rates based on whether a policyholder is a smoker or
high-mileage driver or lives in a household with a smoke alarm),
it is objectionable that insurance companies group policyholders by their gender. For example, under the current system,
no individual woman, regardless of how healthy she is, can ever
overcome the classification and higher prices she pays for health
insurance because she is a woman.

Are all types of insurance based on gender groupings?
No. Federal law[2] prohibits discrimination in any insurance
plan offered *by an employer* if the employer has fifteen or more
employees. (State employment laws may protect employees of
an employer with less than fifteen employees.) That means
that an employer cannot charge male and female employees
different rates or provide different benefits for any type of
insurance—health, life, disability, or pensions. Nor can discrimination occur indirectly via the insurance provider.[3]

Employers also must provide equal treatment to spouses and
dependents of employees in the provision of insurance and
pensions. For example, employers cannot provide spousal coverage of health insurance to spouses of male employees but
refuse to provide such coverage for spouses of female employees (or vice versa).[4]

**Can an employer exclude pregnancy-related costs from
health or disability insurance coverage?**
No. An employer that is subject to Title VII (i.e., one that
employs more than fifteen employees) cannot offer a health
insurance plan that excludes the costs of pregnancy and child-

birth or disability insurance that excludes pregnancy-related benefits.[5]

State employment discrimination laws (see chapter 2) will also apply these principles to employers with less than fifteen employees. There have been court decisions in some states establishing that all health and disability plans offered by employers must include benefits for pregnancy.[6]

Can an employer require women to pay more into pension plans or receive less in pension payments?

No. If an employer requires contributions to a pension plan, male and female employees must be charged the same amount per unit of salary. Also, both male and female workers must receive the same monthly amount of pension benefits for a given pay level when they retire.[7]

What type of insurance does depend on gender groupings?

Except in some states where gender pricing has been prohibited, insurance companies are free to set different prices for men and women for any insurance that is not offered through an employer. However, the general practice is that gender pricing only occurs in health, life, disability, annuity, and auto insurance; it does not usually occur, for example, in property or casualty insurance.

Why do insurance companies use gender rates for these insurance policies?

Because there are statistical differences in the loss experience for men and women, the companies find it administratively convenient to price their product along gender lines. However, the truism that correlation does not prove causation applies here as well. Just because there may be statistical differences between the loss experience for men and women does not mean that those differences are *caused* by gender. For example, women tend to live longer than men, but this can be explained by differences in average female and male behaviors such as smoking, drinking, eating, hazardous work and hobbies, and exercise. Also, studies show that women drivers have fewer accidents than men because they drive less.

If these statistical correlations are true, why is it legally wrong to base prices on them?

There are basically two reasons to oppose gender-based pricing of insurance: a civil rights reason and an economic reason. The civil rights position is that gender, like race or religion, should be an illegal way to classify people, even if there are statistically valid reasons for doing so.

Perhaps the best analogy is a historical one because insurance companies also once based their prices on race and religion. For example, when companies realized that African-Americans as a group had shorter life spans, the companies charged African-Americans higher rates for life insurance.

Insurance companies also charged different rates based on religious characteristics; as recently as 1954, an insurance textbook advised that "for life insurance, Jews are excellent risks. . . . For disability insurance, Jews are expensive." This is because, the textbook explained, on the one hand, "Jew tenacity of life is notorious" and on the other, because "he eats too much, with higher than average incidence of obesity and diabetes."[8]

Most people would readily agree that it would be wrong to base rates on race or religion, even though it is still possible to make some statistically valid generalizations about race and religion.[9] In fact, insurance companies voluntarily abandoned the practice in the 1960s. Sex discrimination is no less objectionable.

An additional reason sex discrimination in insurance is a civil rights issue involves ratemaking practices, which are neither fair nor scientific, contrary to industry claims. Insurers use gender-related actuarial data inconsistently and arbitrarily in every category of gender-based insurance in ways that tend to penalize women. One of many examples involves the use of gender as a rating factor for drivers under the age of twenty-five and not using it for over-25 drivers, when the difference in accident rates between men and women is just as significant over age twenty-five.

What is the economic reason for opposing gender-based insurance pricing?

Although insurance rates based on gender sometimes seem to favor women, the evidence is overwhelming that the overall economic effect is harmful. Data compiled in Montana, where a state law prohibits any insurance pricing based on sex, demonstrates that over the course of their lifetimes, women will benefit economically if all gender-based pricing is eliminated. Before Montana's law took effect, identical auto, major medical, disability income, and whole life insurance and annuity coverage cost women an average of $20,176 more than men over a lifetime in higher premiums and/or lower payouts (dividends and cash value for life insurance and monthly annuity payments). After the law took effect, these same policies purchased gender-free improved $21,859 in lifetime value for women.[10]

Moreover, the "breaks" that companies give to women tend to be insignificant ones. For example, although women may pay less for life insurance, they also receive lower payouts. Likewise, although women generally pay lower rates for auto insurance, they only do so as young adults, generally to the age of twenty-five.

Finally, the sex stereotyping that lies at the base of insurance pricing harms women in the same way that all sex stereotyping harms women.

What are the harmful effects of gender-based pricing?

Perhaps the most serious consequence of gender based insurance pricing is in health insurance. When they are charged more for health insurance, women and children in the ever-growing number of female-headed households suffer adverse health consequences. Concentrated in low-wage, part-time, and small-business jobs, women are less likely than men to receive insurance benefits as employees and are left with purchasing health insurance on the individual insurance market. The higher health insurance rates women face lead them to purchase less comprehensive coverage or no insurance at all. This absence of affordable insurance in turn reduces access to health care to the detriment of women and their children.[11] These effects are particularly severe for women and children of color. For example, African-American children in employed families are far less likely than their white counterparts to be insured.[12]

In addition, current insurance laws allow companies to exclude or charge extra for maternity coverage with major medical policies. Changing the laws to require gender neutrality would provide a significant benefit to women and society, by insuring that women get the health insurance they need for childbirth.

Finally, several major disability insurance companies recently announced that they are raising their rates for women, as they are allowed to do under current law. This is an ominous development for women workers since most purchase disability insurance privately rather than through their employers. Just as with health insurance, prohibitively high costs may leave many families without the protection of wage replacement in times of medical emergency.

What alternatives do insurance companies have for pricing if they are not allowed to use gender?

Companies could use a wide variety of factors for rate setting and reward people more fairly for safe and healthy behavior, regardless of gender. For example, in setting prices for auto insurance, companies could use miles driven, driving experience, driving record, and the type of vehicle used. For health, disability, and life insurance, companies could use such factors as smoking, alcohol use, weight, hazardous work and hobbies, medical history, diet, exercise, and age. Most of these factors are now used inadequately, if at all.

For example, studies by the National Organization for Women have demonstrated that the main reason why women have fewer auto accidents than men is because women on the average drive less than men over the course of their entire lives.[13] Thus, if auto insurance was based in part on miles driven instead of gender, it would benefit more women throughout their whole lives and be more fair. Women who actually do drive many miles would be charged more, and men who drive few miles would be charged less. Both men and women would be charged based on their behavior rather than their gender.

Are there some states in which gender-based pricing is illegal?

Yes. Seven states have acted so far to mandate gender-neutral insurance in one or more lines. In one state, Montana, insurance companies are not permitted to charge gender-based rates for any form of insurance.[14] Five other states, Hawaii, Massachusetts, Michigan, New Jersey, and North Carolina, have laws that prohibit gender discrimination in rates and premiums for auto insurance.[15]

In one state, Pennsylvania, the state appeals court in 1988 interpreted the state equal rights amendment to prohibit gender discrimination in auto insurance.[16] Insurance Commissioner Foster applied the ruling to all lines of insurance. Regulations have been promulgated for auto insurance[17] and are pending for the other forms, such as health insurance.

Are there ways to reform the system in other states?

The easiest method would be to enact a federal law that prohibited all forms of gender-based rating. Such legislation has been introduced several times in Congress.[18] Despite broad support from women's, consumer, labor, and civil rights groups, it has never passed due to vigorous opposition from the insurance lobby. Based on the futile attempts to enact bills, a consensus has emerged among advocates that it is more fruitful to focus on states and pick them off one by one.

State legislation has been introduced and progressed to hearings in many states in the late 1980s and early 1990s, including Illinois, Indiana, Iowa, Minnesota, Missouri, New Hampshire, New York, Oregon, Vermont, Virginia, West Virginia, and Washington. Those who are interested in this issue should contact their local ACLU office or Marcia Youngman at the National Clearinghouse for Ending Sex Discrimination in Insurance, 1214 W. Koch, Bozeman, MT 59715, (406) 587-5704.

NOTES

1. The authors gratefully acknowledge the assistance of MarciaYoungman, director of the National Clearinghouse for Ending Sex Discrimination in Insurance, in the preparation of this chapter.

2. Health insurance and other fringe benefits are "compensation, terms, conditions, or privileges of employment" under Title VII of the 1964 Civil Rights Act, 42 U.S.C. § 2000e-2(a)(1) *et seq.* The Supreme Court applied the principles of Title VII to outlaw discrimination in both contributions to and benefits of pension systems in two cases, *City of Los Angeles, Dep't of Water & Power v. Manhart*, 435 U.S. 702 (1978) and *Arizona Governing Committee v. Norris*, 463 U.S. 1073 (1983). Both *Manhart* and *Norris* are premised on the Title VII principle

that employees must be treated not as members of groups but as individuals.

3. *Arizona Governing Committee v. Norris,* 463 U.S. 1073 (1983).

4. For example, in *Newport News Shipbuilding and Dry Dock Company v. EEOC,* 462 U.S. 669 (1983), the Supreme Court ruled that the employer's hospitalization plan violated Title VII by providing married male employees less comprehensive protection for spousal medical conditions—pregnancy and childbirth—than that afforded married female employees, who received comprehensive spousal coverage.

5. The Pregnancy Discrimination Act (PDA) of 1978, 42 U.S.C. § 2000e(k).

6. *See Colorado Civil Rights Comm'n v. Travelers Insurance Co.,* 759 P.2d 1358 (Colo. 1988); *Massachusetts Elec. Co. v. Massachusetts Comm'n Against Discrimination,* 375 N.E.2d 1192 (Mass. 1978); *Franklin Mfg. Co. v Iowa Civil Rights Comm'n,* 270 N.W.2d 829 (Iowa 1978).

7. The one exception to this is that some women who are already retired or who will retire soon may receive less pension benefits than their male counterparts. This is because the U.S. Supreme Court held that employers would not be forced to equalize pension payments retroactively, that is, they could pay lower benefits to women retirees if those benefits derived from contributions made prior to August 1, 1983, the date of the decision prohibiting discrimination. *Arizona Governing Committee v. Norris,* 463 U.S. 1073 (1983). However, some insurers, like TIAA-CREF, the fund that provides pensions to university employees, equalized all pension benefits to settle sex discrimination lawsuits.

8. H. Dingman, *Risk Appraisal* 116 (1954).

9. For example, an auto insurance company could give a discount to Mormons, who as a group do not drink alcoholic beverages.

10. National Clearinghouse for Ending Sex Discrimination in Insurance, *Ending Sex Discrimination in Insurance: A Fact Sheet* 2 (1990).

11. Babies born to woman without insurance are 30% more likely to die or be seriously ill at birth. *See Babies of Uninsured Parents Found to Be at Risk,* N.Y. Times, Aug. 24, 1989, at B13.

12. More than 30% of African-American children in moderate-income families had no employer coverage in 1986, as compared to less than 20% of similarly situated white children. Children's Defense Fund, "A Vision for America's Future," at 7–9 (1989).

13. Butler, Butler, & Williams, *Sex-Divided Mileage, Accident, and Insurance Cost Data Show That Auto Insurers Overcharge Most Women,* 6 J. of Ins. Reg., pt. I, 243 and pt. II, 373 (1988) (reprints combining the two parts are available from the first author, National

Organization for Women, Suite 700, 1000 16th St., N.W., Washington, D.C. 20036, ph. (202) 331-0066).

14. Montana passed a law in April 1983 that became effective in October 1985; it provides that it is an "unlawful discriminatory practice for any financial institution or person to discriminate solely on the basis of sex or marital status in the issuance or operation of any type of insurance policy, plan, or coverage or in any pension or retirement plan, program or coverage, including discrimination in regard to rates or premiums and payments or benefits." Mont. Code Ann. § 49-2-309.

    In August 1987 the Massachusetts Insurance Commissioner issued a similar regulation, which became effective on September 1, 1988. 211 C.M.R. 35.00. However, in July 1991 the Massachusetts Supreme Judicial Court ruled that the regulation was unlawful because it exceeded the commissioner's statutory authority. *Telles v. Commissioner of Insurance*, 410 Mass. 560, 574 N.E.2d 359 (Mass. 1991).

15. Haw. Rev. Stat. tit. 17, § 294-33; Mich. Comp. Laws § 500.2027(c); N.J. Stat. Ann. § 17:33B-32(b); N.C. Gen. Stat. § 58-3-25(a). *See also* Mass. Gen. L. ch. 175 § 113(b). In a fifth state, California, Insurance Commissioner Gillespie attempted in December 1989 to prohibit the use of gender in auto insurance by promulgating regulations pursuant to Proposition 103. However, the regulations she promulgated were enjoined in a lawsuit brought by insurance companies. *Allstate Insurance Co. v. Gillespie*, 2d Civil No. B050439.

16. *Bartholomew v. Foster*, 541 A.2d 393 (Pa. Commw. 1988), *aff'd per curiam*, 563 A.2d 1390 (Pa. 1989). Also a court in New Jersey suggested that the Legislature should not authorize the state Blue Cross plan to use gender-based rates in health insurance since it would violate New Jersey's equal protection provision. *Matter of Blue Cross and Blue Shield*, 239 N.J. Super. 434, 443, 453 n.6 (App. Div. 1990).

17. 31 Pa. Code §§ 113a.1–.3. This "Genderless Automobile Insurance Rates Statement of Policy" became effective Oct. 15, 1988.

18. Bills introduced in 1982 and 1983, H.R. 100 and S. 372, were the last ones to progress to hearings.

X

Public Accommodations and
Private Clubs

What is a public accommodation?

Public accommodations are all places in the community that are available to the general public without special conditions or restrictions. These include not only public streets, sidewalks, and libraries but also facilities such as hotels, restaurants, and hospitals. Some state laws define public accommodations more broadly. For example, the District of Columbia includes insurance companies in its definition. Lawsuits have also extended the reach of state public accommodations laws. For example, a court in California held that the Boy Scouts are a place of public accommodation under its state law.[1]

Is there a federal law that forbids public bars, restaurants, and hotels to discriminate against women?

No, unfortunately, the federal public accommodations law, Title II, forbids only discrimination based on race, religion, color, and national origin and therefore does not provide any protection to women on a uniform, nationwide basis.

Are there any state or city laws forbidding public bars, restaurants, and hotels to discriminate against women?

Yes. More than twenty states and some cities have passed laws, generally referred to as *public accommodations laws*. More are needed. In the states with such laws, public accommodations are open to all people. In a state without a public accommodations law, the exclusion of women from a public accommodation could be challenged under the Equal Protection Clause or a state ERA. However, as in cases regarding other issues, a showing that there is some "state action" involved in the public accommodation is required before the Equal Protection Clause applies. Convincing courts that there is enough government involvement to amount to state action has been the chief barrier in this area of litigation, although a few suits against discriminatory restaurants have succeeded by relying on state regulation of liquor licenses or use of the city police force to evict women.[2]

Can public accommodations charge different prices to men and women?

It depends. In some states with public accommodation laws, courts have held that offering discounts to one sex, such as reduced prices for "ladies nights," does not violate the public accommodations law because no one is denied admission.[3] However, in most states with public accommodation laws, courts have found that differential prices do discriminate because they deny equal advantages and services to one sex.[4] It is difficult to explain the rationale for these differing results since all public accommodation laws usually contain similar language about "full enjoyment of accommodations" and all the cases involve discrimination against men rather than women.

In a state without a public accommodations law, price and service advantages for one sex could be challenged as a violation of equal protection or a state ERA, similarly to challenging denial of admission as discussed in the question above.

Can civic organizations and private clubs prohibit the admission of women?

It depends. In the many states with public accommodations laws, civic organizations cannot prohibit the admission of women. Thus, for example, the Minnesota Department of Human Rights said that the Jaycee's exclusion of women violated the public accommodations provisions of the Minnesota Human Rights Act. Furthermore, contrary to the arguments of the Jaycees, the United States Supreme Court ruled in 1984 that the admission of women did not violate the Jaycees' First Amendment rights of speech and association.[5] In 1987 the Court also rejected a similar First Amendment challenge by the Rotary Club and thereby permitted the operation of the California Unruh Civil Rights Act (California's public accommodations law) to bar the exclusion of women from Rotary Clubs in California.[6]

Can the rulings in the Jaycees and Rotary cases be extended to other private clubs?

It depends. Although the Court left open the broader question of whether the membership policies of exclusive private clubs could be challenged, the large and nonexclusive character of the Jaycees and Rotary may distinguish them from smaller, more exclusive clubs. Some of the factors to consider are: the size of the club (the smaller it is, the more likely that there are legitimate constitutionally protected rights of association); the process of screening new members; and the extent to which the club permits the public to participate in its activities or eat and drink at the club.

The United States Supreme Court has also upheld against constitutional attack a New York City law, Local Law 63, that prohibits discrimination in private clubs if a club 1) has more than four hundred members, 2) provides regular meal service, and 3) regularly receives payment for dues, fees, use of space, facilities, services, meals or beverages directly or indirectly from or on behalf of nonmembers for the furtherance of trade or business.[7]

It should be remembered that each of these decisions was based on an individual public accommodations law that does not apply in other states. Thus, the first test in any state will be to see whether the local public accommodations law actually prohibits the discrimination. For example, the New Jersey public accommodations law contains an exception for "any institution, bona fide club, or place of accommodation, which is in its nature distinctly private." When a woman challenged the Kiwanis club exclusion of members in New Jersey, the Court determined that the exception applied and the club did not have to admit women.[8] In other states, the result might be different.

What other methods can be used to combat discrimination practiced by private clubs and fraternal orders?

State and federal governments can prohibit certain economic benefits to these groups. Some receive tax-exempt status (which keeps them from having to pay taxes); others are allowed gifts that are tax deductible (thus encouraging gifts), and still others receive direct government grants or subsidies. It is obviously unfair to provide such benefits at public expense to groups that discriminate against women, and women should seek legislation to end the practice on both state and federal levels. Lawsuits can be tried, too. The cases do not force the clubs to stop discriminating, but by removing their tax-exempt status, they increase the cost to the club of discriminating. Thus lawsuits or legislation denying economic benefits to discriminatory clubs provide powerful leverage for change through economic incentive.

This approach was used in Maryland, where a law was enacted that prohibited favorable tax treatment to such clubs; the law was upheld against a challenge by a powerful country club.[9] Also, African-Americans have succeeded with this approach in a number of suits against the Elks.[10]

Why have women tried to gain entry into private clubs?

Women have sought entry into private clubs both to eradicate the stigma associated with being denied admission and to gain the valuable business contacts that often flow from membership in such clubs.[11]

What should a woman do if she thinks she has been discriminated against in a public accommodation?

She should first determine if she lives in a state or city with a public accommodations law. Many of these laws provide for comprehensive enforcement schemes by the same state agency that regulates employment discrimination. It is not possible to explain in this handbook the various procedures under all these laws, but some general advice would be to call the state employment discrimination agency and ask for information about where to go and what to do next. In states without such laws, such a woman might work with other women to pass a new law forbidding the discrimination.

NOTES

1. *Curran v. Mt. Diablo Council of the Boy Scouts of America*, 147 Cal. App. 3d 712, 195 Cal. Rptr. 325 (1983). Cases have also been brought under the federal public accommodations law (which does not apply to discrimination based on sex) to interpret it broadly. For example, a court in Illinois held that the Boy Scouts, depending on factual circumstances, could be a place of public accommodations. *Welsh v. Boy Scouts of America*, No. 90-1671 (N.D. Ill. May 3, 1991) (denying summary judgment to plaintiff); *see Welsh v. Boy Scouts of America*, 742 F. Supp. 1413 (N.D. Ill. 1990) (denying defendant's motion to dismiss).

2.	*Seidenberg v. McSorley's Old Ale House*, 317 F. Supp. 593 (S.D.N.Y. 1970) (state regulation of liquor licenses); *Johnson v. Heinemann Candy Co., Inc.*, 402 F. Supp. 714 (E.D. Wis. 1975) (use of city police force).

3.	*Dock Club, Inc. v. Ill. Liquor Control Comm'n*, 428 N.E.2d 735 (Ill. App. Ct. 1981) ("ladies night" at tavern); *McLean v. First Northwest Industries of America, Inc.*, 635 P.2d 683 (Wash. 1981) ("ladies night" at basketball game.)

4.	*E.g., Ladd v. Iowa West Racing Ass'n*, 438 N.W. 2d 600 (Iowa 1989) ("ladies day" at racetrack); *Koire v. Metro Car Wash*, 707 P.2d 195, 219 Cal. Rptr. 133 (Cal. 1985) (car wash and nightclub discounts to women); *Peppin v. Woodside Delicatessen*, 506 A.2d 263 (Md. App. 1986) (50% discount to any patron wearing a skirt or gown); *Commonwealth of Pennsylvania, Liquor Control Board v. Dobrinoff*, 471 A.2d 941 (Pa. Commw. 1984) (no cover for female patrons of the bar).

5.	*Roberts v. United States Jaycees*, 468 U.S. 609 (1984).

6.	*Board of Directors of Rotary International v. Rotary Club*, 481 U.S. 537 (1987).

7.	*New York State Club Ass'n v. City of New York*, 487 U.S. 1 (1988).

8.	*Kiwanis International v. Ridgewood Kiwanis Club*, 806 F.2d 468 (3d Cir. 1986), *cert. dismissed*, 483 U.S. 1050 (1987). Although the ACLU lost the Kiwanis case, it prevailed in a similar case in New Jersey, when it won a ruling that the eating clubs at Princeton University could no longer exclude women. In that case the "private club" exception did not apply because the New Jersey Supreme Court found that the clubs were inextricably linked with Princeton, itself a place of public accommodation. *Frank v. Ivy Club*, 576 A.2d 241, 117 N.J. 627 (1990), *cert. denied*, 111 S. Ct. 799 (1991).

9.	The law was challenged by the Burning Tree Club but upheld by the Maryland Court of Appeals, the highest court in Maryland. In doing so, the court also invalidated under the Maryland equal rights amendment a provision that exempted clubs that excluded members of one sex at certain days and times. *Maryland v. Burning Tree Club, Inc.*, 554 A.2d 366 (Md. 1989), *cert. denied*, 110 S. Ct. 66 (1989).

	An earlier version of the law contained an exception for clubs that had "the primary purpose . . . to serve or benefit members of a particular sex." The Maryland Court of Appeals also invalidated that exception under the Maryland equal rights amendment. *Burning Tree Club, Inc. v. Bainum*, 501 A.2d 817 (Md. 1985).

10.	*See, e.g., McGlotten v. Connally*, 338 F. Supp. 448 (D.D.C. 1972).

11.	*See generally*, Burns, *The Exclusion of Women from Influential Men's Clubs: The Inner Sanctum and the Myth of Full Equality*, 18 Harv. C.R.-C.L. L. Rev. 321 (1983).

XI

The Military

When President Bush ordered a major American military build-up in the Persian Gulf in the summer and fall of 1990, women comprised 11% of the United States armed forces on active duty. For the first time, politicians referred to "our men and women in uniform," and the media were full of "mom goes to war" stories. Since the advent of the all-volunteer force in 1974, women have played a vital role in the military, which is now unable to do without them. It is also clear that in hostilities women have had an "equal opportunity" to be injured and killed. But do they have an equal opportunity for advancement in the military? Are women viewed as first-class citizens when it comes to national defense? The answers are still no.

In the 1970s and 1980s, women scored major gains in the military and won several important legal cases.[1] First, the armed forces decided to increase significantly the percentages of women in the different services. In 1974 the 2% ceiling on women's enlistment was lifted. And in 1976 the military academies were opened to women for the first time. These new policies yielded results. As of 1989, 10.8% of the United States armed forces were women, including 11% of those on active duty in the army; 10% of those on active duty in the navy; 5% of those on active duty in the marines; 14% of those on active duty in the air force; and 7% of those on active duty in the coast guard.[2]

Although the military now offers women some excellent opportunities, many inequities and problems remain, and women in the military are still second-class citizens in that world. The number of women permitted to join the armed services is still limited to a relatively small percentage of the total force. Women are still precluded from direct combat roles even when they want to serve in that capacity and even when it is vital to their career advancement to do so. The imposition of these restrictions on military women has also affected the careers of women civilian employees of the military. Finally, preferential treatment for veterans, few of whom are women because of the prior quotas and continuing discrimination, magnifies and extends the original inequities well beyond the time of military service. Though deep-rooted, these inequities must be attacked.

Can women be drafted?

Yes, although it is highly unlikely. Nothing in the Constitution prevents Congress from drafting women although it has never taken that option. Indeed, no one has been subject to the draft since 1973 when the draft law expired. The armed forces are now all-volunteer. In February 1980 President Carter asked Congress for legislation and funds to begin draft registration of men and women between the ages of eighteen and twenty. Many members of Congress strongly opposed the registration of women, and only the all-male registration measure passed. The exclusion of women from registration was challenged as a violation of the Equal Protection Clause, but the Supreme Court ruled that this different treatment of men and women was perfectly constitutional.[3] It is decisions such as this, and similar ones which take a generally "hands-off" attitude toward the military, that make it so difficult to launch a constitutional challenge to even the most blatantly discriminatory policies and practices of the military.

Are women excluded from combat roles?

Theoretically, yes. All branches of the armed forces ostensibly prohibit women from serving in direct combat capacities. Until recently women in the air force and navy are prohibited by law from serving on airplanes and ships in direct combat. The army keeps women out of direct combat roles by policy.

A group of female officers and enlisted women in the navy challenged an earlier federal law that absolutely barred the assignment of women to duty at sea, either in combat or noncombat roles. Because navy women were restricted to shore duty, they were excluded from most job classifications and limited in their opportunities for training and promotion. Citing studies that showed women could perform capably in shipboard positions, a federal district court ruled that the statute was unconstitutional, both as to combat and noncombat positions.[4]

Following this decision, however, Congress passed a new statute that prohibited women from serving on aircraft or vessels that were actually engaged in combat missions; it did allow women to be assigned to other navy vessels, but only on a temporary basis if the ship is expected to be assigned a combat mission.[5]

In recognition of the vital role played by women pilots, and based upon a study done by the Air Force, Congress concluded that women can make excellent combat pilots and, therefore, in 1991 repealed the last legal restrictions on women in combat aircraft. The only remaining legal restriction on women in combat is the law prohibiting their service on combat ships. But the law does not require that women be assigned to combat aircraft and the Pentagon has continued a policy of not assigning women to combat positions.

In 1991, Congress also established the Commission on the Assignment of Women in the Armed Forces to study laws and policies restricting the assignment of women in the armed forces and to make a report to the President. The 15 member commission, all appointed by President Bush, focused on issues outside of their mandated scope (military efficiency) and looked at such issues as the social and cultural implications of assigning women to combat. The Commission made its report in November, 1992. It recommended against assigning women to combat positions (with the exception of combat ships other than submarines and amphibious vessels) and actually recommended that Congress reenact the legal restrictions.

Most of these policies are unlikely to be officially changed soon because opposition to women in combat roles is strong and visceral, especially among some military men and members of Congress. But this "protection" is illusory, at best, under the terms of modern warfare, and the exclusion of women from official combat roles severely limits women's opportunities in the military. Also, the services retain wide latitude in defining what is and is not direct combat. Thus, paradoxically, women may serve on supply ships, which are highly vulnerable to attack, but not on destroyers or aircraft carriers, which can more readily defend themselves. It is also clear from the experience in Panama and the Persian Gulf that women have, in fact, been in combat even when their jobs were not defined as direct combat positions. It may be that reality will someday overtake the law and the policy when it becomes clear that women can, and in fact do, perform very well in a whole range of jobs that were once closed to them.

May the "combat exclusion" be used to restrict the jobs of civilian women?

No. Until the mid-1980s, the navy had a policy of not permitting civilian women to go on sea trials of combat ships on which they had performed work. This restriction limited the overtime pay and promotion opportunities of these women. In two separate cases on opposite coasts, Pamella Doviak Celli (an acoustical engineer on submarines) and Glenda Bledsoe (a technician on aircraft carriers) challenged this policy under Title VII of the Civil Rights Act of 1964 and won. The Navy lost its argument that the "hands-off" constitutional approach to service members should also apply to civilians.[6]

Can United States military academies exclude women?

No. In 1976 Congress ordered the military academies to admit women.[7] Women now attend West Point, Annapolis, and the other military academies, though their numbers are limited "consistent with the needs of the services." However, except for this restriction, the same admissions criteria apply to both sexes and, once admitted, women must meet the same academic standards as men.

Do women have the same opportunities as men to enlist in the armed services?

No. Quotas for each branch of the military strictly limit the number of women who may enlist to a level far below the number of women who would enlist if they could. As a result, women are currently required to meet higher educational and trainability requirements (as measured by minimum aptitude tests) then are men. Women, but not men, are required to have high school diplomas (equivalency diplomas will not do), and they must often score higher on the aptitude tests. This discriminatory requirement was temporarily dropped after women began a lawsuit attacking its legality but was reinstated after subsequent higher court rulings indicated that such differential treatment was constitutionally permissible.

Can the armed services refuse to allow single parents of minor children to enlist?

So far, yes. In at least two cases, never-married mothers challenged an army regulation that prohibits the enlistment of unwed parents, unless they give their children up for adoption. (Divorced parents are eligible for enlistment only if they do not have custody of their children.) The plaintiffs, who met all the other criteria for enlistment, argued that this regulation illegally interfered with their constitutional right to marry or not to marry as they chose, with their constitutional right to rear their children, and with family integrity. The courts dismissed the claims on the ground that they lacked authority to review the military's criteria for enlistment.[8] Ironically, if a service member becomes a single parent while already in the military, she or he will be permitted—indeed often required— to remain in the service at least for the term of enlistment.

Must the armed services offer men and women the same salaries, fringe benefits, and opportunities for promotion?

Yes on salaries and fringe benefits; no on promotions. Men and women at any given rank receive the same salaries and benefits, but women's opportunities for promotions are severely limited by the so-called combat exclusion and by quotas at all rank levels. One attempt to compensate for this discrimination is the navy "up or out" statute, which requires that male line officers be discharged from the navy when they are passed over twice for promotion but allows women thirteen years before they are discharged for nonpromotion. A male lieutenant who wanted to stay in the navy long enough to be eligible for retirement pay challenged the statute on equal protection grounds, but the Supreme Court upheld the law, on the theory that its purpose was to compensate women for other disadvantages the navy had imposed on them. Statutory restrictions on women's participation in combat and sea duty made it difficult for female officers to compile service records comparable to those of male officers. A longer period of service before discharge for women officers was therefore necessary to provide them with fair opportunities for advancement, the Court stated.[9] A more logical starting point would have been to rule the whole scheme unconstitutional, beginning with the ban on sea or combat duty for women in the navy. But the male plaintiff did not challenge that discrimination, and it is unlikely that the Court would act on it without an Equal Rights Amendment, and even then such a case might be problematic because of the traditional deference to the military.

As for fringe benefits, Sharron Frontiero, an air force lieutenant, won the right to claim her husband as a dependent for purposes of obtaining increased quarters allowances and medical benefits in a 1973 Supreme Court decision. She challenged a federal statute that permitted a serviceman automatically to claim his wife as a dependent but required a servicewoman to prove that her husband depended on her for more than one-half of his support before she could claim him as a dependent and get the additional fringe benefits. The Court ruled that this scheme was unconstitutional.[10]

May a woman be discharged from the armed services because she is pregnant?

Usually, no. In 1971 Stephanie Crawford, an unmarried woman who had been discharged from the marine corps because she became pregnant, sued to be reinstated as a marine. Five years later, a federal appeals court awarded her back pay for the twenty months that had remained in her tour of duty and declared that the no-pregnancy rule violated the Constitution's equal protection guaranty.[11] Under the marine corps rule, the only temporary physical disability that was cause for automatic discharge was a pregnancy-related disability; all other temporary physical disabilities were considered on an individual basis. The court found this distinction irrational.

After Ms. Crawford began her suit, the marine corps and the other branches of the armed services changed their no-pregnancy rules. The present air force and marine corps regulations provide that a pregnant servicewoman may request a discharge but that otherwise her status is unaffected. The army and navy may waive the discharge of pregnant women and frequently do, except in the case of first term enlistees who have not completed their training. However, the various services will discharge anyone still in training who is physically unable to complete the training for any reason.

Is it legal for federal, state, and local governments to give a job preference to veterans?

Yes. The federal government and most state governments

give some preference to veterans for civil service jobs. Usually the preference consists of the addition of five or ten points to a veteran's score on a civil service exam. However, Massachusetts has an absolute veterans preference system, under which veterans who qualify for state civil-service positions must be considered for appointment ahead of all qualifying nonveterans. The effect of this system is to exclude almost all women from most of the best state civil-service jobs because veterans get them all and so few women are veterans.

Helen Feeney, a state employee and nonveteran, claimed that the Massachusetts veterans preference statute discriminated against women in violation of the Equal Protection Clause. Although Ms. Feeney had ranked at the top in several civil service exams, the jobs for which she was competing were given to lower-scoring male veterans. A federal court agreed that the statute was unconstitutional, but its decision was reversed by the Supreme Court. Although the Court recognized that the veterans preference system had an overwhelmingly adverse impact on women, it upheld the law because the *purpose* of the law was not to discriminate against women but to prefer veterans over nonveterans of either sex.[12] The Supreme Court now refuses to look at the disproportionate and harsh impact of a "neutral" law on women in Equal Protection Clause cases unless the explicit purpose of the law is to hurt women— a standard nearly impossible to prove.

NOTES

1. An excellent source on the role of women in the military in the 1970s is Binkin and Bach, *Women and the Military* (1977). For more recent information see Holm, *Women in the Military: An Unfinished Revolution* (1982) and Stiehm, *Arms and the Enlisted Woman* (1989).
2. Carolyn Becraft, "Facts About: Women in the Military, 1980–1990," is an excellent fact sheet, available from the Women's Research and Education Institute, 1700 18th Street, N.W., Suite 400, Washington, D.C., 20009.
3. *Rostker v. Goldberg*, 453 U.S. 57 (1981).
4. *Owens v. Brown*, 455 F. Supp. 291 (D.D.C. 1978).
5. 10 U.S.C.A. § 6015 (1990).
6. *Celli v. Webb*, C. A. No. 87-0072P (D. Me.), seeking enforcement of

Doviak v. Dept. of the Navy, EEOC Appeal No. 01860381, and *Bledsoe v. Secretary of the Navy*, 839 F.2d 1357 (9th Cir. 1988).

7. Department of Defense Appropriation Authorization Act, 10 U.S.C.A. § 4342 (1977 Supp.).

8. *West v. Brown*, 558 F.2d 757 (5th Cir. 1977), *cert. denied*, 435 U.S. 926 (1978), and *Mack v. Rumsfeld*, 784 F. 2d 438 (2d Cir. 1986), *cert. denied*, 107 S. Ct. 71 (1987).

9. *Schlesinger v. Ballard*, 419 U.S. 498 (1975), *reh'g denied*, 420 U.S. 966 (1975).

10. *Frontiero v. Richardson*, 411 U.S. 677 (1973).

11. *Crawford v. Cushman*, 531 F.2d 1114 (2d Cir. 1976).

12. *Personnel Administrator of Massachusetts v. Feeney*, 442 U.S. 256 (1979).

XII

Homelessness

As the ranks of the poor increased and the availability of low-cost housing decreased during the Reagan-Bush years, a new population emerged : the homeless.[1] Because women and their children comprise the majority of the poor in this country, they have been hit particularly hard. Due to their homelessness, many women have had to surrender their children to foster care or other family members. They have been forced into city-run shelters, where they are often the victims of violence and abuse by shelter workers and mentally-ill shelter residents. It has quickly become evident that the social service system is not equipped to meet their most basic needs—medical care, the attainment of public benefits, drug treatment, and permanent housing. The task for the 1990s is to develop ways to empower these women so that they may leave the ranks of the homeless.

How many people are homeless?

Estimates of the number of homeless vary widely. Most national estimates are based only on the numbers of homeless people who seek help from government agencies while the majority of homeless are in private shelters or on the streets. According to the New York City based Coalition for the Homeless, in 1992 there were 3 million people who were homeless in this country.[2] Over 90,000 of them lived in New York City.[3] Women comprise half of that population.[4] Homeless families, generally headed by women,[5] constitute the fastest-growing segment of the homeless population.[6] Homeless families generally comprise 30% of all those who are homeless.[7]

Who are the homeless women?

They tend to be young and African-American or Hispanic. For example, the Vera Institute of Justice reported in 1979 that of 100 homeless women living in New York City, half were under forty years old, and over half were women of color.[8]

They also tend to be "situationally homeless," which means they have become homeless because they are poor and lack a safety net. For example, the Vera Institute study also found that nearly 50% of the women surveyed had lived in single-room occupancy residences before coming to the shelters.[9] Twenty-five percent had been evicted from their homes.[10] Many have simply been unable to support themselves on the minimum wage. Lack of child care exacerbates the difficulty for single mothers trying to find work in order to pay the rent.

Many homeless women are chronically ill or alcoholic. One author has estimated that one-third of the homeless population is comprised of the mentally ill.[11] This figure includes those who have been released from psychiatric hospitals or diverted from long-term institutional care.[12] Homeless women are more likely than homeless men to be mentally ill.[13]

Finally, many have been victims of violence by their partners, forcing them onto the streets.[14] In fact, the Coalition for the Homeless estimates that in New York City nearly 40% of the women in city shelters have a history of abuse. Yet there are only 392 beds available in battered women's shelters.[15]

What are the principal causes of homelessness?

For many, it is simply the result of poverty. Unemployment and underemployment contribute to poverty, forcing people onto public assistance (Aid to Families with Dependant Children-AFDC), which does not provide adequate benefits to pay the rent.[16] Because shelter allowances are not adequate, many public assistance recipients must pay rent in excess of their allotted shelter allowances.[17]

At the same time, the average value of AFDC benefits has been steadily falling.[18] In the vast majority of states, the shelter portion of the AFDC grant is less than 50% of the federally defined "fair market rent."[19] This means that most, if not all, of AFDC must be used to pay the rent, leaving little or nothing for clothes, food, or other necessities.

Exacerbating these problems is the lack of low-cost housing. The Coalition for the Homeless has observed, "It is the critical shortage of low-cost housing that makes the difference between chronic hardship and outright homelessness."[20] The Coalition reports that since 1981, federal housing for the poor has been cut by 76%.[21] This has greatly diminished the production of affordable housing units as well as the maintenance of existing units. In New York state, the number of low cost rentals fell by over 1.7 million units during the past decade.[22]

Given these problems, lack of a "safety net" is often the deciding factor between staying in a home and becoming homeless. The inadequacy of public benefits and the scarcity of housing forces many families to move in with other families, creating conditions of extreme overcrowding.[23] One study estimates that 200,000 people are living doubled-up in New York City.[24] Eventually, these people land on the streets. One study of New York City shelters found that 50 to 60% of those in shelters had been doubled up before they arrived at the shelter.[25] Eviction alone accounts for 25% of those families that become homeless in New York City.[26]

Are shelters a solution to the problem of homelessness?

No. First, shelter life is often dangerous.[27] In October 1988 a network of women's organizations, shelter residents, and homeless advocates organized an ad hoc task force to assess the extent of abuse and neglect of women living in two New York City shelters. They found that

> . . . the system has failed to provide safe and humane places where women may seek emergency shelter. The lack of an effective administrative system within the shelters creates a system of violence. Consequently, these facilities are out of control. The women complain that the shelter staff and security guards not only fail to appropriately intervene, but also compound the situation by verbally, physically, and at times sexually abusing the shelter residents.[28]

One problem reported is that the staff, including guards, are inadequately trained.[29] Guards are often permitted to interpret curfew policies so restrictively that they refuse women admission into the shelters if they arrive after the curfew, even when beds are available. Guards have been known to turn away women who have arrived after curfew onto dangerous streets, where they risk rape and assault.[30] Guards have also been reported to use crack, alcohol, and other drugs.[31]

Second, shelters do not provide the services that women need to address the problems that caused the homelessness or

that have arisen because of the homelessness. Shelter officials
and social service workers have often failed to advise shelter
residents of entitlements for which they may qualify, and residents may go for weeks without seeing a social worker.[32] Medical care is often unavailable,[33] and there are few programs and
trained social workers available to help mothers and children
who have been separated because of their homelessness to
reunite.[34]

One consequence of these adverse living conditions is that
many women who may already have emotional problems become even more depressed and unable to cope.[35] This can make
it virtually impossible to leave the shelter system. It has been
observed that "self-mobilization and making efforts to extricate
oneself from the shelter system constitute a Herculean task
which, given the dearth of low-income housing, may end in
defeat."[36] Finally, providing shelter is not a final solution. These
women and their families need permanent homes.

**What is the cost of keeping homeless women and families
in shelters?**
In 1992, according to the 1993 Executive Budget of the
Mayor of New York City, New York City spent $223 million on
all shelters for families and $173 million on all shelters for
individuals.[37] The city paid between $1,200 and $3000 per
month to keep one family in a welfare hotel[38] and $1,000 to keep
an individual in a shelter.[39] This is an extraordinary amount
of money that could better be spent developing permanent
housing.

What are the solutions?
At this stage, the solutions are not simple and demand a
reevaluation of our national policies and priorities with regard
to the poor and the homeless. For example, the federal government must reinstate the federal housing budget to build more
low-income housing, and raise the minimum wage and public
assistance grants. However, state and local government and
those in the private sector can also help by providing homeless
women with mental and medical health care, drug treatment,
day care, job training, education, and other social services. For
more information contact:

Coalition for the Homeless
500 8th Avenue
New York, New York 10018
(212) 695-8700

National Coalition for the Homeless
1621 Connecticut Avenue, NW
Washington, D.C. 20009
(202) 265-2371

NOTES

1. The authors gratefully acknowledge Kristin Morse, assistant director for the Coalition for the Homeless, for her assistance.
2. Conversation with K. Morse, June 30, 1992.
3. *Id.*
4. Hagen, J., *Gender and Homelessness,* Social Work 312 (1987) (hereinafter Hagen) at 312.
5. Hagen at 312.
6. *Over the Edge: Homeless Families and the Welfare System.* The National Coalition for the Homeless, July 1988 at l (hereinafter Coalition).
7. Conversation with K. Morse, June 30, 1992.
8. Hagen at 312.
9. *Id.*
10. *Id.*
11. *Id.* at 313.
12. *Id.*
13. *Id.*
14. *Id.*
15. "Coalition for the Homeless Statistics" published by the Coalition for the Homeless.
16. Coalition at 12 (citing U.S. Conference of Mayors, *A Status Report on Homeless Families in America's Cities* p. 21 (1987).
17. Conversation with K. Morse, June 30, 1992.
18. Coalition at 2.
19. *Id.*
20. *Id.* at 13.
21. *Id.* at 2.
22. Conversation with K. Morse, June 30, 1992.
23. Coalition at 22. *See* Institute for Policy Studies, *A Progressive Housing Program for America* (1987).

24. David Dinkins Press Release, Oct. 30, 1990.
25. Coalition for the Homeless Statistics.
26. Hagen at 312.
27. *Victims Again: Homeless Women in the New York City Shelter System* (Homeless Women's Rights Network, Jan. 1989) (hereinafter Victims Again). Copies of the report may be obtained from 105 East 22d Street, Room 519, New York, New York 10010.
28. *Id.* at 2.
29. Victims Again at 3.
30. *Id.*
31. *Id.* at 4.
32. *Id.* at 6.
33. *Id.* at 9.
34. *Id.* at 10.
35. D'Ercole & Struening, *Victimization Among Homeless Women: Implications for Service Delivery,* 18 J. of Community Psychology 141, 148 (1990).
36. *Id.* at 149.
37. Conversation with K. Morse, June 30, 1992.
38. Coalition for the Homeless Statistics.
39. *Id.*

XIII
The Legal System

For many persons, law appears to be magic—an obscure domain that can be fathomed only by the professional initiated into its mysteries. People who might use the law to their advantage sometimes avoid the effort out of awe for its intricacies. But in fact the main lines of the legal system, and of the law in a particular area, can be explained in terms clear to the layperson. The purpose of this short chapter is to outline some important elements of the system.

What does a lawyer mean by saying that a person has a legal right?

Having a right means that society has given a person permission—through the legal system—to secure some action or to act in some way that she or he desires. For example, a woman might have a right to an abortion, a minority person the right to employment free from discrimination, or a person accused of a crime the right to an attorney.

How does one enforce a legal right?

The concept of *enforcing* a right gives meaning to the concept of the right itself. While the abstract right may be significant because it carries some connotation of morality and justice, enforcing the right yields something concrete—the abortion, the job, the attorney.

A person enforces her or his right by going to some appropriate authority—often, a judge—who has the power to take certain action. The judge can order the people who are refusing to grant the right to start doing so, on pain of going to jail if they disobey. The judge can also order the people to pay money to compensate for the loss of the right. Sometimes other authorities, such as federal and state administrative agencies or a labor arbitrator, can take similar remedial action.

The problem with the enforcement process is that it will often be lengthy, time-consuming, expensive, frustrating, and may arouse hostility in others—in short, it may not be worth the effort. On the other hand, in some cases you may not need to go to an enforcement authority in order to implement your right. The concerned persons or officials may not have realized that you have a right and may voluntarily change their actions once you explain your position. Then, too, they may not want to go through the legal process either—it can be as expensive and frustrating for them as it is for you.

Where are legal rights defined?

There are several sources. Rights are defined in the statutes or laws passed by the U.S. Congress and by state and city legislatures. They are also set forth in the written decisions of judges, federal and state. Congress and state and local legislatures have also created institutions called administrative agencies to enforce certain laws, and these agencies interpret the laws in written decisions and rules that further define people's rights.

Are rights always clearly defined and evenly applied to all people?

Not at all, although this is one of the great myths about law. Because so many different sources define people's rights, and because persons of diverse backgrounds and beliefs implement and enforce the law, there is virtually no way to uniformity. Nor do statutes that set forth rights always do so with clarity or specificity. It remains for courts or administrative agencies to interpret and flesh out the details; and in the process of doing so, many of the interpreters differ. Sometimes, two different courts will give completely different answers to the same question. Whether or not a person has a particular right may depend on which state or city he or she lives in.

The more times a particular issue is decided, the more guidance there is in predicting what other judges or administrative personnel will decide. Similarly, the importance of the court or agency deciding a case or the persuasiveness of its reasoning will help determine the effect of the decision. A judge who states thoughtful reasons for a decision will have more influence than one who offers poor reasons.

Law then is not a preordained set of doctrines, applied rigidly and unswervingly in every situation. Rather, law is molded from the arguments and decisions of many persons and institutions. It is very much a human process of trying to convince others—a judge, a jury, an administrator, the lawyer for the other side—that your view of what the law requires is correct.

What is a decision or case?

Lawyers often use these words interchangeably, although technically they do not mean the same thing. A case means the lawsuit started by one person against another, and it can refer to that lawsuit at any time from the moment it is started until the final result is reached. A decision means the written opinion in which the judge declares who wins the lawsuit and why.

What is meant by precedent?

Precedent means past decisions. Lawyers use precedent to influence new decisions. If the facts involved in the prior decision are close to the facts in the present case, a judge will be strongly tempted to follow the former decision. She is not, however, bound to do so and, if persuasive reasons are presented to show that the prior decision was wrong or ill-suited to changed conditions in society, the judge may not follow precedent.

What is the relationship between decisions and statutes?

In our legal system, most legal concepts originally were defined in the decisions of judges. In deciding what legal doctrine to apply to any case, each judge kept building on what other judges had done before him. The body of legal doctrines created in this way is called the common law.

The common law still applies in many situations, but increasingly state legislatures and the Congress pass laws ("statutes") to define the legal concepts that judges or agencies should use in deciding cases. The written decisions of individual judges are still important even where there is a statute because statutes are generally not specific enough to cover every set of facts. Judges have to interpret the meaning of statutes, apply them to the facts at hand, and write a decision; that decision will then be considered by other judges when they deal with these statutes in other cases. Thus it is generally not enough to know what a relevant statute defines as illegal; you also have to know how judges have interpreted the statute in specific situations.

What different kinds of courts are there?

The United States is unique for its variety of courts. Broadly speaking, there are two distinct court systems: federal and state. Both are located throughout the country; each is limited to certain kinds of cases, with substantial areas of overlap. Most crimes are prosecuted in state courts, for instance, although there a number of federal crimes prosecuted in federal court. People must always use state courts to get a divorce (except in the District of Columbia and other federal areas), but they must sue in federal court to establish rights under certain federal laws.

In both federal and state court systems one starts out at the trial court level, where the facts are "tried." This means that a judge or jury listens and watches as the lawyers present evidence of the facts that each side seeks to prove. Evidence can take many forms: written documents, the testimony of a witness on the stand, photographs, charts. Once a judge or jury has listened to or observed all the evidence presented by each side, it will choose the version of the facts it believes, apply the applicable legal doctrine to these facts, and decide which side has won. If either side is unhappy with the result, it may be able to take the case to the next, higher-level court and argue that the judge or the jury applied the wrong legal concept to the facts, or that no reasonable jury or judge could have found the facts as they were found in the trial court, and that the result was therefore wrong.

What are plaintiffs and defendants?

The plaintiff is the person who sues—that is, who *complains* that someone has wronged him or her and asks the court to remedy this situation. The defendant is the person sued—or the one who *defends* herself against the charges of the plaintiff. The legal writing in which the plaintiff articulates her or his basic grievance is the *complaint,* and a lawsuit is generally commenced by filing this document with the clerk at the courthouse. The defendant then responds to these charges in a document appropriately named an *answer.* Some states use different names for these documents.

One refers to a particular lawsuit by giving the names of the plaintiff and defendant. If Mary Jones sues Smith Corporation for refusing to hire her because she is a woman, her case will be called *Jones v. Smith Corporation* (v. stands for versus or against).

What is an administrative agency?

Agencies are institutions established by either state or federal legislatures to administer or enforce a particular law or series of laws and are distinct from both courts and legislature. They often regulate a particular industry. For example, the Federal Communications Commission regulates the broadcasting industry (radio and television stations and networks) and the telephone and telegraph industry, in accordance with the legal standards set forth in the Federal Communications Act; and the Interstate Commerce Commission regulates trucking and railroads.

These agencies establish legal principles, referred to as rules, regulations or guidelines. Rules are interpretations of a statute and are designed to function in the same way as a statute—to define people's rights and obligations on a general scale, detailed fashion than the statute itself. Agencies also issue specific decisions in particular cases, like a judge, applying a law or rule to a factual dispute between particular parties.

How does one find court decisions, statutes, and agency rules and decisions?

All these materials are published and can be found in law libraries. In order to find the item desired, one should understand the system lawyers use for referring to, or citing, these materials. Some examples will help clarify the system. A case might be cited as *Watson v. Limbach Company,* 333 F. Supp. 754 (S.D. Ohio 1971); a statute, as 42 U.S.C. § 1983; a regulation, as 29 C.F.R. § 1604.10(b). The unifying factor in all three citations is that the first number denotes the particular volume in a series of books with the same title; the words or the letters that follow represent the name of the book; and the second number represents either the page or the section in the identified volume. In the examples above, the *Watson* case is found in the 333rd volume of the series of books called *Federal Supplement* at page 754; the statute is found in Volume 42 of the series called the *United States Code* at Section 1983; the regulation is in Volume 29 of the *Code of Federal Regulations* at Section 1604.10(b).

There are similar systems for state court decisions. Once you understand the system, all you need do is find out from the librarian where any particular series of books is kept, then look up the proper volume and page or section. It is also important to look for the same page or section in the material sometimes inserted at the back of a book, since many legal materials are periodically updated. A librarian will tell you what any abbreviations stand for if you are unfamiliar with that series.

Given this basic information, anyone can locate and read important cases, statutes and regulations. Throughout the book, such materials have been cited when deemed particularly important, and women are urged to read them. Although lawyers often use overly technical language, the references cited in this book can be comprehended without serious difficulty, and reading the original legal materials will give women a deeper understanding of their rights.

What is the role of the lawyer in the legal system?

A lawyer understands the intricacies and technicalities of the legal system, can maneuver within it efficiently, and is able to help other people by doing so. Thus, the lawyer knows where to find out about the leading legal doctrines in any given area and how to predict the outcome of your case, based on a knowledge of those doctrines. A lawyer can advise you what to do: forget about the case; take it to an administrative agency; sue in court; make a will; and so on. The lawyer then can help you take the legal actions that you determine are necessary.

How are legal costs determined and how do they affect people's rights?

The cost of using the legal system is predominantly the cost of paying the lawyer for his or her time. Since this has become prohibitive even for middle-class individuals, many people are not able to assert their rights, even though they might ultimately win if they had the money to pay a lawyer for doing the job.

Is legal action the only way to win one's legal rights?

By no means. Negotiation, education, consciousness raising, publicity, demonstrations, organization, and lobbying are all ways to achieve rights, often more effectively that through the standard but costly and time-consuming resort to the courts. In all these areas, it helps to have secure knowledge of the legal underpinning of your rights. One has a great deal more authority if one is protesting illegal action. The refrain "That's illegal" may move some people in and of itself; or it may convince those with whom you are dealing that you're serious enough to do something about the situation—by starting a lawsuit, for instance.